*J.K. LASSE*

# GUIDE FOR TOUGH TIMES

*J.K. LASSER'S*™

# GUIDE FOR TOUGH TIMES

## Tax and Financial Solutions to See You Through

Barbara Weltman

John Wiley & Sons, Inc.

Published by John Wiley & Sons, Inc., Hoboken, New Jersey.
Published simultaneously in Canada.

For general information on our other products and services or for technical support, please contact our Customer Care Department within the United States at (800) 762-2974, outside the United States at (317) 572-3993 or fax (317) 572-4002.

Wiley also publishes its books in a variety of electronic formats. Some content that appears in print may not be available in electronic books. For more information about Wiley products, visit our web site at www.wiley.com.

***Library of Congress Cataloging-in-Publication Data:***

Weltman, Barbara.
   J.K. Lasser's guide for tough times : tax and financial solutions to see you through / Barbara Weltman.
      p. cm.
   Includes index.
   ISBN 978-0-470-40232-0 (pbk.)
  1. Finance, Personal–United States–Popular works.   2. Income tax–United States–Popular works.   3. Investments–United States–Popular works.   4. Taxation–United States.   I. J.K. Lasser Tax Institute.   II. Title.   III. Title: Guide for tough times.
   HG179.W4657 2009
  332.02400973–dc22

                                   2008032269

Printed in the United States of America.

10  9  8  7  6  5  4  3  2  1

# Contents

# Acknowledgments

I would like to thank members of the J.K. Lasser team, Elliott Eiss, Esq. and David Pugh, for their assistance in the preparation of this book. Like me, they are dedicated to ensuring that information is reliable, helpful, and easily understandable. I would also like to thank Christina Verigan, who did a careful job in editing this book.

# Introduction

Charles Dickens' opening sentence in *A Tale of Two Cities* described the era of the French Revolution as "It was the best of times, it was the worst of times." That description fits today's economic climate as well. It's the best of times because there is virtually unlimited opportunity for advancement in a job or to start a business, there's technology that helps you stay in touch and up to date, and you have access to information about every aspect of your financial life—the so-called American Dream (a belief that anyone can achieve his or her goals) is alive and well for many people. But now is the worst of times for so many other reasons; soaring gasoline and food prices, increasing unemployment, rising inflation, uncertain tax rules, and a growing number of home foreclosures are some of the big economic problems plaguing us today.

Today it seems that everyone is feeling a little nervous about what is going on in world markets and how they are impacted personally. When the stock market (a term that usually refers to the Dow Jones Industrial Average, or the Dow, which is comprised of just 30 stocks) goes up, many believe that the economy has turned a corner; when it goes down, that's more proof that tough times are with us. Your feelings of anxiety about the economy are not out of place, given what is happening with prices, jobs, and other key financial indicators. There is a lot of uncertainty. You're right to be concerned with what's going on and how you can weather this economic storm.

Dramatic financial changes in your life, which are indeed happening to many people today, can create stress levels that are so high as to impact your health. Stress can manifest itself in headaches, sleep disorders, difficulty concentrating, short temper, stomach upset, and feelings of anxiety and depression, and can lead to serious illnesses, including diabetes, asthma and arthritis flare-ups, irritable bowel syndrome, and clinical depression. In 1967, two psychiatrists, Thomas Holmes and Richard Rahe, developed their Stress Scale, a scoring test that measures how much certain life events contribute to stress and when stress levels put you at risk for illness. Some of the biggest stress causers are dismissal from work, changes in your financial state, divorce, and mortgage foreclosure. All of these events are happening today with increased frequency.

Serious life event changes can also wreak havoc with your financial security and personal wealth. You may be strapped to pay for ordinary living expenses, such as home heating oil or filling up your car's gas tank. Many today are living paycheck to paycheck, with no financial cushion, so that the slightest money setback can push them over the edge into economic disaster. For instance, a homeowner who experiences an illness that keeps him or her from working can easily fall behind in mortgage payments and, if this continues, could lose the home to foreclosure. Others today are facing choices about whether to purchase gas in order to get to work or buy groceries. Millions of Americans (an estimated 45.7 million) are without health coverage, so just about any medical issue can lead to onerous debt.

If there is a bright side to a dark economy, it's that good times will return. No one knows when, so the wait feels infinite. Like astronauts seeing only blackness when they're on the dark side of the moon, history shows that light (and economic prosperity) will return; economic downs don't last forever. Bad times are recessions, defined as two consecutive quarterly declines in the gross domestic product (GDP); depressions (economic downturns that last at least several years); or just short-term economic slowdowns. Are we technically experiencing a recession? It doesn't matter from the consumer's perspective, because any economic slowdown creates a personal financial impact. Regardless of how you label the current economic situation, it probably won't last long. Of the 11 recessions seen since World War II, each has been progressively shorter; the last two ran only eight months each. However, the consequences of a slowdown can last a lot longer for some, such as those who lose a job or their home; but for most people, good times are just around the corner.

Another bright side to today's tough times is that using smart strategies, including maximizing all tax breaks to which you are entitled, can get you through. You can find ways to stretch your dollar, get more income, reduce your expenses, and avoid an irreversible catastrophe, such as losing your home, by taking advantage of numerous tax rules. Simple actions can produce big and immediate results to ease your financial pain.

And yet another good thing that can come out of getting through tough economic times is learning (maybe the hard way) good financial habits. This will help you avoid problems when the next downturn occurs, as will inevitably happen. You'll have learned to create safeguards that will insulate you to some extent from future bad economies. And you'll have learned how tax rules impact just about every aspect of your life and can help alleviate some of the financial pain or discomfort that comes with losses and other adverse economic events. The information is here; it's up to you to act upon it.

## How to Use This Book

The book covers the topics that affect your personal and economic life—your home, everyday expenses, your investments, your job or business, school, credit card debt, medical issues, storm damage, divorce, and death. Each chapter provides insights into some of the problems that can arise with respect to these topics and suggests practical strategies you can use to get out of difficulties or avoid them entirely. The "What to Do Now" boxes give you specific steps to follow for resolving specific issues or problems.

Throughout the book you'll find resources that you can use to learn more. The web sites were correct when the book went to print, but I caution you that sites change and I can't help that. There's also a Glossary that you can view to understand some difficult or unfamiliar tax and financial terminology.

You will note that there are many instances throughout the book that point to pending changes at the time of publication. Congress, states, and other entities are continually considering or taking action that can impact your economic situation. Even though there was a stimulus package in early 2008 to spur the economy, there may be additional measures adopted later in 2008 or in coming years that could help to bring down the price of gas, assist troubled homeowners to keep from falling into foreclosure, or provide breaks for other market sectors in need of recovery. Stay alert to changes (you'll find tax law changes at JKLasser.com (www.jklasser.com).

If you want to get on my e-mail list to receive my free Idea of the Day[SM] and monthly e-newsletter, *Big Ideas for Small Business*®, or want to contact me directly (I try to respond to all inquiries), go to www.barbaraweltman.com.

# CHAPTER 1

# Challenges in Today's Economy

You probably don't need an expert or piles of statistics to tell you that these are troubling economic times. Every trip to the gas station or the supermarket confirms the challenges you face. Many families face tough choices today about where to spend their limited income—paying the mortgage or rent, heating costs, food, gas for the car, health insurance premiums, and on and on. For some, routine concerns about rising costs are compounded by uncertainty about their job security or whether their business will be able to survive for much longer.

You don't have to become an economics professor to understand the forces at work in today's marketplace that impact your pocketbook, but it's helpful to get some perspective about the economy we're in and what you can do to ride out bad times. It's also important to remain nimble and optimistic; understand your options, and recognize that things will surely get better (as they always do).

In this chapter, you will learn about the current economic conditions, prospects for the future, and what you can do now in areas including:

- High fuel costs
- Volatile stock markets
- Problems in the housing market
- Rising unemployment
- Uncertain tax rules

- Low U.S. dollar
- Prospects for recovery

## High Fuel Costs

Who cares what the cost of crude oil is on the spot market? You do. Rising crude oil prices, which are of particular interest mainly to commodity traders and oil-producing countries, eventually trickle down to consumers and are felt at the gas pump and in home heating oil prices.

The price of a barrel of oil has hit a new high. In July 2008, oil topped $147 a barrel and, despite a pullback of the price into the $120s in early August, many were predicting $150 or even $200 a barrel within weeks or months. The rise in crude oil prices is unprecedented. From 1869 through 2006, the price of a barrel of crude oil averaged about $21 (adjusted for inflation); the price spiked in war years and other periods of conflict in the Middle East.

Why are oil prices so high? There's no simple or single answer. There are many contributing factors, including increased world demand for oil supplies (especially from countries with growing economies such as China and India), a weak U.S. dollar, and speculators (although some experts dispute the ability of speculators to influence prices). Whatever the reason, the price of crude oil continues to climb.

What about the future? No one has a crystal ball, and experts differ on prospects for the future. Some optimists say the price could drop back to $50 a barrel, while others see $200 a barrel with no limit in sight. The Energy Information Administration (www.eia.doe.gov/steo), which provides official energy statistics from the U.S. government, posts the short-term outlook for energy, and the numbers aren't good. Even if the U.S. begins offshore drilling, a measure that has been made possible by the lifting of a presidential ban, it might be years before the positive effects of this activity would be felt. In the interim, world fuel consumption, a factor in driving up the price of oil, is projected to grow by a million barrels per day, even as U.S. consumption is predicted to decline. Natural gas, which is used for homes, was $7.17 per thousand cubic feet (Mcf) in 2007, but it is expected to average about $11 per Mcf in both 2008 and 2009. The point of these numbers is to make you think about how you are directly impacted—at the pump and in your home.

### Gasoline Prices

Everyone who drives a car or truck knows that prices at the pump for gasoline and diesel fuel have skyrocketed within a relatively short period of time.

Who or what is responsible for the price increases? Again, several factors may be at work. Refining capacity (the ability to take crude oil and turn it into gasoline for vehicles) is severely limited (no new refinery has been constructed in the United States since 1976 and the number of refineries within the country has declined since that time by half). Any weather disruptions, such as a hurricane, reduce refinery production. Less supply means higher prices.

Gasoline taxes are another factor (although some would argue it's a small one). There are the federal excise tax (18.4¢ per gallon), the state excise taxes (averaging 18.2¢ per gallon), and other state and local taxes, including sales taxes, gross receipts taxes, oil inspection fees, underground storage tank fees, and other miscellaneous environmental fees (averaging 10.4¢ per gallon). The idea of a federal gas tax holiday has so far been rejected by Congress.

Some states, including Connecticut and Michigan, had considered a temporary holiday on their taxes on gasoline. There has been only mild support for a federal excise tax holiday; even if enacted it would save only 18.4¢ per gallon. Any tax holiday would merely provide temporary relief and is not a long-term solution to higher gasoline prices.

### Home Heating Prices

Like gas at the pump, the price of home heating oil is dependent on the cost of crude oil. Some experts are predicting that the cost of the 2008–2009 home heating oil season could be 25 to 50 percent more than it was in the 2007–2008 season. Someone paying $2,000 in the winter of 2008 to heat a home might pay $3,000 in the winter of 2009. For instance, in June 2007, the average gallon of home heating oil in New York was $2.68 a gallon; in July 2008, it was $4.68 a gallon, a 75 percent increase in under a year.

Homes heated by natural gas (rather than oil or electricity) are not exempt from higher prices. Prices for natural gas have also risen dramatically this year and could continue to rise in the near future.

## What to Do Now

Consider locking in heating oil prices by contracting with your oil company as soon as possible for your oil needs in the upcoming winter season. This will let you obtain the lowest price possible if the price of heating oil rises and will enable you to budget for this expenditure during the heating oil season. (However, if you anticipate prices will fall, then you might prefer to continue to pay as you use oil throughout the winter to benefit from possible price declines.)

Consider obtaining a home energy audit so that you can learn ways to reduce your heating and cooling costs. Most local utilities providers perform these audits for you free of charge or work with third parties to do them for you. Then, if you need and want to make energy-saving improvements (such as adding insulation or upgrading your furnace), you may qualify for very low-interest loans. There may also be state tax breaks for these improvements.

There's more about dealing with energy costs, including tax breaks for making energy improvements, in Chapters 2 and 5.

## Volatile Stock Markets

Why should the average person care about the stock market? There are a couple of reasons. First, more than half of all U.S. households own stocks—directly or through company retirement plans and/or individual retirement accounts (IRAs). Second, stock market data, such as the Dow Jones Industrial Average (comprised of 30 stocks), is headline news every day, creating a psychological impact on consumers who pay attention to this information.

The stock market never moves in a straight line; the prices of stocks go up and down. There have been and will probably be days to come when the market drops significantly in a single day, causing serious concerns that more bad days are in the offing. It is hoped that the trend of the stock market is up over the long term.

Many believe that the stock market can be used as an indicator of when the economy has turned the corner. Historically, the stock market rebounds about six months before the economy as a whole. So when you see stocks going up fairly steadily for weeks (not just a day or two), you can assume, if you believe the pundits, that the worst may have passed.

Will there be a stock market collapse like the one experienced in 1929 that was followed by the Great Depression? According to Milton Friedman, one of the leading economists in the past 100 years, the answer is no, because of current actions by the Federal Reserve (the Fed) and other factors. Today, unlike in 1929, there are some controls in place that will minimize a market collapse.

- The government is committed to using tools at its disposal to ensure that financial institutions can weather certain market activity, such as letting banks and brokerage firms borrow money from the Fed, insuring (for one year) money market funds, banning short selling of hundreds of financial stocks, and giving the U.S. Treasury the ability to buy illiquid mortgage assets from financial institutions. Dr. Friedman argues that the Fed's actions and blunders during the 1920s and especially following the stock market crash of 1929 are the main reason for the depth and length of the depression in the 1930s.

- The stock market has rules in place to halt trading at specific points for specific amounts of time if the market is falling dramatically. This gives investors and speculators in the market a chance to cool down and act more rationally. And the Commodity Futures Trading Commission (CFTC) has introduced new initiatives to address speculative activity.

- Investors' accounts are protected through insurance from the Securities Investor Protection Corporation (SIPC). While this insurance does not protect investors from their own bad investment decisions, it does provide protection in case brokerage firms experience financial difficulties.

reached 6.1 percent. This is still a historically low number (it reached a high of 10.2 percent in November 1982), but troubling for those who make up this statistic.

The increase in the three-month average of the unemployment rate by 0.3 percentage points has historically been a signal that the economy is in a recession or is about to enter one. This benchmark was met in December 2007, and many take this as an indication that the economy is in serious trouble.

What does the future hold? No one knows whether there will be more layoffs or whether the Economic Stimulus package and other measures will avert higher unemployment. When this book was being prepared, Congress was considering legislation that would enable states to extend the usual 26-week term for unemployment benefits by 13 weeks (by 26 weeks in some hard-hit areas).

If you are laid off, spring into action. Be prepared to spend time every day doing something that will advance your chances of finding a job. This can include networking with family, friends, and former business associates (good thing you already revised your resume). Use technology, such as blogging, which can help you gain visibility and establish your credentials where appropriate. See Chapter 8 for more information about dealing with problems on the job.

## Uncertain Tax Rules

Never has there been a time when tax rules have been more uncertain than now. This is due to a confluence of events:

- *Expiring laws*. The tax cuts set in motion in 2001 and 2002 legislation are set to expire at the end of 2010, with old rules scheduled be back in effect in 2011.
- *Changing administration and new Congress*. A presidential election and a new Congress may bring a new tax philosophy to bear on future legislation.
- *Recurring extensions*. Certain persistent problems have not received permanent fixes, but merely annual attention. For instance, the alternative minimum tax (AMT), which could affect 30 million taxpayers or more if nothing is done, has been undergoing annual patches to prevent this occurrence.
- *Budget deficits*. The continued budget deficit and the need for revenue to service the wars in Iraq and Afghanistan, make stimulus payments (explained later in this chapter), and fund entitlement programs, such as Social Security and Medicare, put ever-increasing demands on the tax system.

In recent years, Congress has taken a band-aid approach to tax policy—fix what must be done now and let major problems and policies wait for another day.

### What to Do Now

Now is the time to revisit tried-and-true investment strategies to see you through this uncertain time.

- *Don't panic*. Don't let emotions govern your investment decisions. Remember, you don't have an actual loss until you sell (unless, of course, the company goes under). If you wait while the market as a whole recovers, your particular investments may ride the up wave. By the same token, however, don't form an emotional attachment to losing stocks that have no chance of recovery.
- *Invest for the long run*. Don't try to be a market timer—even experts are often wrong. Instead, make patient and prudent investment decisions.
- *Diversify*. If you don't have all your eggs in one basket, your risk of significant loss is minimized. It's rare for all market sectors to decline at once. A well-balanced portfolio can cushion you during volatile market activity.
- *Buy on the cheap*. Recognize that a down market is a buying opportunity to pick up quality stocks at fire-sale prices.

There's more about investment strategies in a volatile market in Chapter 3.

## Problems in the Housing Market

Fannie Mae and Freddie Mac, the nation's two largest mortgage finance companies, were seized by the federal government in September 2008 in an effort to help stabilize the housing market. The long-term impact of this action is unknown. There are three key indicators of the housing market: home prices, the number of home sales, and the number of foreclosures.

### Home Prices

Home prices are important for a number of reasons. They affect what current sellers can receive for their homes. They impact the availability of home equity that can be borrowed by homeowners through home equity loans and lines of credit. They influence how wealthy (or poor) homeowners feel, which can translate into consumer spending (if homeowners feel poor, they may not be inclined to spend money even if there is money on hand to spend).

Housing prices in most parts of the country are down, and some experts predict that declines could last into 2010. Prices of homes in Las Vegas, for example, have already dropped by more than 20 percent. Some pundits are predicting declines of as much as 50 percent in some areas. Of course, there are still some bright spots in the housing market, such as New York City and Portland, Oregon, where housing prices have continued to rise in these uncertain economic times.

Someone's bad news is always someone else's good news. Declining home prices may be bad news for homeowners, especially those trying to sell their homes now. But it's good news for home buyers, who can get into the market at attractive prices.

Even home sellers should not necessarily look at the current housing market as a setback. Those looking to trade up or relocate will benefit when they are on the buying end, so even if they don't maximize their return when they sell, they will do so when they buy a new home.

### What to Do Now

Your action depends on whether you are a buyer or a seller. If you're a buyer, you're in the catbird seat. Sellers are willing to accommodate reasonable requests and negotiate better terms to clinch a sale. Combine lower housing prices with continued low mortgage interest rates for qualified buyers and you have the formula for great opportunity for many prospective home buyers. And there's a bonus to make things even more affordable: A refundable federal tax credit of up to $7,500 for first-time homebuyers ($3,750 for married persons filing separately). The credit, however, applies only for homes bought on or after April 9, 2008, and before July 1, 2009, and the credit, which is effectively an interest-free loan from Uncle Sam, is repaid to the federal government over 15 years starting in the second year after the year of purchase. For example, if you buy your first home in December 2008 and claim the $7,500 credit on your 2008 return, you must include $500 on your return each year, starting in 2010.

If you're a seller, you'll have to be realistic in the face of today's home prices. Forget what you could have gotten for your home a year or two ago. Look at comparable *recent* sales in your area to determine current value. If you aren't willing to part with your home at today's price and you can afford to stay put, you can wait out the current housing market and hope for better times to come. No one knows for sure when that will be; some experts are predicting that it could take several years for the housing market to rebound.

### Home Sales

The National Association of Realtors (NAR) reported that in April 2008, home sales were down 13.1 percent from the same period the year before, and off 29 percent from the peak in the housing market in April 2005.

### Foreclosures

The number of foreclosures and near-foreclosures is alarmingly high. More than 1.5 million homeowners have experienced foreclosure during this current housing crisis. Somewhere between 10 and 30 percent of homeowners are now *underwater*, which means their home is worth less than their outstanding mortgage. Once a homeowner is underwater and has no equity, there is a high probability of foreclosure. RealtyTrac (www.realtytrac.com) reported that in April 2008 one in 519 homeowners received a foreclosure notice, and that foreclosures were up 65 percent over the number just one year ago. In July 2008, when Congress enacted the Housing and Economic Recovery Act of 2008, more than 400,000 homeowners were on the brink of foreclosure. The tax implications for homeowners in foreclosure are discussed in Chapter 2.

## Rising Unemployment

Because of job layoffs, particularly in certain industries (such as airlines, automakers, and financial companies), everyone in the job market is a little jittery. Those with the least seniority may have the greatest concerns because typically the last one hired is the first one fired. In May 2008, the jobless rate reached 5.5 percent and persisted at this rate through July 2008; in August 2008 it

### What to Do Now

Depending on how long or how severe the economic turndown is, no one's job is 100 percent safe. Develop a plan to help keep your job, as well as what to do if, despite your best efforts, you lose it.

- *Improve your job skills*. The more you know and can do, the more likely it is that your employer will keep you. The skills you gain can help you on your current job and, should you need it, to find a new position.

- *Review and revise your resume*. It's always a good idea to have your resume up to date and ready to go, just in case you need it. Also, keep your ear to the ground so you'll know as early as possible whether your job may be in jeopardy; this will enable you to leap into action if it becomes necessary.

- *Understand what a layoff means*. What benefits would you be entitled to from your employer? Could you continue your medical coverage for 18 months under the Consolidated Omnibus Budget Reconciliation Act (COBRA)? If so, what would this cost you? How much could you receive in unemployment benefits? Would you be entitled to any supplemental unemployment benefits from a union? Having this information at your fingertips may relieve some anxiety about the shaky job situation.

- *Develop another income stream*. If you're concerned about job security, it couldn't hurt to have a backup plan to carry you through. This can be done by starting a sideline business. Even though times may be tough, there's always room in the marketplace for new ideas and products, and start-ups can succeed.

## What to Do Now

Stay alert to developments so you can take action when they become official. There may be many proposals discussed in the media, but until they become law, you might not want or need to take any action.

- *Follow tax news and information.* Don't wait until you buy your annual income tax guide or meet with a tax professional who prepares your annual return to learn about new tax breaks and opportunities that apply to you. Use JKLasser.com (www.jklasser.com) for up-to-the-minute information and insight into law changes so you can decide what steps you can take to benefit from them. Also visit the Internal Revenue Service (IRS) web site (www.irs.gov) and your state tax department web site to find out about tax law changes.

- *Factor into your current decisions any potential future tax changes.* For example, if you believe that tax rates will rise in the future, then don't opt to defer income now If you have the opportunity to do so. Take the income now and pay the tax with the expectation that it will be a smaller tax bite than if you delay receipt of the money

- *Take political action.* Let your U.S. senator and representative know how you feel about proposed tax changes that will affect you. Find them at Congress.org (www.congress.org) by entering your zip code in the search box.

## Low U.S. Dollar

When is a dollar not a dollar? When you use it to buy goods and services overseas. Then the value of the dollar is dependent on what it is worth relative to other currencies, such as the euro (used by most members of the European Union), the pound (Great Britain), and the yen (Japan). Over the past several years, the value of the dollar has declined (it is down about 50 percent compared with the euro), which means that your dollar does not go as far as it used to when buying things abroad.

If you don't travel overseas, you might think you aren't impacted by the value of the dollar. Again, economics come into play. Many experts, for example, believe that part of the reason for soaring gasoline prices is the low dollar since oil is, at least for the present, denominated in dollars. Also, foreign investment within the United States is transforming ownership of America because companies and properties here are cheap when priced in foreign currencies. For instance, Anheuser-Busch, a beer company owned by U.S. families for 143 years, is becoming a Belgian company, and a majority interest in the Chrysler

Building in New York City is now owned by an investment arm of the Abu Dhabi government.

Of course, some view the low dollar as a boon to the U.S. economy because it makes our exports more attractive to foreign buyers. This helps the U.S. trade deficit, which measures the amount of U.S. dollars going overseas versus money coming into our economy.

The bottom line to you is that unless you vacation abroad, you may not be directly impacted by a change in the value of a dollar. Just understand that it could, however, impact the prices of items you buy that have been shipped here from other countries.

---

### What to Do Now

When shopping online, pay attention to whether items are listed in dollars or another currency (with the Internet, it's easy to wind up at a distant site that uses another currency). Determine whether something is really a bargain after you convert the price into dollars.

---

## Prospects for Recovery

Business cycles—expansions (good times) and contractions (bad times)—are a normal part of our economy. Arthur Burns, a noted economist and former Federal Reserve chairman, wrote in 1947, "For well over a century, business cycles have run an unceasing round. They have persisted through vast economic and social changes; they have withstood countless experiments in industry, agriculture, banking, industrial relations, and public policy; they have confounded forecasters without number, belied repeated prophecies of a 'new era of prosperity' and outlived repeated forebodings of 'chronic depression.'" What's changed today, more than half a century later?

Fortunately, the downturns don't usually last nearly as long as the upswings. Recessions, defined as two consecutive quarters of declines in the gross domestic product (GDP), occur from time to time. There have been 11 recessions since World War II (the last one in 2001), but these have lasted for shorter periods than in prior times. In the first half of the twentieth century, recessions lasted an average of 18 months; now they typically run only about eight months. The Great Depression, which was a monster recession, lasted 43 months!

The seriousness of recessions has also subsided in the past 50 years. The impact of a recession is judged by two things: loss of jobs and loss of income. During the recession of 1981–1982, the unemployment rate hit 10 percent; in 2001 it was 6 percent. In early 2008, the unemployment rate was just 5 percent. Similarly, the drop in national income (not your individual pocketbook) usually runs about 1 percent to 1.5 percent. Compare these two factors (job loss and income loss) with declines during the Great Depression—unemployment then was as high as 25 percent and income loss was at 30 percent.

Of course, these statistics are no comfort to you if you have been directly impacted by a job termination or mortgage foreclosure. Things couldn't be more serious or difficult to handle. For most people, the key to getting through difficult economic times is having some perspective, optimism, and good tax and financial strategies. This book is designed to provide you with steps you can take to ease your financial burdens and position yourself for the coming economic upturn.

### Congressional Efforts for Recovery

In February 2008, Congress passed the Economic Stimulus Act of 2008, a $152 billion tax package intended to jump-start the economy. The highlight of the package was the payment of rebate checks (called stimulus payments or checks), which totaled more than $100 billion in payments to an estimated 130 million taxpayers.

### What to Do Now

No checks were sent until 2007 income tax returns were filed. Taxpayers who requested filing extensions had to wait to receive their checks. Many who were not otherwise required to file 2007 income tax returns, such as low-income earners, certain seniors, and certain veterans, could still obtain refund checks by filing a return for this purpose (file a special version of Form 1040A for this purpose).

If you moved after filing your 2007 return and did not tell the IRS about your new address, your check may have gone undelivered (unless you used direct deposit for your income tax refund so that the stimulus check was also deposited directly into your bank or other designated account). Tell the IRS about your new address by filing Form 8822, Change of Address.

If you believe you are entitled to a payment but haven't received yours yet, you can call a special toll-free hotline created by the IRS to answer questions about stimulus payments at 866–234–2942.

Technically, the rebate checks are advance payments of an additional new tax credit on your 2008 taxes. They are not taxable; they are not added to your income for 2008; and they do not impact eligibility for any federal benefits, such as food stamps, Supplemental Security Income (SSI), or temporary assistance for needy families. If you received a rebate check but, based on your 2008 income, would not have been eligible for it, look at it as a gift from your Uncle Sam; you don't have to pay it back. If you did not receive a stimulus payment or the one you received based on your 2007 return was less than what you are eligible for based on your 2008 return, claim it as a tax credit on your 2008 return. Use an IRS worksheet in the instructions to the 2008 Form 1040 to reconcile these disparities.

The checks, which began to be sent in May 2008, were expected to produce positive results in the economy within about six months. Retail sales in May 2008 had already reflected the $57 billion in stimulus payments sent out during the month by having a solid 1 percent overall gain (compared with a 0.4 percent gain in April). And the Commerce Department reported in August that the spending of stimulus checks contributed to the 1.9 percent annual growth rate of the Gross Domestic Product (GDP). Is this a sign for optimism? Who knows?

### HOUSING RELIEF

In July 2008, Congress passed the Housing and Economic Recovery Act of 2008 to help those at risk of foreclosure avoid this result. The measure lets eligible homeowners trade their high-cost adjustable rate mortgages (ARMs) for lower-cost 30-year fixed rate loans. Participating lenders who want to have FHA loan guarantees can offer new mortgages on no more than 87 percent of the home's current value. For more details, see Chapter 2.

### What to Do Now

If you currently have an adjustable rate mortgage, check with your lender immediately to determine eligibility for the new program. If eligible—you must be financially able to pay the mortgage—you may be able to reduce the amount of your outstanding mortgage and replace your current mortgage with a fixed rate 30-year loan.

### INVESTOR AND TAXPAYER RELIEF

In October 2008, Congress passed the massive $700 billion Emergency Economic Stimulus Stabilization Act of 2008 to help loosen up the tight credit market by enabling the U.S. Treasury to buy "toxic" investments from certain financial institutions; this will help them clean up their books and start to lend money that will stimulate the economy. The measure also provides significant financial and tax help to consumers, including a temporary increase in FDIC limits and extensions of many favorable tax breaks through 2009.

# CHAPTER 2

# Managing Your Home

Today, almost 68 percent of Americans own homes. If you're one of them, your home may be your biggest financial asset, but it may mean much more to you than money. Your home is the place to hang your hat, raise a family, and be a part of a community.

Unfortunately, difficult economic times can make home ownership a financial challenge. These days, property taxes and the cost of heating and cooling a home are continually on the rise. Those with adjustable-rate mortgages (ARMs) may be facing a reset of their interest rates to be higher than they're currently paying. Many ARMs are subprime mortgages that were granted to individuals with credit histories that were not strong enough for a conventional mortgage. How can home ownership remain affordable?

Some homeowners have already experienced disaster; their homes have been lost to foreclosure. The federal government has provided some tax assistance to those afflicted. The tax assistance supplements a massive new housing law designed to prevent foreclosures, for example by encouraging lenders to refinance ARMs to fixed-rate loans while reducing the outstanding loan balance and by delaying the foreclosure of returning soldiers.

There are some steps you can take to reduce certain outlays for home ownership. Some of these measures have tax results. In this chapter, you will find information about:

- Home equity loans
- Refinancing existing mortgages
- Reverse mortgages

- Selling your home at a loss
- Foreclosures and repossessions
- Mortgage workouts
- Short sales
- Property tax relief
- Energy consumption for your home

For information about reducing monthly utility costs for your home, see Chapter 5.

## Home Equity Loans

Equity in your home is the amount you would pocket on a sale after paying off any existing mortgages. Equity in your home grows in two ways: by paying down an existing loan and by property appreciation (growth in property values).

### Example

Say you bought your home for $250,000, putting $50,000 cash down and obtaining a $200,000 mortgage (7 percent for 30 years); your starting equity is $50,000. Now, 10 years later, your loan balance is about $170,000. But property values have also increased in 10 years, so your original $250,000 home may now be worth $400,000 (even with recent property value declines). Your equity today is $230,000 ($400,000 – $170,000).

### *Tapping Out Home Equity*

If you have a home equity line of credit (HELOC) in place, you have an important source of borrowing. You can use the money in your line when and to the extent you choose; you don't have to tell the lender what you're using the money for. Many homeowners use their lines of credit to pay personal expenses, such as a child's education, a vacation, or credit card debt. Others use the money to make repairs or improvements to the home. A home equity line typically runs for a set number of years, such as 10 or 15 years. Thereafter, either it is renewed or whatever is outstanding becomes a fixed obligation (you can't borrow any more and must repay the remaining balance over a set period).

**CAUTION**

A home equity line of credit is secured by your home, so be cautious when you use the funds. If you fail to repay the loan, you risk losing your home.

With a HELOC, you pay interest only when and to the extent to you tap into your line. For instance, if you have a line of $100,000 and you use $10,000 to replace your roof, you pay interest on only the $10,000. As you pay off the

$10,000, you increase your credit line and reduce the amount on which you pay interest.

Home equity lines of credit typically bear a variable rate of interest, which may reset monthly or at some other interval. As interest rates rise, the cost of borrowing becomes more expensive. You can check prevailing interest rates on home equity lines of credit at various places, including Bankrate.com (www.bankrate.com) and MortgageLoan.com (www.mortgageloan.com).

---

### What to Do Now

If there is equity in your home and you don't yet have a home equity line of credit, you might consider obtaining one now. This will give you access to money if you need it quickly for any purpose, such as paying your property tax bill, making a repair to your home, or meeting a medical expense not covered by insurance. Usually, there are no costs associated with obtaining a home equity line of credit (but shop around for the best credit terms, including a waiver of any prepayment penalties if you settle your outstanding loan balance within a set time, and understand what costs you may have, if any).

---

### Limit on Deducting Home Equity Interest

While interest on a mortgage used to buy or build a home (called acquisition indebtedness) is fully deductible if the debt doesn't exceed $1 million, a more modest limit applies to home equity interest. Interest on a home equity line is deductible only if total borrowing does not exceed $100,000 ($50,000 for a married person filing a separate return).

However, this limit can be exceeded if the HELOC borrowing is used:

- To substantially improve the home (then it's part of home acquisition indebtedness).
- To refinance an existing acquisition debt.
- For investment or business purposes.

### Freezes on Home Equity Lines

Home equity lines are based in part on the value of the home. Generally, a bank will give you a home equity line so that total borrowing on the home (your primary mortgage if any, plus the full extent of the home equity line of credit) does not exceed a certain percentage of the home's value (typically about 75 percent). For example, if you home is worth $300,000 and your outstanding mortgage is $150,000, you may be able to get a home equity line of credit up to $75,000.

In today's environment, home prices in most areas are declining. This means that the equity against which the line was made has shrunk or disappeared. Beware of freezes on home equity lines. To protect themselves, some banks have opted to freeze existing home equity lines of credit by reducing borrowing power or canceling the lines altogether.

---

### What to Do Now

If you already have a HELOC, it is not clear whether a bank can impose a freeze on a line it has previously authorized. If you find yourself in this position, contact an attorney to discuss your options.

---

## Refinancing Existing Mortgages

Refinancing—getting a new mortgage to replace an old one—is a common practice of homeowners who want to accomplish certain goals, such as lowering their monthly payments or converting an adjustable-rate mortgage to a fixed-rate loan.

With interest rates low and a new law change in place, it makes sense for some homeowners to refinance their current mortgages now. Doing this will reduce the size of the monthly payments and the total amount of interest over the life of the loan.

### Improved Credit Rating

Interest rates on mortgages are usually based in part on a homeowner's credit rating (Fair Isaac Corporation's FICO score). If you had less than an excellent credit rating when you first obtained a mortgage but your credit rating has improved since then, you may qualify for a better interest rate. The higher your credit rating, the lower the interest rate you'll pay (see Table 2.1).

**TABLE 2.1** How FICO Scores Affect Mortgage Rates

| FICO Score | Interest Rate |
| --- | --- |
| 760–850 | 5.780% |
| 700–759 | 6.002% |
| 660–699 | 6.286% |
| 620–659 | 7.096% |
| 580–619 | 8.583% |
| 500–579 | 9.494% |

*Source:* Bankrate.com.

> ### Example
>
> A homeowner with a FICO score of 650 takes out a $200,000 30-year mortgage with an interest rate of 7 percent. Monthly payments are $1,330.64. Now assume that the homeowner's FICO score improves to 760 so he can obtain a mortgage at a 5.75 percent rate (the loan balance is now $195,000). His monthly payments for a new 30-year mortgage would be $1,226.77, for an annual savings of $1,246.20.

## REFINANCING JUMBO MORTGAGES

A jumbo mortgage is one that exceeds the limits for loans issued by certain federal agencies that issue mortgages. Interest on loans that fall below jumbo limits are generally lower than the rates for larger loans. Some homeowners who currently have jumbo loans may be able to refinance and obtain a new mortgage that is below the new jumbo loan limits, thereby cutting their interest rate and monthly mortgage payments. The U.S. Department of Housing and Urban Development (HUD) has predicted that a quarter of a million people in 2008 might be eligible to refinance their existing mortgages and benefit from lower interest rates.

Under the Economic Stimulus Act of 2008, the cap on the principal for mortgages issued by the Federal National Mortgage Association (Fannie Mae) and the Federal Home Loan Mortgage Corporation (Freddie Mac) is $729,750 (up from the prior $417,000 limit). The higher limit applies to mortgages originated between July 1, 2007, and December 31, 2008. It also applies to mortgages approved during this period that are used for home purchases completed after December 31, 2008.

The Federal Housing Administration (FHA) is allowed to issue higher loan amounts as well—up to 125 percent of the area median price (increased from the prior 95 percent limit). This means the new limit for most parts of the United States is $271,050 (up from the previous limit of $200,160). For 75 high-priced metropolitan areas in the country, including Los Angeles, New York City, San Francisco, and Washington, D.C., the limit is up to $729,750 (up from $362,790). The new limits went into effect on March 6, 2008, and apply only through December 31, 2008.

The Housing and Economic Recovery Act of 2008 permanently increases the cap on mortgages guaranteed by Fannie Mae and Freddie Mac to $625,000. The same limit applies for FHA-guaranteed mortgages. This means the old $417,000

> **CAUTION**
>
> The U.S. Department of Veterans Affairs (VA), which also issues mortgages, does not yet have a higher limit. Pending legislation (H.R. 5625) would allow a higher limit for mortgages issued through the end of 2008. Under proposed legislation, the VA's higher limit would match the FHA limits.

cap that had been scheduled to apply after December 31, 2008, will not; instead the cap will remain at $625,000.

## Tax Consequences of Refinancing

Whether interest on the new loan is fully deductible or subject to limits depends on the refinancing.

- If you merely replace the old loan, which was used to buy, build, or substantially improve the home, with a new loan that is not greater than the old loan balance, then all interest payments on the new loan are treated as arising from acquisition indebtedness. As long as the original loan was not more than $1 million, all of the interest is fully deductible.

- If you replace the old loan with a larger loan (you refinance the old loan balance *and* take out equity), the portion of interest related to the refinancing is acquisition indebtedness, while the tax treatment of interest on the balance depends on what the proceeds are used for. If the loan proceeds are used for a substantial renovation, then this portion is also acquisition indebtedness. But if the proceeds are used for other personal purposes, such as taking a vacation or paying education or medical bills, then interest is deductible only if the proceeds don't exceed $100,000.

## Reverse Mortgages

Ever hear the expression "House rich, cash poor"? It means that on paper you may have considerable wealth because of the value of your home, but it does you little good. You don't have the cash needed to pay your expenses. Those who are at least 62 years old have an option to stay in their home but cash out on some of their equity by obtaining a reverse mortgage. The money can be used for anything, such as paying property taxes, heating costs and home repairs, medical expenses, or a vacation.

With a reverse mortgage, the lender pays you, usually as a lump sum or as a line of credit you can draw upon. There's no repayment requirement while you continue to live in the home. If you sell the home or when you die, then the lender collects what's outstanding (principal plus interest); anything left over belongs to you (or your estate). To qualify for a reverse mortgage, you must:

- Be at least 62 years old,
- Own and live in your home (it must be your principal residence),

- Have no mortgage or one so small that can be paid off with the proceeds of the reverse mortgage, and
- Receive consumer counseling from an agency approved by the U.S. Housing and Urban Development Department.

The amount of the reverse mortgage you can obtain depends on several factors: Your age, the value of your home, and FHA mortgage limits in your area. As a rule of thumb, the older you are and the more valuable your home, the larger the reverse mortgage. Use an online calculator from AARP (www.rmaarp.com) to see approximately what you could expect from a reverse mortgage.

The new housing act limits loan origination fees on reverse mortgages to 2 percent of any loan up to $200,000, plus 1 percent on any loan over that limit, up to a maximum of $6,000. The new law also prohibits the lender from forcing you into purchasing a financial or insurance product as a condition of qualifying for a reverse mortgage.

There are two federally-insured reverse mortgage programs: "Home Equity Conversion Mortgage" (HECM) (www.hud.gov/offices/hsg/sfh/hecm/hecmhomc.cfm) and Home Keeper Mortgage from Fannie Mae (https://www.efanniemae.com/sf/mortgageproducts/reverse/homekeeper.jsp).

## Selling Your Home at a Loss

Selling a home in today's real estate environment can be challenging. Prices in many areas are declining, and homes are remaining on the market longer and longer. Motivated sellers may be forced to discount homes even more than prevailing prices in order to secure qualified buyers.

If you can sell your home, it may not fetch a price that equals what you put into the home. Fix-up costs and real estate agent's fees to sell the home eat into what you net.

### Tax Consequences of Home Sale

If you have a loss on the sale of your home, you cannot deduct it. A home is a personal asset, even though you may have hoped or expected it to appreciate in value and prove profitable in the long run. No tax loss is allowed on the sale of a personal asset. (The rules for a short sale, where the sale price is insufficient to cover the full outstanding balance of the mortgage, are discussed later in this chapter.) You do not have to report the sale on your tax return if you have a loss.

#### FIGURE GAIN OR LOSS

Gain or loss on the sale of a home is the difference between the amount realized on the sale (see Figure 2.1) and your adjusted basis in the home (see Figure 2.2).

Worksheet. **Gain (or Loss), Exclusion, and Taxable Gain**

| | | |
|---|---|---|
| **Part 1** – Gain (or Loss) on Sale | | |
| 1. | Selling price of home . . . . . . . . . . . . . . . . . . . . . . . . . . . . . . . . . . . . . . . . . . . . . . . . . . . . . | **1.** _____ |
| 2. | Selling expenses . . . . . . . . . . . . . . . . . . . . . . . . . . . . . . . . . . . . . . . . . . . . . . . . . . . . . . . . | **2.** _____ |
| 3. | Subtract line 2. from line 1 . . . . . . . . . . . . . . . . . . . . . . . . . . . . . . . . . . . . . . . . . . . . . . . . | **3.** _____ |
| 4. | Adjusted basis of home sold (from Figure 2.2) . . . . . . . . . . . . . . . . . . . . . . . . . . . . . . . . . . | **4.** _____ |
| 5. | Subtract line 4 from line 3. This is the **gain (or loss)** on the sale. If this is a loss, stop here . . . . . . . . . . . . . . . . . . | **5.** _____ |
| **Part 2** – Exclusion and Taxable Gain | | |
| 6. | Enter any depreciation allowed or allowable on the property for peridos after May 6, 1997. If none, enter zoro | **6.** _____ |
| 7. | Subtract line 6 from line 5. (If the result is less than zero, enter zero.) . . . . . . . . . . . . . . . . . . . . . . | **7.** _____ |
| 8. | If you quality to exclude gain on the sale, enter your maximum exclusion. If you do not quality to exclude gain, enter -0- . . . . . . . . . . . . . . . . . . . . . . . . . . . . . . . . . . . . . . . . . . . . . . . . . . . . . . . . | **8.** _____ |
| 9. | Enter the smaller of line 7 or line 8. This is your exclusion . . . . . . . . . . . . . . . . . . . . . . . . . . . . . . . . . . . | **9.** _____ |
| 10. | Subtract line 9 from line 5. This is your **taxable gain**. Report it on Line 1 or B or Schedule Dcepending on how long you owned the residence. Use Form 6252, if reporting the gain on the settlement sale method; enter any exclusion from Line 9 on Line 15 of Form 6252. If the amount on this line is zero, do not report the sale or exclusion on you tax return. If the amount on Line 6 is more than zero, complete Line 11 . . . . . . . . . . . . . . . . . . . . | **10.** _____ |
| 11. | Enter the smaller of line 5 or line 10. Enter this amount on line 12 of the *Unrecaptured Section 1250 Gain Worksheet* in the instructions for Schedule D (Form 1040) . . . . . . . . . . | **11.** _____ |

**FIGURE 2.1** Gain or Loss

## CONVERTING YOUR HOME TO RENTAL PROPERTY

If you are trying to sell your home and home prices are continuing to slip, you can take action that will allow you to deduct some of your loss. You can convert your personal residence into rental property and put the home up for rent at a fair price (you'll have to live elsewhere).

Worksheet. **Adjusted Basis of Home Sold**

| | | |
|---|---|---|
| 1. | Enter the purchase price of the home sold. (If you filed Form 2119 when you originaly acquire d that home to postpone gain on the sale of a previous home before May 7, 1997, enter the adjusted basis of the new home from that Form 2119.) . . . . . . . . . . . . . . . . . . . . . . . . . . . . . . . . . . . . . . . . . . . . . . . . . | **1.** _____ |
| 2. | Seller paid points for home bought alter 1990. Do not include any seller-paid points you already subtracted to arrive at the amount entered on line 1 . . . . . . . . . . . . . . . . . . . . . . | **2.** _____ |
| 3. | Subtract line 2 from line 1 . . . . . . . . . . . . . . . . . . . . . . . . . . . . . . . . . . . . . . . . . . . . . . | **3.** _____ |
| 4. | Settlement fees or closing costs. If line 1 includes the adjusted basis of the new home from Form 2119, go to line 6. | |
| a. | Abstract and recording fees . . . . . . . . . . . . . . . . . . . . . . . . . . . . . . . . . . . . . . . . **4a.** _____ | |
| b. | Legal fees (including title search and preparing documents) . . . . . . . . . . . . . . . . . . . . . . **4b.** _____ | |
| c. | Surveys . . . . . . . . . . . . . . . . . . . . . . . . . . . . . . . . . . . . . . . . . . . . . . . . . . . . . . **4c.** _____ | |
| d. | Title insurance . . . . . . . . . . . . . . . . . . . . . . . . . . . . . . . . . . . . . . . . . . . . . . . . . **4d.** _____ | |
| e. | Transfer or stamp taxes . . . . . . . . . . . . . . . . . . . . . . . . . . . . . . . . . . . . . . . . . . . **4e.** _____ | |
| f. | Amounts that the seller owed that you agreed to pay (back taxes or interest, recording or mortgage fees, and sales commissions) . . . . . . . . . . . . . . . . . . . . . . . . . . . . . . . . . . . **4f.** _____ | |
| g. | Other . . . . . . . . . . . . . . . . . . . . . . . . . . . . . . . . . . . . . . . . . . . . . . . . . . . . . . . **4g.** _____ | |
| 5. | Add lines 4a through 4g . . . . . . . . . . . . . . . . . . . . . . . . . . . . . . . . . . . . . . . . . . . . . . . . . | **5.** _____ |
| 6. | Cost of additions and improvements. Do not include any additions and improvements included on line 1 . . . . | **6.** _____ |
| 7. | Special tax assessments paid for local improvements, such as streets and sidewalks . . . . . . . . . . . . . . | **7.** _____ |
| 8. | Other increases to basis . . . . . . . . . . . . . . . . . . . . . . . . . . . . . . . . . . . . . . . . . . . . . . . . . | **8.** _____ |
| 9. | Add lines 3, 5, 6, 7, and 6 . . . . . . . . . . . . . . . . . . . . . . . . . . . . . . . . . . . . . . . . . . . . . . | **9.** _____ |
| 10. | Depreciation, related to the business use or rental of the home, claimed (for allowable) . . . . . . **10.** _____ | |
| 11. | Other decreases to basis . . . . . . . . . . . . . . . . . . . . . . . . . . . . . . . . . . . . . . . . . **11.** _____ | |
| 12. | Add lines 10 and 11 . . . . . . . . . . . . . . . . . . . . . . . . . . . . . . . . . . . . . . . . . . . . . . . . . . . **12.** _____ | |
| 13. | **ADJUSTED BASIS OF HOME SOLD.** Subtract line 12 from line 9. Enter here and on Worksheet 29-3, line. 4. | **13.** _____ |

**FIGURE 2.2** Your Home's Adjusted Basis

*Transaction 1: A sale of property.* Gain or loss is the difference between the adjusted basis and the amount realized (including any canceled debt up to the fair market value of the property).

*Transaction 2: The receipt of ordinary income for cancellation of the debt.* You generally have cancellation of debt income equal to the excess of the canceled debt over the fair market value of the property (unless the tax-free exclusion rule applies, as explained later in the chapter for mortgage workouts).

## Example

A homeowner bought a residence for $285,000. He paid $57,000 (20 percent down) and took out a mortgage loan for $228,000 for which he was personally liable. When the loan balance had been reduced to $200,000, he defaulted on the mortgage. The lender accepted his voluntary conveyance of the property in full satisfaction of the loan; the home was worth $196,000 at the time. He has a loss of $89,000 (the difference between his adjusted basis of $285,000 and the home's fair market value of $196,000). The loss is not deductible, because the home was held for personal use. He also has income on the cancellation of the loan, because the amount of the debt ($200,000) exceeded the fair market value of the home ($196,000) by $4,000. This amount is taxable unless the homeowner qualifies for the special break explained later in this chapter.

### Tax Reporting

The lender will report the foreclosure to you and to the Internal Revenue Service (IRS). If the mortgage is foreclosed or the home is repossessed, or you simply abandon the property, the lender will issue a Form 1099-A, Acquisition or Abandonment of Secured Property.

If the lender cancels some or all of the outstanding loan balance and it is at least $600, the lender will issue Form 1099-C, Cancellation of Debt. Starting in 2009, Form 1099-C will include the lender's telephone number, making it easier for the debtor to contact the lender if any information on the form is in dispute.

## Mortgage Workouts

As adjustable-rate mortgages reset to higher interest rates, homeowners may have difficulty making the monthly payments. Some homeowners may choose to sell their homes to get out from under their mortgage obligations. Others may try to work things out with the lender to reduce the monthly payments. Lenders are often willing to restructure the debt so they don't have to go through foreclosure.

## What to Do Now

If you're having difficulty making your mortgage payments, don't wait until your home goes into foreclosure to take action. As soon as possible see what help may be available to you from Uncle Sam:

- *FHASecure.* In August 2007, a new federal program was created to help homeowners avert foreclosure. FHASecure (www.fha.gov and click on "FHASecure") gives the Federal Housing Administration (FHA) the ability to offer refinancing to homeowners who have good credit histories but who cannot afford their current payments. The FHA estimates that it will help more than 300,000 families to refinance their mortgages and keep their homes.

- *HOPE NOW.* In February 2008, the Economic Stimulus Act created a cooperative effort among mortgage counselors, servicers, investors, and lenders called HOPE NOW (www.hopenow.com) to help homeowners refinance into new mortgages or receive mortgage modifications. This program covers about 90 percent of the subprime mortgage market.

- *FHA relief.* In July 2008, the Housing and Economic Recovery Act created a comprehensive program for homeowners to convert their high-interest rate adjustable mortgages into affordable 30-year fixed rate loans. This program for participating lenders reduces the outstanding loan balance so the new loan is based on the home's current market value (which may be below its original value).

A number of states have enacted their own relief for homeowners. For example, 20 states have created intervention programs, 14 states have task forces working on the home mortgage situation, 13 states have counseling hotlines, and 9 states have set up funds for emergency loans totaling $450 million. Some states have enacted tighter underwriting requirements to avert the situation in which numerous homeowners can't make their payments. Ohio, for example, has a bevy of attorneys working for free to represent homeowners in modifying their mortgages with lenders.

---

If your lender agrees to accept a reduced payment by forgiving some of the loan principal, usually this debt forgiveness is taxable. However, under the Mortgage Debt Relief Act of 2007, there is a special tax break for debt forgiveness (called discharge of indebtedness) related to a principal home in 2007 through 2012.

Up to $2 million of debt forgiveness is tax free if certain conditions are met:

- The loan that is reduced must be secured by a principal residence.
- The loan must have been incurred for the purchase, construction, or substantial improvement of the principal residence.

### Partial Tax-Free Relief

If only part of the loan is qualified principal residence indebtedness, only part of debt forgiveness may be tax free. There's an ordering rule, which limits the exclusion (the amount that's tax free) to the amount of the discharged debt that exceeds the amount that is not qualified debt. In other words, only a discharge in excess of nonqualified debt can produce any tax-free income; the discharge must be offset by nonqualified debt first.

---

**Example**

A home is secured by a debt of $1 million, $800,000 of which is qualified principal residence debt. The home is sold for $700,000 and the lender discharges $300,000. Only $100,000 of the discharged debt is tax free ($300,000 discharged debt minus $200,000 of nonqualified debt). The balance, $200,000, is potentially taxable.

---

### Basis of the Home

The basis of the home must be reduced by any debt forgiveness that is not recognized as income. The basis reduction will increase the amount of gain realized on the future sale of the home. However, as a practical matter, if you do have a gain on a later sale, all or most of it may be tax free because of the home sale exclusion (you are not taxed on gain up to $250,000, or $500,000 on a joint return, if you sell a home that was owned and used as your principal residence for two out of five years before the date of sale).

> **CAUTION**
> Discharged debt related to investment property or a vacation home is taxable. It does not qualify for this special tax-free treatment available to principal residences in 2007–2012.

### Mechanics of Debt Forgiveness

When a lender forgives debt, you will receive a Form 1099-C, Cancellation of Debt. This lets the IRS know the amount of debt forgiveness that is potentially taxable. Then, if you meet the conditions for tax-free treatment of this debt, you must complete Form 982 (see Figure 2.3), Reduction of Tax Attributes Due to Discharge of Indebtedness (and Section 1082 Basis Adjustment). You only need to complete three lines on the form:

- Line 1e, which is the discharge of qualified principal residence indebtedness (assuming you did not experience the discharge through bankruptcy but merely had debt forgiven by the lender).
- Line 2, which is the total amount of discharged indebtedness excluded from gross income.
- Line 10b, which is the smaller of the amount on line 2 or the basis of the home (generally your cost plus capital improvements to the home).

<table>
<tr><td>Form 982<br/>(Rev. February 2008)<br/>Department of the Treasury<br/>Internal Revenue Service</td><td>Reduction of Tax Attributes Due to Discharge of Indebtedness (and Section 1082 Basis Adjustment)<br/>▶ Attach this form to your income tax return.</td><td>OMB No. 1545-0046<br/><br/>Attachment<br/>Sequence No. 94</td></tr>
</table>

| Name shown on return | Identifying number |
|---|---|

---

**Part I**   General Information (see instructions)

**1** Amount excluded is due to (check applicable box(es)):

**a** Discharge of indebtedness in a title 11 case . . . . . . . . . . . . . . . . . ☐

**b** Discharge of indebtedness to the extent insolvent (not in a title 11 case) . . . . . . . ☐

**c** Discharge of qualified farm indebtedness . . . . . . . . . . . . . . . . . ☐

**d** Discharge of qualified real property business indebtedness . . . . . . . . . . . . ☐

**e** Discharge of qualified principal residence indebtedness . . . . . . . . . . . . . ☐

**2** Total amount of discharged indebtedness excluded from gross income . . . . . . | **2** |

**3** Do you elect to treat all real property described in section 1221(a)(1), relating to property held for sale to customers in the ordinary course of a trade or business, as if it were depreciable property? . . . . ☐ Yes ☐ No

---

Form 982 (Rev. 2-2008)                                                                 Page **2**

# General Instructions

*Section references are to the Internal Revenue Code unless otherwise noted.*

## What's New

• The Mortgage Forgiveness Debt Relief Act of 2007 allows individuals to exclude from gross income any discharges of qualified principal residence indebtedness. This exclusion applies to discharges made after 2006 and before 2010 and is entered on line 1e. Additionally, the basis of the principal residence must be reduced (but not below zero) by the amount excluded from gross income. The basis reduction is entered on line 10b. See *How To Complete the Form* below for more information.

• The exclusion for discharge of certain indebtedness of a qualified individual by reason of Hurricane Katrina expired for discharges after 2006.

## Purpose of Form

Generally, the amount by which you benefit from the discharge of indebtedness is included in your gross income. However, under certain circumstances described in section 108, you may exclude the amount of discharged indebtedness from your gross income.

You must file Form 982 to report the exclusion and the reduction of certain tax attributes either dollar for dollar or 33⅓ cents per dollar (as explained below).

 *Certain individuals may need to complete only a few lines on Form 982. For example, if you are completing this form because of a discharge of indebtedness on a personal loan (such as a car loan or credit card debt) or a loan for the purchase of your principal residence, follow the chart below to see which lines you need to complete.*

## How To Complete the Form

| IF the discharged debt you are excluding is . . . | THEN follow these steps . . . |
|---|---|
| Qualified principal residence indebtedness | **1.** Be sure to read the definition of qualified principal residence indebtedness in the instructions for line 1e on page 4. Part or all of your debt may not qualify for the exclusion on line 1e but may qualify for one of the other exclusions.<br/><br/>**2.** Check the box on line 1e.<br/><br/>**3.** Include on line 2 the amount of discharged qualified principal residence indebtedness that is excluded from gross income. Any amount in excess of the excluded amount may result in taxable income. See *Canceled Debts* in Pub. 525, Taxable and Nontaxable Income, for more information. If you disposed of your residence, you may also be required to recognize a gain on its disposition. For details, see Pub. 523, Selling Your Home.<br/><br/>**4.** Enter on line 10b the smaller of (a) the amount of qualified principal residence indebtedness included on line 2 or (b) the basis (generally, your cost plus improvements) of your principal residence.<br/><br/>⚠ **CAUTION** *If the discharge occurs in a title 11 case, you may not check box 1e. You must check box 1a and complete the form as discussed below under A nonbusiness debt. If you are insolvent (and not in a title 11 case), you can elect to follow the insolvency rules by checking box 1b instead of box 1e and completing the form as discussed below under A nonbusiness debt.* |
| A nonbusiness debt (other than qualified principal residence indebtedness, such as a car loan or credit card debt) | Follow these instructions if you do not have any of the tax attributes listed in Part II (other than a basis in nondepreciable property). Otherwise, follow the instructions for *Any other debt* below.<br/><br/>**1.** Check the box on line 1a if the discharge was made in a title 11 case (see the definition on page 3) or the box on line 1b if the discharge occurred when you were insolvent (see the definition in the instructions for line 1b on page 3).<br/><br/>**2.** Include on line 2 the amount of discharged nonbusiness debt that is excluded from gross income. If you were insolvent, do not include more than the excess of your liabilities over the fair market value of your assets.<br/><br/>**3.** Include on line 10a the smallest of (a) the basis of your nondepreciable property, (b) the amount of the nonbusiness debt included on line 2, or (c) the excess of the aggregate bases of the property and the amount of money you held immediately after the discharge over your aggregate liabilities immediately after the discharge. |
| Any other debt | Use *Part I* of Form 982 to indicate why any amount received from the discharge of indebtedness should be excluded from gross income and the amount excluded.<br/><br/>Use *Part II* to report your reduction of tax attributes. The reduction must be made in the following order unless you check the box on line 1d for qualified real property business indebtedness or make the election on line 5 to reduce basis of depreciable property first.<br/><br/>**1.** Any net operating loss (NOL) for the tax year of the discharge (and any NOL carryover to that year) (dollar for dollar);<br/><br/>**2.** Any general business credit carryover to or from the tax year of the discharge (33 ⅓ cents per dollar);<br/><br/>**3.** Any minimum tax credit as of the beginning of the tax year immediately after the tax year of the discharge (33 ⅓ cents per dollar);<br/><br/>**4.** Any net capital loss for the tax year of the discharge (and any capital loss carryover to that tax year) (dollar for dollar);<br/><br/>**5.** The basis of property (dollar for dollar);<br/><br/>**6.** Any passive activity loss (dollar for dollar) and credit (33⅓ cents per dollar) carryovers from the tax year of the discharge; and<br/><br/>**7.** Any foreign tax credit carryover to or from the tax year of the discharge (33 ⅓ cents per dollar).<br/><br/>Use *Part III* to exclude from gross income under section 1081(b) any amounts of income attributable to the transfer of property described in that section. |

**FIGURE 2.3** Form 982

## Definitions

**Title 11 case.** A *title 11 case* is a case under title 11 of the United States Code (relating to bankruptcy), but only if you are under the jurisdiction of the court in the case and the discharge of indebtedness is granted by the court or is under a plan approved by the court.

**Discharge of indebtedness.** The term *discharge of indebtedness* conveys forgiveness of, or release from, an obligation to repay.

## When To File

File Form 982 with your federal income tax return for a year a discharge of indebtedness is excluded from your income under section 108(a).

The election to reduce the basis of depreciable property under section 108(b)(5) and the election made on line 1d of Part I regarding the discharge of qualified real property business indebtedness must be made on a timely-filed return (including extensions) and may be revoked only with the consent of the IRS.

If you timely filed your tax return without making either of these elections, you can still make either election by filing an amended return within 6 months of the due date of the return (excluding extensions). Write "Filed pursuant to section 301.9100-2" on the amended return and file it at the same place you filed the original return.

## Specific Instructions

### Part I

**Lines 1a through 1c.** If you check any of these boxes, you may elect, by completing line 5, to apply all or a part of the debt discharge amount to first reduce the basis of depreciable property (including property you elected on line 3 to treat as depreciable property). Any balance of the debt discharge amount will then be applied to reduce the tax attributes in the order listed on lines 6 through 13 (excluding line 10b). For lines 1a and 1b only, if after reducing the tax attributes there remains a balance of the debt discharge, the excess is permanently excluded from your gross income. You must attach a statement describing the transactions that resulted in the reduction in basis and identifying the property for which you reduced the basis. If you do not make the election on line 5, complete lines 6 through 13 (excluding line 10b) to reduce your attributes. See section 1017(b)(2) and (c) for limitations of reductions in basis on line 10a.

**Line 1b.** The insolvency exclusion does not apply to any discharge that occurs in a title 11 case. It also does not apply to a discharge of qualified principal residence indebtedness (see the instructions for line 1e on page 4) unless you elect to have the insolvency exclusion apply instead of the exclusion for qualified principal residence indebtedness.

Check the box on line 1b if the discharge of indebtedness occurred while you were insolvent. You were insolvent to the extent that your liabilities exceeded the fair market value (FMV) of your assets immediately before the discharge. For details, see Pub. 908, Bankruptcy Tax Guide.

**Example.** You were released from your obligation to pay your credit card debt in the amount of $5,000. The FMV of your assets immediately before the discharge was $7,000 and your liabilities were $10,000. You were insolvent to the extent of $3,000 ($10,000 of total liabilities minus $7,000 of total assets). Check the box on line 1b and include $3,000 on line 2.

**Line 1c.** Check this box if the income you exclude is from the discharge of qualified farm indebtedness. The exclusion relating to qualified farm indebtedness does not apply to a discharge that occurs in a title 11 case or to the extent you were insolvent.

*Qualified farm indebtedness* is the amount of indebtedness incurred directly in connection with the trade or business of farming. In addition, 50% or more of your aggregate gross receipts for the 3 tax years preceding the tax year in which the discharge of such indebtedness occurs must be from the trade or business of farming. For more information, see sections 108(g) and 1017(b)(4).

The discharge must have been made by a qualified person. Generally, a *qualified person* is an individual, organization, etc., who is actively and regularly engaged in the business of lending money. This person cannot be related to you, be the person from whom you acquired the property, or be a person who receives a fee with respect to your investment in the property. Also, a qualified person includes any federal, state, or local government or agency or instrumentality thereof.

If you checked line 1c and did not make the election on line 5, the debt discharge amount will be applied to reduce the tax attributes in the order listed on lines 6 through 9. Any remaining amount will be applied to reduce the tax attributes in the order listed on lines 11a through 13.

You cannot exclude more than the total of your: (a) tax attributes (determined under section 108(g)(3)(B)); and (b) basis of property used or held for use in a trade or business or for the production of income. Any excess is included in income.

**Line 1d.** If you check this box, the discharge of qualified real property business indebtedness is applied to reduce the basis of depreciable real property on line 4. The exclusion relating to qualified real property business indebtedness does not apply to a discharge that occurs in a title 11 case or to the extent you were insolvent.

*Qualified real property business indebtedness* is indebtedness (other than qualified farm indebtedness) that: (a) is incurred or assumed in connection with real property used in a trade or business; (b) is secured by that real property; and (c) with respect to which you have made an election under this provision. This provision does not apply to a corporation (other than an S corporation).

Indebtedness incurred or assumed after 1992 is not qualified real property business indebtedness unless it is either (a) debt incurred to refinance a qualified real property business indebtedness incurred or assumed before 1993 (but only to the extent the amount of such debt does not exceed the amount of debt being refinanced) or (b) qualified acquisition indebtedness.

*Qualified acquisition indebtedness* is (a) debt incurred or assumed to acquire, construct, reconstruct, or substantially improve real property that is secured by such debt; and (b) debt resulting from the refinancing of qualified acquisition indebtedness, to the extent the amount of such debt does not exceed the amount of debt being refinanced.

You cannot exclude more than the excess of the outstanding principal amount of the debt (immediately before the discharge) over the net FMV (as of that time) of the property securing the debt, reduced by the outstanding principal amount of other qualified real property business indebtedness secured by that property (as of that time). The amount excluded is further limited to the aggregate adjusted basis (as of the first day of the next tax year, or if earlier, the date of disposition) of depreciable real property (determined after any reductions under sections 108(b) and (g)) you held immediately before the discharge (other than property acquired in contemplation of the discharge). Any excess is included in income.

**FIGURE 2.3** *(Continued)*

**Line 1e.** Check this box if the income you exclude is from discharge of qualified principal residence indebtedness. Also, be sure you complete line 2 and line 10b. However, if the discharge occurs in a title 11 case, you must check the box on line 1a and not this box. If you are insolvent (and not in a title 11 case), you can elect to follow the insolvency rules by checking box 1b instead of checking this box.

*Principal residence.* Your *principal residence* is the home where you ordinarily live most of the time. You can have only one principal residence at any one time.

*Qualified principal residence indebtedness.* This indebtedness is a mortgage you took out to buy, build, or substantially improve your principal residence. It also must be secured by your principal residence. If the amount of your original mortgage is more than the cost of your principal residence plus the cost of any substantial improvements, only the debt that is **not** more than the cost of your principal residence plus improvements is qualified principal residence indebtedness. Any debt secured by your principal residence that you use to refinance qualified principal residence indebtedness is treated as qualified principal residence indebtedness, but only up to the amount of the old mortgage principal just before the refinancing. Any additional debt you incurred to substantially improve your principal residence is also treated as qualified principal residence indebtedness.

*Amount eligible for the exclusion.* The exclusion applies only to debt discharged after 2006 and before 2010. The maximum amount you can treat as qualified principal residence indebtedness is $2 million ($1 million if married filing separately). You cannot exclude from gross income discharge of qualified principal residence indebtedness if the discharge was for services performed for the lender or on account of any other factor not directly related to a decline in the value of your residence or to your financial condition.

*Ordering rule.* If only a part of a loan is qualified principal residence indebtedness, the exclusion applies only to the extent the amount discharged exceeds the amount of the loan (immediately before the discharge) that is **not** qualified principal residence indebtedness. For example, assume your principal residence is secured by a debt of $1 million, of which $800,000 is qualified principal residence indebtedness. If your residence is sold for $700,000 and $300,000 of debt is discharged, only $100,000 of the debt discharged may be excluded (the $300,000 that was discharged minus the $200,000 of nonqualified debt). The remaining $200,000 of nonqualified debt may qualify in whole or in part for one of the other exclusions, such as the insolvency exclusion.

**Line 2.** Enter the total amount excluded from your gross income due to discharge of indebtedness under section 108. If you checked any box on lines 1b through 1e, do not enter more than the limit explained in the instructions for those lines. If you checked line 1a, 1b, or 1c, this amount will not necessarily equal the total reductions on lines 5 through 13 (excluding line 10b) because the debt discharge amount may exceed the total tax attributes.

See section 382(l)(5) for a special rule regarding a reduction of a corporation's tax attributes after certain ownership changes.

**Line 3.** You may elect under section 1017(b)(3)(E) to treat all real property held primarily for sale to customers in the ordinary course of a trade or business as if it were depreciable property. This election does not apply to the discharge of qualified real property business indebtedness. To make the election, check the "Yes" box.

**Part II**

**Line 7.** If you have a general business credit carryover to or from the tax year of the discharge, you must reduce that carryover by 33⅓ cents for each dollar excluded from gross income. See Form 3800, General Business Credit, for more details on the general business credit, including rules for figuring any carryforward or carryback.

**Line 10a.** In the case of a title 11 case or insolvency (except when an election under section 108(b)(5) is made), the reduction in basis is limited to the aggregate of the basis of your property immediately after the discharge over the aggregate of your liabilities immediately after the discharge.

**Line 10b.** If box 1e is checked, enter the smaller of:

● The part of line 2 that is attributable to the exclusion of qualified principal residence indebtedness, or

● The basis of your principal residence.

**Part III**

**Adjustment to basis.** Unless it specifically states otherwise, the corporation, by filing this form, agrees to apply the general rule for adjusting the basis of property (as described in Regulations section 1.1082-3(b)).

If the corporation desires to have the basis of its property adjusted in a manner different from the general rule, it must attach a request for variation from the general rule. The request must show the precise method used and the allocation of amounts.

Consent to the request for variation from the general rule will be effective only if it is incorporated in a closing agreement entered into by the corporation and the Commissioner of Internal Revenue under the rules of section 7121. If no agreement is entered into, then the general rule will apply in determining the basis of the corporation's property.

**Paperwork Reduction Act Notice.** We ask for the information on this form to carry out the Internal Revenue laws of the United States. We are required to give us the information. We need it to ensure that you are complying with these laws and to allow us to figure and collect the right amount of tax.

You are not required to provide the information requested on a form that is subject to the Paperwork Reduction Act unless the form displays a valid OMB control number. Books or records relating to a form or its instructions must be retained as long as their contents may become material in the administration of any Internal Revenue law. Generally, tax returns and return information are confidential, as required by section 6103.

The time needed to complete and file this form will vary depending on individual circumstances. The estimated burden for individual taxpayers filing this form is approved under OMB control number 1545-0074 and is included in the estimates shown in the instructions for their individual income tax return. The estimated burden for all other taxpayers who file this form is shown as follows: **Recordkeeping,** 5 hr., 58 min.; **Learning about the law or the form,** 2 hr., 17 min.; **Preparing and sending the form to the IRS,** 2 hr., 28 min.

If you have comments concerning the accuracy of these time estimates or suggestions for making this form simpler, we would be happy to hear from you. See the instructions for the tax return with which this form is filed.

**FIGURE 2.3** (*Continued*)

## INSOLVENCY OR BANKRUPTCY

If a homeowner's debt is discharged at a time when he or she is insolvent (the homeowner's total liabilities exceed his or her assets), then the debt forgiven is not taxable. This rule applies to any home, including a vacation home or investment property.

**What to Do Now**

If you are falling behind in your mortgage, don't wait until the situation is dire. Immediately contact the lender to discuss your situation. Maybe you're experiencing a temporary problem, such as a medical condition that has kept you out of work but you expect to be better soon.

If the reason for your trouble is that your adjustable mortgage has re-set or is about to re-set at an interest rate too high to be affordable, your lender may participate in a new federal program to reduce and convert your debt into an affordable fixed rate loan. Recognize that some lenders may not be in a position to offer any restructuring. They may have sold your mortgage to the secondary market (who knows who is holding your mortgage now) and are powerless to help you.

## Short Sales

The term *short sale* is often used in connection with stock traders who effectively bet that a stock will decline in value. However, short sales have a different meaning when it comes to real estate. A short sale occurs when the sale price of the home is lower than the outstanding mortgage balance. The lender agrees to let the home pass to the new owner; the lender takes the loss while the new owner receives good title and is not obligated in any way to make good on the former owner's loan.

### Tax Consequences of Short Sale

From the seller's perspective, the amount of the mortgage that's forgiven is discharge of indebtedness income. Like such income incurred during a mortgage workout, discharge of indebtedness income on a short sale in 2007 through 2009 can be tax free (see the rules in the preceding section).

## Property Tax Relief

Localities are hungry for revenue, and one of their main sources is property taxes. In many areas, these taxes have been growing at unbelievably high rates each year. How is a homeowner to keep up and afford to remain in the neighborhood?

Homeowners who itemize their deductions can write off their property taxes, which helps to lower their income tax bills each year. This deduction applies to your primary residence as well as any vacation home(s). The value of the deduction for property taxes depends on the homeowner's tax bracket, so a $1,000 deduction saves a homeowner only $250 if he or she is in the 25 percent tax bracket. *Note:* For 2008 and 2009 (unless Congress extends the law), homeowners who don't itemize can deduct property taxes up to $500 ($1,000 on a joint return).

Beyond the basic tax deduction for paying property taxes, there may be special relief for certain homeowners.

## Relief Programs

Some localities offer a variety of tax relief programs for special homeowners. Here are some options:

- *Property tax exemptions.* Localities may reduce the property taxes on homes held by certain individuals, such as senior citizens, disabled individuals, and veterans.

- *State homeowners tax relief programs.* In New York, for example, there is the School Tax Relief (STAR) program (www.orps.state.ny.us/star). All homeowners in New York are eligible for some relief with respect to their primary residences; there is enhanced relief for seniors with income below set amounts (a similar program applies in Pennsylvania). Other states, such as Maine and New Hampshire, offer relief only to those with income below set amounts.

- *Property tax freezes.* Some localities delay the payment of any property taxes for certain homeowners until the home is sold. For instance, in South Dakota, the freeze applies to a homeowner age 70 or older who meets residency and income tests. The unpaid taxes are a lien on the property and must be paid, plus interest, when the home is transferred (sold or inherited). Others, such as New Jersey, freeze the property taxes for low-income seniors and disabled individuals to a base amount; eligible homeowners receive a rebate of taxes over the base amount.

- *Rebates or reductions.* Volunteer emergency responders may be given a cut in their property taxes or money back because of their volunteer work for the community. The tax implications of these rebates or reductions are explained next.

## Income Tax Relief for Volunteers

For 2008, 2009, and 2010, volunteer emergency responders such as firefighters and emergency medical technicians (EMTs) can exclude from income up to $360 per year ($30 per month multiplied by the number of months for providing services as a volunteer emergency responder during the year) in property or income tax cuts by state or local government. However, any charitable deduction for expenses paid by a responder in connection with performing these services must be reduced by any payment excluded from income.

### What to Do Now

Check into property tax relief that may apply to you by contacting your municipality. You usually must fill out paperwork with your city or town to enjoy this tax relief.

### Reduced Assessments

You may be overpaying your property taxes. These taxes are based on the assessed value of your home, and as many as 50 percent to 60 percent of homes are overassessed. Your home may be overvalued for various reasons:

- *Errors.* Your municipality may have a home listed with four bedrooms but the home has only three or may say that the property sits on 11 acres when there's really only one acre. Check carefully that your assessment reports the correct number of rooms and square footage of your home.
- *Overvaluations.* You may believe that your home's value is too high relative to comparable homes in your area. Compare your home's value to similar homes using Zillow.com or RealEstate.com's Home Price Check. If your home is overassessed by 10 percent or more, take action.

---

**What to Do Now**

Challenge your assessment where warranted (to correct a mistake or an overassessment). The International Association of Assessing Officers says that more than 50 percent of owners who challenge their assessments get them reduced. Find out the rules for challenging assessments in your locality. Typically, there's limited window of opportunity during the year to bring your case up for consideration. You'll need proof, such as photos of the home showing that you don't have a garage even though the assessment lists one. If necessary, work with an attorney who handles property assessment challenges.

---

## Energy Consumption for Your Home

The cost of heating and cooling your home and electricity to run lights, appliances, and other electrical items is skyrocketing. The amount you pay for utilities depends on a number of factors—your home's energy efficiency, your personal habits (how careful you are to turn off lights and maintain temperatures at optimum-conservation levels), and your location (e.g., total energy expenditures on average are highest in the Northeast and lowest in the West).

### Federal Tax Credits

If you make certain improvements to your home, you may qualify for a federal income tax credit. Every dollar of a tax credit reduces the amount of taxes you otherwise would owe.

**CAUTION**

A general decline in property values within an area does not mean you can expect your property taxes to decline; all homeowners in the area are in the same position, and the tax rate is usually increased to compensate for the reduced tax base.

- Solar panels, solar water heaters, and fuel cell power plants—30 percent of the cost up to a top credit of $2,000 per type of improvement. The credit also applies to residential wind property.

- Insulation to walls and ceilings; storm doors and windows (including skylights); metal roofs with a special pigmented coating; high-efficiency water heaters, furnaces, and boilers; and high-efficiency central air-conditioning—up to set limits (depending on the type of improvement). This tax credit expires at the end of 2008 but may be extended by Congress.

### State Tax Breaks

States have enacted several ways to encourage homeowners to make energy-saving improvements that add efficiency or rely on renewable energy sources, such as solar and wind power. The types of incentives, some of which are offered by state or local government and others by local utility companies, include:

- Grants to make energy improvements (e.g., for caulking, weather-stripping, and insulation).

- Low-interest loans for making improvements.

- Property tax exemptions for certain improvements that add to the value of a home.

- Rebates for certain equipment purchases (e.g., certain water heaters).

- Sales tax exemptions for energy-related purchases (e.g., solar-related items).

- Tax credits for purchases of qualified equipment and improvements (e.g., solar energy panels).

View the tax incentives available to homeowners in your state by going to the Database for State Incentives for Renewables & Efficiency (www.dsire.org). Check back often, as new breaks are continually being created.

---

### What to Do Now

Determine the payback term for making energy improvements to your home. This is the time it takes for you to recover your investment through energy savings and tax incentives. For instance, if you add new storm windows at a cost of $8,000 and enjoy an initial tax break of $1,000, plus annual energy consumption savings of $1,000, it will take seven years to recoup your investment; each year after that you can enjoy continued energy savings. If you expect to be in your home more than seven years, it makes sense.

## *Energy Conservation*

The math is simple—use less energy and you'll save money. Doing this, of course, is not so simple. It requires thought and changing habits that may be difficult to break. Suggestions for energy conservation can be found in Chapter 5.

# CHAPTER 3

# Investment Choices Today

In today's frenetic markets, investors are wary. Dramatic swings of the stock market—up 200 points one day, down 300 the next—are all too common and can keep you up at night with worry that your hard-earned money may evaporate in the blink of an eye.

Fortunately, there are some good reasons why you need *not* worry that the stock market will have the kind of collapse it had during the Great Depression. Since then, the government has put many controls in place to maintain some sanity in the market. For instance, prior to 1929, many stocks were fully leveraged; instead of paying cash, investors borrowed to the hilt and when stock prices went south they didn't have the money to meet their loan requirements. Today, buying on margin (borrowing against existing securities in a brokerage account) generally is limited to no more than 50 percent of the value of stock and 70 percent of the value of bonds (90 percent for Treasuries). And there are some government-created insurance safety nets for certain investments.

In order to make the most of the money you have to invest, it's important to act smartly. To do this, you need to learn the lingo and understand forces at work that can erode the buying power of your money, what investment choices to choose from, how markets work, and what protections you can rely on to cushion any unforeseen financial disasters. Then you can apply this information to your unique situation, factoring in today's economic and market conditions.

You may want to work with an investment adviser, such as a stockbroker or financial planner, to help you make your investment decisions.

As you look at the information in this chapter, some points may be familiar to you or seem simplistic; but because they're important, they bear repeating for all readers. In this chapter you will find information on:

- Why go for yield
- Investment options
- Investment strategies for bull and bear markets
- FDIC and SIPC protection
- Investment safety nets
- Protecting retirement savings

## Why Go for Yield?

Ask people how much income or gains they want to earn on an investment and they're likely to reply, "As much as I can." Who doesn't share this view? But this response doesn't go far enough in answering the question. The truth is that you need to earn a certain amount in order to meet your goals. These goals include:

- Maintaining your buying power (see impact of inflation, discussed next).
- Saving for future needs, such as a child's education, starting a business, or funding retirement.

Your investment returns don't come in a vacuum. They have to be evaluated after taking into account two potentially devastating factors: inflation and taxes. Inflation and taxes aren't just difficult and complex numbers and formulas that you can dismiss; they are real players in your daily economic life. Take the time now to understand how inflation and taxes impact you directly so you can then formulate an investment strategy that works for you.

### Impact of Inflation

Inflation is always a problem. It pushes up the cost of the goods and services you need or want to buy, eroding the buying power of your dollar. Table 3.1 shows the rate of inflation, measured by the consumer price index (CPI), over the past 12 years.

The average inflation rate runs about 2.5 percent to 3 percent annually. However, these are tough times; the inflation rate for 2008 is projected to be substantially higher than the average annual rate—probably around 5 percent.

To keep pace with inflation, your investment returns must at least equal the inflation rate each year. Inflation year after year has historically averaged 3 percent. However, the total inflation rate since 1982 is 95 percent. This means

**TABLE 3.1** Historic Rates of Inflation

| Year | Rate | Year | Rate |
|------|------|------|------|
| 1996 | 2.93% | 2002 | 1.59% |
| 1997 | 2.34% | 2003 | 2.27% |
| 1998 | 1.55% | 2004 | 2.68% |
| 1999 | 2.19% | 2005 | 3.39% |
| 2000 | 3.38% | 2006 | 3.24% |
| 2001 | 2.83% | 2007 | 2.85% |

*Source:* U.S. Bureau of Labor Statistics.

that an item costing $1 in 1982 would cost you $1.95 today. In other words, you'd need almost twice the income to pay for the same items today.

These inflation figures are based on the Consumer Price Index for All Urban Consumers (CPI-U) compiled by the U.S. Bureau of Labor Statistics. Table 3.2 shows you the items that are part of the CPI-U for the nation as a whole (there are regional indexes not covered here) and how much weight they carry with respect to the full index.

However, your personal inflation index may be much higher. How much have your property taxes risen year after year? How much more do you pay for medical coverage than you did previously? What does it cost to fill up your car's gas tank today compared with a year ago? Two years ago?

Maybe medical care is a more significant portion of your annual expenses than 6.231 percent (this tends to be true the older you get). If your medical costs rise faster than the rate factored into the overall rate of inflation, then your *personal* inflation index is higher than the national CPI-U. To keep pace with your higher personal inflation rate, your investments must perform even better!

**TABLE 3.2** Components of the CPI-U

| Item | Weight in CPI-U |
|------|-----------------|
| Housing | 42.427% |
| Transportation | 17.688% |
| Food and beverages | 14.914% |
| Medical care | 6.231% |
| Education and communication | 6.086% |
| Recreation | 5.647% |
| Clothing | 3.731% |
| Other goods and services | 3.277% |

*Source:* U.S. Bureau of Labor Statistics.

You may have heard about *stagflation* and wondered what this is and how it might affect you. Stagflation is the worst of all possible worlds: It is a time of rising prices (high inflation) and high unemployment without a rising economy or during a recessionary economy (defined as at least two consecutive quarters when the gross domestic product (GDP) is down). Stagflation occurred in the late 1970s when there were high gasoline prices and high unemployment but only modest economic growth. Some economists are predicting stagflation today—there are already high gasoline prices and slower economic growth, but unemployment is still relatively low. When stagflation hits, it is challenging for many to keep up with higher prices, especially if they are on the unemployment rolls.

### Impact of Taxes

In addition to inflation, you must factor in the impact that taxes have on your investment earnings—only your after-tax income matters when it comes to buying power.

In deciding on investments, consider the tax consequences that result from your choices. There are four basic ways your investments are taxed (reflecting tax rates for 2008:)

1. *Ordinary income.* This income is taxed at your regular tax rate, which may be as high as 35 percent. *Examples:* Interest on bank savings account deposits and certificates of deposit (CDs); profit on the sale or exchange of property held one year or less (short-term capital gain).

2. *Capital gains.* Profits on the sale or exchange of property held more than one year (long-term capital gain) as well as qualified dividends are subject to lower tax rates than those imposed on ordinary income. The top basic capital gain rate is 15 percent; the rate is 25 percent for unrecaptured depreciation on sales of realty and 28 percent on gains from collectibles or certain small business stock. Those in the 10 percent or 15 percent tax bracket pay *no* tax on long-term capital gains for sales and dividends in 2008 through 2010. *Examples:* Gain on the sale of stock held long-term, capital gain distributions from mutual funds, and ordinary dividends paid on stocks.

**CAUTION**

The tax rates on capital gains and ordinary income are not carved in stone. Congress may increase the rates in 2009.

3. *Tax-deferred income.* This income isn't taxed currently; it becomes taxable at some time in the future. Because there is no reduction in the investment for current taxes, you can accumulate more over time. *Examples:* Commercial annuities, 401(k) plans, and regular individual retirement accounts (IRAs).

4. *Tax-free income.* This income is not subject to tax now or in the future. Tax-free income may be in the form of exclusions or exemptions from tax and, in many cases, need not even be reported on your tax return. *Examples:* Interest on municipal bonds, distributions from Roth IRAs and Roth 401(k)s, and the first $250,000 ($500,000 on a joint return) of gain on the sale of a principal residence.

## Investment Options

There seems to be an ever-increasing array of assets you can invest in. This is so for a personal portfolio as well as within a retirement plan, such as a 401(k) plan and an IRA. Obviously, some of your choices are limited by your pocketbook. For instance, you may want to invest in commercial real estate but don't have the millions of dollars on hand to get started. You can, however, find investment solutions to meet any of your goals that are within your resources. If you can't afford to purchase an entire commercial building, you could still invest in this type of asset with a modest amount of money by buying an interest in a limited partnership or a real estate investment trust (REIT).

And, whatever amount of salary you commit to your employer's retirement plan, such as a 401(k), it's up to you to make wise investment decisions with that money, along with employer's matching contributions, so you can maximize your retirement dollars. Each plan has a menu of investment options to choose from; you do this by allocating your contributions to the investments selected from the menu.

### Investment Asset Classes

The three main asset classes are stocks, bonds, and cash. Other asset classes include real estate, commodities, and collectibles. Investments in these classes can be highly specialized and are not discussed in detail here. Here is some information about the three main asset classes and what you could hope to gain from them:

1. *Stocks.* With these investments you become a part owner in a corporation. Stock is held primarily for appreciation; you hope that the price of the stock goes up over time. Stocks may also pay dividends, which essentially are a distribution of profits. You can purchase shares of stock or obtain ownership through a stock mutual fund. You can also play the market with options (puts and calls).

2. *Bonds.* These are loans an investor makes to the issuer for the face amount of the instrument (you become a creditor). You make money from the interest paid on the bonds and, if you sell prior to the bond's maturity, on any market appreciation (explained under "Bond Risk" at the end of this section). You can buy individual bonds or an interest in a bond portfolio through a bond mutual fund.

3. *Cash.* Keeping money in bank savings accounts and money market funds is referred to as a cash investment. The money in a bank account is easily accessible and the value of the deposit doesn't change, other than for additions of interest. Cash in money market mutual funds are similar to bank deposits (they are easily accessible), except that the value of a share in the fund can decline below $1, which happened to one fund in September 2008. In response, the federal government is insuring all money market funds for investments as of September 19, 2008, for one year (so new deposits and interest earned after this date don't enjoy the same protection).

## Mutual Funds

Mutual funds may hold any or all types of investments from these three asset classes. A mutual fund is an investment vehicle run by an investment company. In an open-end mutual fund (which most funds are), investors' dollars are pooled to make the investments; investors hold shares in the fund. The benefits to mutual fund investors include:

- *Diversity.* You have the opportunity to own a portion of multiple investments (more than a single individual could afford to buy). For example, a $2,500 investment in a stock mutual fund gives an investor an interest in, say, 20 or more stocks. In contrast, that same $2,500 could likely buy only a few shares in a few different companies.

- *Professional management.* A team of experts decides what the fund should buy, own, or sell.

- *Liquidity.* Mutual fund shares can be easily sold to receive cash proceeds.

**CAUTION**

Mutual funds may be load (with up-front purchase costs) or no-load (with fewer fees); all mutual fund returns are diminished by some fees to pay their investment advisers, administrative costs, and other expenses. When considering any mutual fund investment, always look not only at the fund's performance over time but also at its fees.

Mutual funds don't trade on any exchange (although fund performance for many funds is listed in the daily newspapers near the stock exchange listings). Shares are purchased directly from a mutual fund company, such as Fidelity and Vanguard, or through brokerage firms.

## Exchange-Traded Funds

Exchange-traded funds (ETFs) are a little like mutual funds and a little like stocks. They are a bundle of securities that trade like stocks on the American Stock Exchange (currently there are more than 700 listed ETFs). They can be traded at any time that the market is open and typically have lower expenses compared with mutual funds. Exchange-traded funds are called tax efficient because you can buy or sell them with a view to the tax results (compared with mutual funds, which report their tax results to you at the end of the year). The vast majority of ETFs represent an index, such as the S&P 500.

Exchange-traded funds are purchased like individual stocks, so there are commissions for buying and selling them. Some ETFs have incremental requirements (you have to buy them in lots of 100).

It's usually a good idea to restrict your investments to those you fully understand. Even sophisticated investors can be easily duped or lose money because of crafty promoters touting the newest investment on the block.

Having an understanding of the need to receive a certain amount of return in order to just stay even (after inflation and taxes) doesn't necessarily help you decide which types of investments to own. Investment choices depend not only on your desire for yield, but also on your tolerance for risk.

### Risk Tolerance

How much risk are you willing to bear? Although there are no guarantees, it's assumed that the higher the risk, the higher the potential reward (investment return potential). Conversely, lower returns usually come with lower risk.

The risk scale, with 1 being the lowest risk and 10 being the highest risk, can be used to assess your tolerance. Depending on how you see yourself, you'll want to have a mix of investments, with your total portfolio holding a little of each class of assets reflecting different levels of risk. Low-risk assets tend to have low volatility (there is little change in prices over time), while high-risk assets are very volatile (there can be dramatic price fluctuations). Table 3.3 shows your investment approach, rated from 1 to 10, and the types of investments that correlate to that style.

**TABLE 3.3** Your Investment Style

| Low Risk | Low to Medium Risk | Medium Risk | Medium to High Risk | High Risk |
|---|---|---|---|---|
| 1–2 | 3–4 | 5–6 | 7–8 | 9–10 |
| Savings accounts | Fixed annuities | Balanced mutual funds | Common stocks | Futures |
| CDs | Municipal bonds | Preferred stock | Growth mutual funds | Options |
| Money market funds | High-grade muni bond funds | Corporate bonds | Stock ETFs | Junk (high-yield) bonds |
| Treasury securities (including U.S. savings bonds) | | | Real estate investments International funds | Sector funds Derivatives Hedge funds |

If you decide that your investment style is low to medium risk, that doesn't mean you hold *only* assets within that investment style category. Instead, a significant portion of your portfolio would be made up of assets with the low-risk and low-to-medium-risk investment style classes and only a small amount of assets from the other investment style classes. For instance, if your investment style is low to medium risk, you might have 40 percent of your holdings in assets in the low-risk class, 30 percent in the low-to-medium-risk class, 20 percent in the medium-risk class, and 10 percent in the medium-to-high-risk class. Your yield would probably be relatively modest, because the types of investments in the bulk of your portfolio usually provide only modest returns.

In contrast, someone who has a high tolerance for risk might invest heavily in assets in the high-risk and medium-to-high-risk investment style classes, while still holding some assets from the lower-risk categories. This person could expect to receive higher returns from most of his or her portfolio, but might experience some losses that could erode overall returns.

### Assessing Your Investment Style

How do you assess your investment style? It depends on several factors, including:

- *Age.* The younger you are, the more you can afford to take some risk, because you'll have time to make up any losses. As you near retirement age or when you are already retired, your risk tolerance may decline because your primary concern is preserving your capital.

- *Overall wealth.* The more you have, the more you can afford to risk. Those of modest means usually take a more conservative approach because each loss is more significant relative to their total holdings. Wealthier individuals can afford to risk assets, the loss of which would not impair their lifestyle.

- *Personality.* Regardless of age and wealth, decide whether you can sleep at night or are kept awake thinking about your holdings. Many wealthy individuals maintain a conservative portfolio because they don't like to lose anything.

### What to Do Now

Determine your investment style so you can create an appropriate investment plan. Be honest about your personal feelings and your economic situation. Choose a style you can live with comfortably. If your situation changes (e.g., you come into a large sum of money unexpectedly), you can change your investment style and adapt your portfolio accordingly. It's helpful to work with a professional—a stockbroker or financial planner—who can review your investment style and investment options with you.

## Market Forces

Even after you know your investment style, you still have to factor in what's going on in the market. These factors include:

- *Interest rates.* Rates on bank CDs and money market mutual funds generally follow the rates fixed by the Federal Reserve. As the federal funds rate goes up, interest rates on investments tend to rise; as the fed funds rate is cut, interest rates on investments decline.

- *Value of the dollar.* The value of the U.S. dollar relative to other currencies, such as the euro (€), the pound (£), and the yen (¥), changes constantly. It is usually assumed that a low dollar means that U.S. exports can grow, but a higher U.S. dollar gives us better buying power. For instance, it is believed that the current low value of the U.S. dollar is partly responsible for the high cost of oil, since oil is presently priced in dollars.

- *Commodity prices.* The cost of commodities (physical substances such as grains and metals) impacts the cost of nearly everything. Today, the U.S. economy is experiencing exceptionally high commodity prices, which are raising the cost of food, building materials, and just about everything else.

## Interplay between Stocks and Bonds

Stocks and bonds are both investment classes, but they are very different types of assets. Stocks (as well as stock mutual funds and stock ETFs) represent investments (equity). An investor in equity hopes to make money from the appreciation in the stock, along with any dividends that may be paid from the corporation. Bonds, in contrast, are loans—an investor is the creditor of the bond issuer. Bonds have a fixed maturity; during the life of the bond, the investor usually receives interest income, and at the end of the bond's maturity, the investor is paid the principal owed on the bond.

It is a general rule that when stocks are down, bonds usually are up (and vice versa). For example, in the 12-month period from April 1, 2007, through March 31, 2008, the stock market declined by 5 percent while bonds returned over 8 percent. Of course, there are sometimes exceptions to this rule.

## Stock Risk

Investments in common stock have practically no protection. As an investor you hope that the value of the stock will appreciate. You may also be entitled to receive dividends payable on the stock from time to time. However, neither stock appreciation nor dividend payments are guaranteed in any way. Risks include:

- *Dividend cuts.* If a corporation experiences financial difficulties, it may reduce or even eliminate its dividend for the quarter or permanently.

- *Bankruptcy.* If the corporation goes belly-up, common stock shareholders are at the end of the line when it comes to a share of the corporation's liquidated value. Or a corporation may have a serious collapse and try to reorganize for the future or become a takeover target—either way the value of shares in these situations is usually nearly but not wholly worthless. (Enron and WorldCom are examples of bankruptcies.) Investors may be able to write off their losses (see Chapter 4).

### Bond Risk

Bonds generally are considered relatively safe investments, but they're not without some risks. These risks include:

- *Market risk.* If you hold a bond to maturity, you receive the face amount (you get back your principal). However, if you must sell the bond prior to maturity, the money you receive depends on the price of the bond in a secondary market. When interest rates rise, the value of a bond usually declines; when interest rates decline, the value of a bond increases.
- *Callability.* Other than Treasuries, bonds usually can be called before maturity; the issuer redeems the bonds and pays off the principal owed to investors. The risk to investors is the inability to lock into an interest rate for the initial life of the bond. If the bonds are called (something that happens when interest rates drop and issuers believe they can refinance their debt at lower cost to them), you receive your money but are faced with reinvesting it in a lower-interest-rate market.
- *Credit risk.* The credit rating of the bond issuer may be downgraded (credit ratings are discussed later in this chapter) and when this happens, the value of the bond declines.
- *Default.* In rare instances, issuers cannot pay back investors; they default on their obligations. When this happens, investors, who are creditors of the issuers, have a loss (the tax treatment of losses is discussed Chapter 4). However, if the bond is insured (see later in the chapter), investors may get their money back.

## Investment Strategies for Bull and Bear Markets

The stock market is constantly in flux. When the stock market is rising, this is called a bull market. When the naysayers are in control and the market is tumbling, this is called a bear market (technically, a bear market is signaled by a drop in a market index such as the Dow Jones Industrial Average or Standard & Poor's 500 index by more than 20 percent). Historically, bull markets have lasted much longer than intervening bear markets. Bull markets have increased by an average of 189 percent over about three years and seven months. In contrast, bear markets have on average decreased by 32.7 percent and lasted one year and two months.

For most long-term investors who can afford to stay the course, money that is in solid investments will recover from any downturns and appreciate over time. However, during bear markets, some corporations may go under, leaving their investors with nothing.

### Bull Market Strategies

Everyone hopes for a bull market, with prices rising. But this scenario can present problems for investors. Many hesitate to buy stocks they want because they believe the price is too high.

It's conventional wisdom not to try to catch a stock, or even a stock sector (such as technology), that seems to be spiraling upward out of control. Just remember the dot-com bubble earlier this decade.

### Bear Market Strategies

Bear markets require brave investors. In reality, bear markets present an opportunity to buy good companies at fire-sale prices. When do you want to buy designer clothes at a department store—when they raise prices or put them on sale? The same thinking should apply to stocks in solid companies. Of course, discounted prices alone don't make the stocks good picks; choose only those stocks that show promise for the long term.

The key to riding out a bear market is not to panic. Recognize that the down market will eventually turn around and rise. If you stay the course, you'll avoid any commissions to buy and sell. You may also avoid taxable gains; even though prices of stocks may be down, they may not be down to the level at which you made your investments, so selling would produce gains, albeit smaller than you had hoped.

Use the bear market to:

- *Harvest losses.* Even though the market will eventually recover, some stocks will not. Sell losing stocks that you no longer believe in for the long term. Use these losses for tax advantage (explained in Chapter 4).

- *Look over your asset allocation.* You may have allocated a set percentage of your holdings to stocks and another part to bonds, but when the market declines, it can throw your allocation out of whack. You may want to reallocate assets (e.g., by putting your next investment in the appropriate asset class to rebalance your portfolio). If you're unsure about where to put new money, consider staying in cash (e.g., putting the proceeds from sales and any new investment money into a money market fund) until you can make a decision that you're comfortable with

**What to Do Now**

Determine whether this is a bull or bear market (or close to it); often this isn't easy to do and even experts can disagree. Then craft your investment strategies for the near future. Carefully monitor changes in the marketplace so you can modify your strategies accordingly.

## FDIC and SIPC Protection

During the Great Depression, there was a run on the banks—depositors tried to withdraw their savings all at once. The result: Banks couldn't satisfy all of the claims and went under, leaving depositors without their money. In the wake of this financial disaster, the federal government created the Federal Deposit Insurance Corporation (FDIC at www.fdic.gov) to provide a safety net to bank depositors. Since the FDIC started on January 1, 1934, no depositor has lost any money as a result of a bank failure. When California's IndyMac Bank depositors withdrew $1.3 billion over an 11-day period in June and July 2008 and the bank failed (it was taken over by federal regulators), investors with deposits covered by the FDIC did not lose one penny.

The Securities Investor Protection Corporation (SIPC at www.sipc.org) was created in 1970 to restore to investors their assets that were in the hands of bankrupt or other financially troubled brokerage firms. It does not provide the same type of broad protection as the FDIC.

### Federal Deposit Insurance Corporation

The Federal Deposit Insurance Corporation (FDIC) is an independent federal agency that is funded by premiums paid by banks and thrift institutions under FDIC coverage. Current funding on hand is $49 billion to protect $3 trillion in deposits.

How much protection do your accounts enjoy? Your savings, checking, and other deposit accounts, as well as certificates of deposit (CDs) are insured to $100,000 per depositor in each bank or thrift that the FDIC insures; $250,000 through 2009. For example, you can have (if you're wealthy enough) $250,000 in Bank A and another $250,000 in Bank B, and both accounts are fully insured.

Deposits held in different categories of ownership, such as single or joint accounts, can be separately insured. A single category includes accounts held in your own name, accounts for which you are a custodian, a business account for a sole proprietorship doing business as (d/b/a) its business name. A joint ownership category includes accounts on which two or more people have equal rights; each owner's share is taken into account and added to any personal accounts when determining the extent of insurance coverage. For example, if you have a personal savings account with $125,000 and a joint account with your parent with a balance of $250,000, you are fully insured ($125,000 personal account plus one-half of the $250,000 joint account). Reordering names on the joint account or listing different Social Security numbers first won't increase your FDIC coverage.

Informal and formal revocable trusts that allow the owner to change the beneficiary at any time until his or her death are treated as the owner's account and usually the $100,000 limit applies. These include Totten trusts, accounts payable on death (POD) to a named beneficiary, an account in trust for (ITF) a named beneficiary, and accounts titled as trustee for (ATF) a named beneficiary. Formal revocable trusts, referred to as "living trusts," also belong to the owner and are usually limited to the $100,000 cap even though there is a named beneficiary.

However, the owner of an account can be insured, based on the number of beneficiaries, if the beneficiaries are "qualified" (a spouse, children, grandchildren, parents, grandparents, and siblings). Thus, a father with a POD account for his two children can be insured up to $200,000 ($100,000 for each qualified beneficiary).

Also, there is separate coverage under the FDIC for retirement accounts, such as individual retirement accounts (IRAs), simplified employee pensions (SEPs), savings incentive match plans for employees (SIMPLEs), and self-directed 401(k) plans. The coverage limit for these accounts is up to $250,000 in the aggregate, even after 2009. For example, if you have a Roth IRA with $25,000 and a traditional IRA with $50,000, the maximum you can have in your SEP in the same bank is $175,000 ($25,000 + $50,000 + $175,000 = $250,000). The fact that you've named multiple beneficiaries on your retirement accounts does not increase the insurance limit.

> **CAUTION**
>
> Coverdell education savings accounts (ESAs), health savings accounts (HSAs), and Archer medical savings accounts (MSAs) are not part of the retirement account category eligible for the $250,000 insurance limit after 2009. Also, defined benefit (pension) plans are not covered by this limit, although there may be coverage under the Pension Benefit Guaranty Corporation (PBGC) (see "PBGC Protection" later in this chapter).

## NONINSURED INVESTMENTS

Not all investments made at or held by banks have FDIC protection.

- Investments, such as mutual funds and annuities, purchased through a bank-owned investment company (a broker/dealer) are not FDIC insured. Even though the broker from the bank-owned investment company sits in the FDIC-insured bank, these accounts are not covered by FDIC insurance. These investments, however, may enjoy SIPC protection (discussed in the next section).

- The contents of a safe-deposit box at a bank are not FDIC insured. Your homeowner's insurance policy may cover the contents of your box, or you may need to purchase a separate policy for this purpose.

- Treasury securities such as Treasury bills (T-bills) purchased through the bank are not covered by FDIC protection, because they don't have to be. Treasuries are backed by the full faith and credit of the U.S. government. Even if the bank goes under, your Treasuries are still held in an account (book entry) for you by the federal government; the bank is merely a custodian. You can contact your nearest Federal Reserve bank and show proof of ownership to reclaim securities from banks that go under.

---

### What to Do Now

Figure the extent of your protection using an interactive online tool called the Electronic Deposit Insurance Estimator (EDIE) at www2.fdic.gov/edie. When banks merge, you may need to take additional action to preserve the maximum coverage for your money. If a bank in which you have one or more accounts merges with another bank in which you also have one or more accounts, the separate coverage continues only for six months. After that time, FDIC coverage limits apply to all accounts held in different branches of the same bank. *Note:* Members of credit unions may enjoy similar protection for their deposits through the National Credit Union Administration (NCUA).

---

### Securities Investor Protection Corporation

The SIPC, like the FDIC, is an independent agency created by the federal government. But that's where the similarity with the FDIC ends. The SIPC only covers investor assets when a brokerage firm experiences severe financial distress.

In such a case, an investor's assets held by the brokerage firm are insured up to $500,000 per customer, including a maximum of $100,000 for cash claims (e.g., money market accounts). The assets are valued as of the date that the firm asks a bank to put it in liquidation (ups or downs in an account after this date have no impact on the investor's recovery). Additional funds may be available to satisfy the remainder of customer claims after the cost of liquidating the brokerage firm is taken into account. Investors can anticipate recovery of their assets within one to three months following the liquidation proceeding.

#### NONINSURED LOSSES

The SIPC coverage does not extend to all losses in brokerage accounts. Not covered are:

- *Losses resulting from your investment choices.* You alone bear this risk of loss. Tax breaks may alleviate some of the pain of these losses (see Chapter 4).

- *Losses resulting from certain activities of your broker.* If a broker steals from a client's account or fails to follow an investor's instructions, the brokerage firm may be liable for any losses. Typically, the firm carries its own insurance to cover these losses. Most firms provide coverage of up to $50 million per account.

## Investment Safety Nets

In addition to government-provided protection under the FDIC and SIPC for certain types of losses, there are other ways to protect yourself from loss.

### Diversification

The best way to minimize any investment losses is to follow the old adage and don't put all your eggs in one basket. If you have a mix of assets from different asset classes—some interest-bearing bank accounts, stocks or stock mutual funds, bonds or bond funds, and so on—you probably won't be vulnerable to a complete washout. Some assets may decline in value or even, in some cases, become worthless. But overall, your mix of holdings will be preserved and, it is hoped, increase in value over time.

Also consider diversifying within your asset class. Buying an index mutual fund—one that tracks the Dow Jones Industrial Average or Standard & Poor's 500 Index—gives you an interest in 30 stocks or 500 stocks, respectively. Most investors can't afford to hold a sufficient number of individual stocks to achieve sufficient diversity. Other ways to diversify is by investing through other mutual finds and/or EFTs. For instance, you can diversify your bond holdings through a mutual fund. You may not hit a home run, something you could do if you picked just the right stock, but at least you'll get on base and eventually score.

### Bond Protection

There are several types of bonds: Treasury securities (e.g., the 10-year Treasury bond); agency bonds issued by federally chartered corporations or agencies (e.g., Fannie Mae and Freddie Mac); municipal bonds issued by states and local governments and their agencies (munis); and corporate bonds issued by corporations traded on a U.S. exchange.

#### BOND RATINGS

Bonds are reviewed by independent companies that assign a rating. The two major rating services are Moody's Investors Service and Standard & Poor's (S&P). Investment-grade bonds range from a high rating of AAA from S&P (Aaa from Moody's) to a low rating of BBB– from S&P (Baa3 from Moody's). Bonds below investment grade (junk bonds) have a rating from BB+ from S&P (Ba1 from Moody's) to as low as CCC– (Ca). Bonds that may soon be or are already in default have a rating of D from S&P (C from Moody's).

When you find out that a bond rating has been downgraded, it means that a rating company has reviewed the issuer and decided that the prospects have become riskier. When a rating is upgraded, things are looking better.

### BOND INSURANCE

Treasuries don't need any outside insurer to provide protection for investors. These instruments are backed by the full faith and credit of the U.S. government. Agency bonds such as Fannie Mae and Freddie Mac, which are issued by federally chartered corporations or agencies, technically don't have the same security; as a practical matter it is doubtful whether the government would let these agency bonds fail, so outside insurance is unnecessary.

But municipal bonds can improve their ratings by having outside companies provide insurance protection to investors. Today, more than half of these bonds carry insurance. Investors pay more for insured bonds than for uninsured bonds paying the same interest rate and having the same maturity. Major insurers include MBIA Corporation, Ambac Financial Group, Financial Guaranty Insurance Corporation (FGIC), and Financial Security Assurance Inc. (FSA); traditionally insured bonds have carried an AAA (Aaa) rating.

**CAUTION**

The value of having bond insurance may not mean as much today as it did previously. The financial soundness of some bond insurers has been called into question recently, and the rating of some of these insured bonds is no longer AAA (Aaa). However, it should be remembered that a default in a municipal bond is rare. A recent study by S&P of over 10,000 munis issued since 1986 found that there were no defaults for bonds with a rating of AAA and AA, and the default rate for bonds with an A rating was only 0.16 percent.

## Financial Markets Bailout Plan

On October 3, 2008, a $700 billion package to rescue Wall Street and Main Street became law. It enables the U.S. Treasury to infuse billions of dollars into financial institutions by buying "toxic" investments from them. This should provide liquidity for these institutions to lend money, which, hopefully, will stimulate the economy.

## Protecting Retirement Savings

Retirement savings in qualified retirement plans and IRAs (including Roth IRAs) are important to your future financial security. You accumulate these investments for a specific purpose and want to conserve these assets.

### Choosing Investments

Depending on the type of plan, you may have a wide range of investment options in which to put your retirement savings. For example, the typical corporate 401(k) plan today has a menu of investment options that includes stock mutual funds, bond mutual funds, balanced funds, targeted funds (the investment mix depends on your age), and money market funds—you may have a dozen or so choices.

You don't have to put all your money in a single investment vehicle; you can choose, for example, to put 25 percent each into four different investments. This can be three different types of stock funds and one bond fund, or any other mix you select.

The closer you get to retirement age, the more careful you probably want to become in making investment decisions affecting retirement assets. Also, in most cases, you cannot deduct any losses on trades you make, so you would be more conservative in investment choices for retirement plans than you might be in your personal (nonretirement) portfolio. Also factor in the types of investments you own outside of your retirement plans so you can take a comprehensive view on all your holdings and won't duplicate your efforts; for example, you don't want to own the same stock fund in your personal account that you hold in your 401(k).

## What to Do Now

Refer to Table 3.3 earlier in this chapter. It may be helpful for purposes of choosing investments for your retirement plan to correlate the investment style with your age. The younger you are, the more risk you can afford to tolerate; as you near or are in retirement, the lower the risk should be for these assets.

### Limiting Exposure to Employer Stock

Many who participate in company-sponsored 401(k) plans receive employer contributions that are often made with corporate stock. Over the years, you can build up a significant holding in employer stock.

Conventional wisdom suggests that you limit your holdings of employer stock to no more than 10 percent to 15 percent of your retirement plan's portfolio. This limit makes sense in light of major corporate collapses in recent years, including Enron, WorldCom, and, most recently, Bear Stearns. Still, one survey by *Pensions and Investments* found that 26 percent of assets in the 65 largest corporate plans was still in employer stock, and at some companies, including General Electric and Chevron, employees' accounts were more than 50 percent employer stock (even though the price of GE stock has done nothing in nearly five years).

## What to Do Now

Learn from your plan administrator when you are permitted to sell your shares of employer stock and reinvest the proceeds in alternative investments. By law, you must be allowed to sell the stock after three years of service, although some plans allow you to do so immediately after the employer contribution is made.

### PBGC Protection

The Pension Benefit Guaranty Corporation (PBGC, based online at www.pbgc.gov) is a federal corporation that was created to protect the pensions of American workers. It provides protection *only* for participants in defined benefit (pension) plans; it does not give any help to participants in profit-sharing plans, 401(k) plans, or other defined contribution plans, and it does not provide any payments for health and welfare benefits, vacation pay, or severance pay.

If a company whose plan is covered by the PBGC goes bankrupt, its retirement plan terminates and the PBGC takes it over. The PBGC will pay a monthly pension to participants. The maximum monthly payment for a pension based solely on the life of the participant in 2008 is $4,312.50 ($3,881.25 for a joint and 50 percent survivor annuity). The monthly limit changes annually.

Once the PBGC takes over the defunct pension plan, it sends out notices to participants and retirees, informing them of their estimated benefits. These benefits may be the same as they had been receiving or expected to receive, but in some cases it may be less.

# CHAPTER 4

# Handling Investment Losses

L osses in investments are inevitable from time to time. You try to make good investment decisions, but despite your best efforts, you're bound to have losses—but only infrequently, it is hoped. In today's economic environment, some securities may be up, but many may have declined in value since you acquired them. In fact, because of several market crises, including the collapse of the dot-com bubble in 2000, terrorist attacks in 2001, and corporate scandals in 2002 (Enron and WorldCom), not to mention the recent subprime mortgage debacle, returns on stocks for the past decade (through May 30, 2008), are down—the S&P 500 is off by 4.7 percent and the NASDAQ is off by 38 percent. Of course, there are also many winners in stocks—and you may be holding them. And many experts are optimistic about a market recovery later in 2008 or in 2009.

Still, if you have losing positions, it may be time to face the music, sell these holdings, and reinvest for better potential. Fortunately, you may be in a position to turn lemons into lemonade by taking advantage of certain tax breaks that can lessen the pain of these losses. By claiming deductions for losses, you reduce amount of income that is taxed, so deductible losses save you tax dollars.

Declines in the value or prices of your assets can result from a number of market conditions and other factors. For example, as the price of oil rises, the prices of shares in companies highly dependent on oil, such as airlines, tend to fall, while the prices of oil companies' stock tend to rise. As interest rates rise, the prices of bonds usually fall.

As a general rule, as long as you hold on to securities that have declined in value, you don't really have any loss; you may feel poorer but you don't have a tax write-off. In order to report a loss for tax purposes, you need more than a mere decline in an asset's value or price; you have to take an action, such as selling a security. The only exception to this general rule is when an investment becomes totally worthless—a corporation goes bankrupt and liquidates, with no assets for shareholders, or a borrower defaults on a bond and can't pay what is due.

In this chapter you will learn about how and to what extent you can deduct losses on stocks, bonds, and other assets:

- Rules for capital losses
- Wash sale rule
- Section 1244 losses
- Worthless securities
- Penalty on early withdrawal of savings
- Bank deposit losses

## Rules for Capital Losses

The market goes up and down, and as you watch the prices of the stocks you own decline, you have a *potential* loss (called a paper loss). After all, the prices of the stocks can go up again while you hold on to your shares. If you ride out the bad times and your holdings recover, you don't have any losses to report. You must actualize your losses to claim a tax loss. Until you *sell* the stocks or they become totally worthless, you may feel like you've lost money, but you don't have any losses for tax purposes.

When you sell assets held for investment at a loss, you can claim a capital loss deduction. For instance, if you sell stock that has dropped in price since you bought it, you can deduct the loss. You can't take a capital loss deduction for assets held for personal purposes. This includes a loss on the sale of your home (see Chapter 2), vacation property, or your personal car.

### Holding Period

The capital loss may be short-term or long-term, depending on your holding period for the asset sold. The holding period is usually based on how long you've owned an asset. If you owned the asset for 12 months or less, the loss is short-term. If you owned the asset for more than 12 months, the loss is long-term.

Why does the holding period matter? The tax law requires that capital losses offset capital gains in a certain order. Capital losses first offset capital gains within the same holding period group (short-term or long-term) and within the same tax rate group (15 percent for most capital gains for most taxpayers, 25 percent for depreciation recapture, and 28 percent for gains on collectibles and small business stocks).

## Example

If a person has a $10,000 short-term gain, a $20,000 long-term gain, and a $15,000 short-term capital loss as her only transactions for the year, the capital loss would first offset the short-term gain and then $5,000 of the long-term gain. If the capital loss were long-term, it would offset $15,000 of the long-term gain. (See Figure 4.1.)

| SCHEDULE D (Form 1040) Department of the Treasury Internal Revenue Service | Capital Gains and Losses ▶ Attach to Form 1040 or Form 1040NR.   ▶ See Instructions for Schedule D (Form 1040). ▶ Use Schedule D-1 to list additional transactions for lines 1 and 8. | OMB No. 1545-0074 2008 Attachment Sequence No. 12 |
|---|---|---|
| Name(s) shown on return | | Your social security number |

**Part I    Short-Term Capital Gains and Losses—Assets Held One Year or Less**

| | (a) Description of property (Example: 100 sh. XYZ Co.) | (b) Date acquired (Mo., day, yr.) | (c) Date sold (Mo., day, yr.) | (d) Sales price (see page D-7 of the instructions) | (e) Cost or other basis (see page D-7 of the instructions) | (f) Gain or (loss) Subtract (e) from (d) |
|---|---|---|---|---|---|---|
| 1 | | | | | | |
| | | | | | | |
| | | | | | | |
| | | | | | | |
| | | | | | | |
| 2 | Enter your short-term totals, if any, from Schedule D-1, line 2 | | 2 | | | |
| 3 | Total short-term sales price amounts. Add lines 1 and 2 in column (d) | | 3 | | | |
| 4 | Short-term gain from Form 6252 and short-term gain or (loss) from Forms 4684, 6781, and 8824 | | | 4 | | |
| 5 | Net short-term gain or (loss) from partnerships, S corporations, estates, and trusts from Schedule(s) K-1 | | | 5 | | |
| 6 | Short-term capital loss carryover. Enter the amount, if any, from line 10 of your **Capital Loss Carryover Worksheet** on page D-7 of the instructions | | | 6 ( | | ) |
| 7 | **Net short-term capital gain or (loss).** Combine lines 1 through 6 in column (f) | | | 7 | | |

**Part II    Long-Term Capital Gains and Losses—Assets Held More Than One Year**

| | (a) Description of property (Example: 100 sh. XYZ Co.) | (b) Date acquired (Mo., day, yr.) | (c) Date sold (Mo., day, yr.) | (d) Sales price (see page D-7 of the instructions) | (e) Cost or other basis (see page D-7 of the instructions) | (f) Gain or (loss) Subtract (e) from (d) |
|---|---|---|---|---|---|---|
| 8 | | | | | | |
| | | | | | | |
| | | | | | | |
| | | | | | | |
| | | | | | | |
| 9 | Enter your long-term totals, if any, from Schedule D-1, line 9 | | 9 | | | |
| 10 | Total long-term sales price amounts. Add lines 8 and 9 in column (d) | | 10 | | | |
| 11 | Gain from Form 4797, Part I; long-term gain from Forms 2439 and 6252; and long-term gain or (loss) from Forms 4684, 6781, and 8824 | | | 11 | | |
| 12 | Net long-term gain or (loss) from partnerships, S corporations, estates, and trusts from Schedule(s) K-1 | | | 12 | | |
| 13 | Capital gain distributions. See page D-2 of the instructions | | | 13 | | |
| 14 | Long-term capital loss carryover. Enter the amount, if any, from line 15 of your **Capital Loss Carryover Worksheet** on page D-7 of the instructions | | | 14 ( | | ) |
| 15 | **Net long-term capital gain or (loss).** Combine lines 8 through 14 in column (f). Then go to Part III on the back | | | 15 | | |

For Paperwork Reduction Act Notice, see Form 1040 or Form 1040NR instructions.    Cat. No. 11338H    Schedule D (Form 1040) 2008

**FIGURE 4.1  Schedule D**

*(continued)*

*(Continued)*

Schedule D (Form 1040) 2007           Page **2**

| Part III | Summary |
| --- | --- |

**16**   Combine lines 7 and 15 and enter the result .   .   .   .   .   .   .   .   .   .   .     | **16** |

If line 16 is:
- A **gain**, enter the amount from line 16 on Form 1040, line 13, or Form 1040NR, line 14. Then go to line 17 below.
- A **loss**, skip lines 17 through 20 below. Then go to line 21. Also be sure to complete line 22.
- **Zero**, skip lines 17 through 21 below and enter -0- on Form 1040, line 13, or Form 1040NR, line 14. Then go to line 22.

**17**   Are lines 15 and 16 **both** gains?
☐ **Yes.** Go to line 18.
☐ **No.** Skip lines 18 through 21, and go to line 22.

**18**   Enter the amount, if any, from line 7 of the **28% Rate Gain Worksheet** on page D-8 of the instructions .   .   .   .   .   .   .   .   .   .   .   .   .   .   ▶ | **18** |

**19**   Enter the amount, if any, from line 18 of the **Unrecaptured Section 1250 Gain Worksheet** on page D-9 of the instructions .   .   .   .   .   .   .   .   .   .   .   .   ▶ | **19** |

**20**   Are lines 18 and 19 **both** zero or blank?
☐ **Yes.** Complete Form 1040 through line 43, or Form 1040NR through line 40. Then complete the **Qualified Dividends and Capital Gain Tax Worksheet** on page 35 of the Instructions for Form 1040 (or in the Instructions for Form 1040NR). **Do not** complete lines 21 and 22 below.

☐ **No.** Complete Form 1040 through line 43, or Form 1040NR through line 40. Then complete the **Schedule D Tax Worksheet** on page D-10 of the instructions. **Do not** complete lines 21 and 22 below.

**21**   If line 16 is a loss, enter here and on Form 1040, line 13, or Form 1040NR, line 14, the **smaller** of:

- The loss on line 16 or
- ($3,000), or if married filing separately, ($1,500)   }   .   .   .   .   .   .   .   .   .   . | **21** (         ) |

**Note.** When figuring which amount is smaller, treat both amounts as positive numbers.

**22**   Do you have qualified dividends on Form 1040, line 9b, or Form 1040NR, line 10b?
☐ **Yes.** Complete Form 1040 through line 43, or Form 1040NR through line 40. Then complete the **Qualified Dividends and Capital Gain Tax Worksheet** on page 35 of the Instructions for Form 1040 (or in the Instructions for Form 1040NR).
☐ **No.** Complete the rest of Form 1040 or Form 1040NR.

Schedule D (Form 1040) 2007

**FIGURE 4.1**

## Capital Loss Limit

Capital losses can offset capital gains dollar for dollar. For instance, if you have $5,000 of capital gains for the year and $5,000 of capital losses, you won't have any net gains on which to pay tax.

Capital losses in excess of capital gains for the year can offset ordinary income, such as salary and interest income, up to $3,000 ($1,500 for a married person filing a separate return).

Capital losses in excess of capital gains and the $3,000 deduction allowance can be carried forward and used in a following year. There is no time limit on capital loss carryforwards for individuals. Capital losses cannot be carried back to offset gains in previous years.

When couples file jointly, it doesn't matter which spouse had the loss, because it is reported on their Schedule D. However, if couples file separate returns, any capital loss carryover belongs solely to the spouse who was the owner of the asset that generated the loss. One spouse can't use the capital losses of the other on his or her separate return.

When a person dies, capital losses die, too. Any such losses belong solely to the deceased individual; any capital losses that incurred in the year of death, plus any capital loss carryovers, can be reported only on the deceased individual's final income tax return. Capital losses that are not used up here are lost forever; they cannot be used by a surviving spouse on his or her return following the year of death. (See Figure 4.2.)

### Sales to Related Parties

If you sell an asset to a person who is considered a related party, no loss deduction is allowed. A related party for purposes of the capital loss restriction includes most close relatives, such as a spouse, child, grandchild, great-grandchild, parent, grandparent, great-grandparent, or sibling. It doesn't include other relatives, no matter how close you feel to them, such as in-laws, aunts and uncles, nieces and nephews.

The capital loss restriction cannot be avoided by selling to a person not in the related-party list if that person is acting as a nominee of a related person.

---

**Capital Loss Carryover Worksheet—Lines 6 and 14**     *Keep for Your Records*

Use this worksheet to figure your capital loss carryovers from 2007 to 2008 if your 2007 Schedule D, line 21, is a loss and **(a)** that loss is a smaller loss than the loss on your 2007 Schedule D, line 16, **or (b)** the amount on your 2007 Form 1040, line 41 (or your 2007 Form 1040NR, line 38, if applicable), reduced by any amount on your 2007 Form 8914, line 6, is less than zero. Otherwise, you do not have any carryovers.

1. Enter the amount from your 2007 Form 1040, line 41, or Form 1040NR, line 38. If a loss, enclose the amount in parentheses . . . . . . . . . . . . . . . . . . . . . . . . . . . . . . . . . . . . . . . . . . . . . . . . . . . . . . . . . . . . . . . . . . . . . . .   **1.** _____

2. Did you file Form 8914 (to claim an exemption amount for housing someone displaced by Hurricane Katrina) for 2007?
   ☐ **No.** Enter -0-.
   ☐ **Yes.** Enter the amount from your 2007 Form 8914, line 6 . . . . . . . . . . . . . . . . . . . . . . . . . . . .   **2.** _____

3. Subtract line 2 from line 1. If the result is less than zero, enclose it in parentheses . . . . . . . . . . . . . . . . . .   **3.** _____
4. Enter the loss from your 2007 Schedule D, line 21, as a positive amount . . . . . . . . . . . . . . . . . . . . . . . . . .   **4.** _____
5. Combine lines 3 and 4. If zero or less, enter -0- . . . . . . . . . . . . . . . . . . . . . . . . . . . . . . . . . . . . . . . . . . . .   **5.** _____
6. Enter the **smaller** of line 4 or line 5 . . . . . . . . . . . . . . . . . . . . . . . . . . . . . . . . . . . . . . . . . . . . . . . . . . . .   **6.** _____
   **If line 7 of your 2007 Schedule D is a loss, go to line 7; otherwise, enter -0- on line 7 and go to line 11.**
7. Enter the loss from your 2007 Schedule D, line 7, as a positive amount . . . . . . . . . . . . . . . . . . . . . . . . . . . .   **7.** _____
8. Enter any gain from your 2007 Schedule D, line 15. If a loss, enter -0- . . . . . . . . . . .     **8.** _____
9. Add lines 6 and 8 . . . . . . . . . . . . . . . . . . . . . . . . . . . . . . . . . . . . . . . . . . . . . . . . . . . . . . . . . . . . . . . . . .   **9.** _____
10. **Short-term capital loss carryover for 2008.** Subtract line 9 from line 7. If zero or less, enter -0-. If more than zero, also enter this amount on Schedule D, line 6 . . . . . . . . . . . . . . . . . . . . . . . . . . . . . . . . . . . . . . . .   **10.** _____
    **If line 15 of your 2007 Schedule D is a loss, go to line 11; otherwise, skip lines 11 through 15.**
11. Enter the loss from your 2007 Schedule D, line 15, as a positive amount . . . . . . . . . . . . . . . . . . . . . . . . . . .   **11.** _____
12. Enter any gain from your 2007 Schedule D, line 7. If a loss, enter -0- . . . . . . . . . . . .     **12.** _____
13. Subtract line 7 from line 6. If zero or less, enter -0- . . . . . . . . . . . . . . . . . . . . . .     **13.** _____
14. Add lines 12 and 13 . . . . . . . . . . . . . . . . . . . . . . . . . . . . . . . . . . . . . . . . . . . . . . . . . . . . . . . . . . . . . . .   **14.** _____
15. **Long-term capital loss carryover for 2008.** Subtract line 14 from line 11. If zero or less, enter -0-. If more than zero, also enter this amount on Schedule D, line 14 . . . . . . . . . . . . . . . . . . . . . . . . . . . . . . . . . . . . .   **15.** _____

---

**FIGURE 4.2** Capital Loss Worksheet for Figuring Carryovers

## What to Do Now

Take a hard look at your holdings and weed out your losers. Not only does this make good financial sense, but it also enables you to take a deduction for your losses. From a tax perspective you may want to take these steps:

*Step 1:* Look at any gains or losses you've already taken during the year. Include any gains or losses that are passed through to you from pass-through entities (S corporations, partnerships, or limited liability companies), trusts, and estates in which you have an interest.

*Step 2:* Check last year's return for any capital loss carryover you can apply this year.

*Step 3:* Actualize short-term losses first to offset any short-term capital gains you've already taken. If you're not holding any potential short-term losses, then actualize long-term capital losses to offset your short-term capital gains.

*Step 4:* If you've fully offset short-term gains with capital losses, consider taking additional losses to offset any long-term capital gains, *plus* an additional $3,000 ($1,500 if you are married and file a separate return).

### CAUTION

**Never let tax considerations alone dictate your actions; be sure to make sound financial decisions after factoring in the tax treatment for your decisions.**

For instance, if you sell property at a loss to a brother-in-law who is acting as the nominee of your sister, you can't recognize your loss.

The rule that restricts your ability to report a loss on a sale to a related party isn't limited to sales to your relatives. It also applies to sales to a related corporation (one in which you own more than 50 percent of the value of the stock) and certain other controlled entities, such as trusts and estates.

The disallowed loss can be salvaged if the related party then sells the asset at a profit. The portion of the gain that reflects your loss is not taxed to the related party. Of course, you don't benefit from the disallowed loss; you can't deduct the loss when the related party sells the asset at a gain.

## Example

You bought stock for $10,000 and sell it to your father two years later when it is priced at $8,000. If your father sells the stock for $9,000, he need not report this gain because he can use part of your $2,000 loss to offset it. If he sells the stock for $11,000, his taxable gain is $1,000, the portion of the gain in excess of your $2,000 loss that was disallowed.

## Losses in Retirement Plan Accounts

As a general rule, you can't deduct losses on assets held by a tax-deferred or tax-free account, such as a 401(k) or a Roth IRA. This fact—that losses aren't deductible—should be remembered when making investment decisions in these retirement accounts.

However, under very special situations, losses on investments made through these retirement accounts can be recognized.

- *Traditional individual retirement accounts (IRAs)*. Recognize any unrecovered basis (nondeductible contributions) when all the funds in all of your accounts have been distributed to you. No loss can ever be claimed with respect to deductible funds contributed to your IRA. If after meeting this rule you have any losses, deduct them as a miscellaneous itemized deduction on Schedule A of Form 1040; the loss is allowed only to the extent that miscellaneous itemized deductions exceed 2 percent of your adjusted gross income (AGI).

- *Roth IRAs*. If you have a loss on your Roth IRA investments, you can recognize it only when all amounts have been distributed from all your Roth IRAs and the total distributions are less than your unrecovered basis (the after-tax contributions you made to the Roth IRAs). Like losses in traditional IRAs, recognized losses in Roth IRAs can be claimed only as a miscellaneous itemized deduction.

**CAUTION**

If losses from a traditional IRA or Roth IRA are deducted as a miscellaneous itemized deduction, they must be added back to income for purposes of figuring the alternative minimum tax (AMT). In effect, anyone subject to the AMT cannot benefit from these tax losses.

## Losses in 529 Plans

While losses usually are not deductible, you can write off losses if you withdraw all the funds from the account and this is less than your contributions.

### Example

You contribute $2,000 to a nondeductible IRA in 2006, and by the end of 2007 the account has earned $400 in income. If you received a distribution in 2007 of $600 (comprised of one-fourth of the basis from the contribution and one-fourth of the income or $500 of basis + $100 of income), your basis in the IRA is $1,800 ($2,000 + $400– $600). In 2008, the account suffers a $500 loss. Your basis is now $1,500 ($2,000—$500). If you take a distribution of the remaining balance of $1,300, you can claim a loss of $200 (basis of $1,500, less the distribution of account balance of $1,300).

## Losses on Inherited Property

When you inherit property, your basis is the property's estate tax value, usually its value on the date of death. This is so even if the deceased person from whom you inherited the property paid more for the property than it was worth at the time of his or her death. The decline in the value of a deceased person's assets does not create any tax breaks—for the deceased person or for the person who inherits the assets.

### Example

Your uncle bought 100 shares of Z Inc. for $25,000. At the time of his death, they had declined to a total value of $12,000; he left the shares to you. Since he didn't sell them before he died, the loss cannot be reported on his final income tax return. Your basis in the shares is $12,000; you can't factor in the amount he paid for the shares to increase your basis.

## Maximizing Tax Losses

Don't underreport your losses by not properly adding to your basis certain costs or expenses that relate to the asset or the sale. The higher your tax basis, the greater your tax-deductible loss. Take into account:

- Stock dividends you reinvested in the same company. If, for example, you participate in a dividend reinvestment plan for stock or mutual fund shares, remember to include the reinvested dividends as part of your basis. If you don't, you'll effectively pay twice on the same income—once when you receive the dividends and again if you fail to include them in basis so that you overreport your gain or underreport your loss.

- Brokers' commissions to buy and sell shares.

- Acquisition costs, such as an attorney's fees to handle the purchase of realty.

- Selling costs for realty, such as the real estate broker's fees.

Use the specific identification method to maximize losses when selling a portion of your holdings in a particular stock or mutual fund if you acquired your interests in these investments at different times. This will enable you to designate which shares you're selling so you can optimize your tax results. If you don't earmark which shares you're selling, the tax law assumes you are selling the first shares you acquired (first in, first out).

### Example

You bought shares in P Corp., a pharmaceutical company, over time. In 1998, you bought 50 shares at $87 each and in 2001 you bought 100 shares at $95 each. The stock is now trading at $75 and you don't have much confidence that it will recover, but you only want to sell 100 shares. Without any action on your part, the first-in, first-out rule applies, so that the 100 shares sold would be deemed to be 50 from the first lot and 50 from the second lot, for a tax loss of $1,600: 100 × $75 = $7,500; (50 × $87) + (50 × $95) = $9,100; $9,100 − $7,500 = $1,600. If you earmark the shares you're selling, you can designate that you're selling 100 shares of the second lot, so your loss is $2,000 ($7,500 sales proceeds minus $9,500 basis of the second lot).

To use the specific identification method, you must give instructions to your broker about which shares to sell and receive a written confirmation of your instructions from the broker or transfer agent within a reasonable time.

## Wash Sale Rule

The tax law doesn't want you to be able to churn your holdings solely for tax advantage without really changing your economic position. To this end, there is a restriction in the tax law called the wash sale rule. This rule prevents you from recognizing a loss on the sale of a security if you acquire a substantially identical one within 30 days before or after the date of sale. For instance, if you sell 10 shares of Y Corp. at a loss on May 1 and two weeks later on May 15 you buy 10 shares of Y Corp., you cannot deduct the loss on the May 1 sale.

The wash sale rule has no applicability to gains. You can sell for profit as often as you want (each gain must be reported). However, the wash sale rule applies to short sales. If you incur a loss when you close a short sale within 30 days before or after another similar short sale, the loss cannot be recognized.

### Substantially Identical Securities

The wash sale rule applies to stocks, bonds, and mutual fund shares that are the same or substantially identical. Selling stock in Hewlett-Packard (HP) at a loss and buying shares in Apple Inc. within the wash sale period are not subject to the wash sale rule. Although HP and Apple are both technology companies and each sells computers, they are not viewed as substantially identical.

Similarly, selling shares in a Vanguard S&P mutual fund at a loss and buying shares in a Fidelity S&P mutual fund within the wash sale period does not fall within the wash sale rule, because these funds have different fees and other differences that keep them from being substantially identical. Shares in different funds within the same mutual fund family are, of course, different securities and are not subject to the wash sale rules. If you sell shares from a Fidelity stock fund at a loss and buy shares in a Fidelity bond fund within the wash sale period, the loss can be recognized.

Bonds are not viewed as substantially identical, even if they are from the same issuer, if there is any difference in interest rates. However, differences in maturity or interest payment dates do not create significant differences, and bonds bearing these small differences will be treated as substantially identical securities subject to the wash sale rules.

The wash sale rule applies to any option you buy to acquire a substantially identical security within the wash sale period.

The wash sale rule cannot be avoided by having a controlled person acquire a substantially identical security within the wash sale period. A controlled person for this purpose is a spouse or a corporation you control.

### Basis Adjustment

The loss from a wash sale generally is not lost forever; it is preserved in the basis of the newly acquired security. Thus, the fact that you really suffered an economic loss when you made the sale is taken into account. You add the disallowed loss to the basis of the new security, so that when the newly acquired security is sold, the deferred loss will be recognized (or the gain will be minimized to the extent of the deferred loss).

### Example

You own 100 shares of X Inc. that cost you $1,000. You sell these shares for $800 and, within 30 days from the sale, you buy 100 shares of the same stock for $850. Because you bought substantially identical stock, you cannot deduct your loss of $200 on the sale. However, the disallowed loss of $200 is added to the cost of the new stock, $850, to obtain your basis in the new stock, which is $1,050. If you later sell the new stock for $1,050, you have no recognized tax gain even though the stock cost you only $850.

The holding period of the newly acquired security includes the holding period of the old security. However, if there is time between the date you sold the old security and the date you purchased a new security, don't add the intervening time to your holding period; include only the actual holding period of the old security as part of the holding period for the newly acquired security.

### Rule Applies to All Accounts

In the past, some tax experts believed that you could get around the wash sale rule by selling a security within a taxable account and then acquiring the same security during the wash sale period in a tax-deferred account, such as an IRA or a Roth IRA. However, the IRS has ruled that the wash sale rule applies when you sell in your taxable account and then cause your tax-deferred account (IRA) to acquire a substantially identical security during the wash sale period. Even worse, the basis of the IRA cannot be increased by the loss that is disallowed under the wash sale rule; it is lost forever.

**What to Do Now**

If you want to take a tax loss while avoiding the wash sale rule, there are various steps you can take if you want to preserve your investment position in the same security:

- Wait out the wash sale period before reacquiring the same security.
- Use a technique called doubling up. You buy the same number of shares in the company you're currently holding and then, after the wash sale period has expired, sell off the old shares, leaving you with the same number of new shares in the same stock.
- Play an industry rather than a company. If you believe in a particular industry, you can sell your losing shares and immediately buy shares in a competing company without triggering the wash sale rule. Of course, the competing companies may be worlds apart because no two companies are identical (though both may benefit or be hurt by conditions within their industry).
- Buy bonds that are similar but have slightly different interest rates. If interest rates are different, the bonds are not substantially identical.
- Acquire a smaller number of shares in the same security during the wash sale period. You'll be able to recognize a portion of the loss in this case. For example, if you sell 100 shares and within the wash sale period you buy 50 shares of the same corporation, only half of your loss is disallowed; the other half can be recognized.

The wash sale rule can be a positive rather than a penalty. You can use the wash sale rule to your advantage in timing year-end transactions. Say, for example, that you're in negotiations to sell an asset at the end of the year for a profit but aren't sure when the deal will close. You can sell losing stock late in December to create a deductible loss. If the profitable deal closes in December, then you've created an offset to your gain. If the deal doesn't close until January, be sure to buy back the losing stock within the 30-day wash sale period to trigger the wash sale rule, and again sell, but this time wait out the wash sale period. This will enable you to defer the loss from December to the following year when the gain is reported.

## Section 1244 Losses

Usually, a loss on the sale or exchange of stock is a capital loss. However, there's a special tax rule that applies to certain stock in a closely held corporation. If the stock is considered to be Section 1244 stock, then loss up to $50,000 ($100,000 on a joint return) is treated as an ordinary loss. Having the loss treated as an ordinary loss rather than a capital loss is more favorable because the loss isn't limited by the extent of capital gains for the year plus the $3,000 maximum ordinary loss limit.

Certain rules come into play to determine whether you sold stock that meets the requirements for Section 1244 treatment. Forget about any publicly traded stock being Section 1244 stock; only stock in a closely held corporation can qualify because of the capitalization limit. To qualify as Section 1244 stock, the stock must have been issued by a small corporation (one whose capitalization does not exceed $1 million).

The corporation must be an operating business and not a holding company. During the corporation's five most recent tax years before the stock is sold or becomes worthless, more than 50 percent of the corporation's income must have been derived from operating revenues (not passive investments). You aren't required to attach any documents to your return showing the corporation's revenues or other information. Keep this information, though, in case the IRS wants to see it.

You must have acquired the stock in exchange for money or property. You can treat stock that you received for performing services as Section 1244 stock. Section 1244 stock can be common or preferred stock.

You must be the original owner of the stock and must have acquired the stock directly from the corporation. Stock you acquire from another shareholder doesn't qualify as Section 1244 stock.

### Losses over the Section 1244 Limit

Any losses on qualified stock in excess of the Section 1244 limit are treated as capital losses. The excess loss can be used to offset capital gains and then up to $3,000 of ordinary income.

**Example**

Several years ago you invested $150,000 in your corporation and, in 2008, it went bankrupt, so you entire investment is lost. If your stock qualifies as Section 1244 stock and you and your spouse file a joint return, you can report $100,000 as an ordinary loss and $50,000 as a capital loss. If you have no capital gains for the year, your total deduction is $103,000 ($100,000 Section 1244 loss plus $3,000 ordinary loss). You have a capital loss carryforward of $47,000.

## Worthless Securities

Stocks and bonds, whether publicly traded or privately held, can lose all of their value. As long as you can show that your securities had *some* value at the end of the previous year but become totally worthless this year, you can write off the loss. Your loss write-off is limited to your basis in the security (usually what you paid for it, plus any transaction costs). The fact that you may have watched the security soar in price at one time before plummeting does not increase your tax write-off.

Securities that become completely worthless during the year are treated as having become worthless on the last day of the year (December 31). This deemed date of worthlessness determines whether your loss is short-term or long-term.

The loss deduction is allowed only in the year you can show that the security is completely worthless. Usually, this requires an identifiable event to establish worthlessness, such as a liquidation of the corporation following bankruptcy, with no assets available to pay shareholders. Even *some* small value prevents a loss deduction because the security is not totally worthless.

You may be able to nail down a loss for a worthless security by abandoning it. A new regulation allows a loss in this case. Under the final regulation, although you do not have to relinquish legal title to the security in all cases to establish abandonment, you do have to permanently surrender and relinquish all rights in the security and receive no consideration in exchange for the security.

---

### What to Do Now

Determine when a security has become totally worthless so you can take the loss on the proper tax return. Do this by checking the year-end statements from brokerage firm that is holding your stock. If you hold publicly traded stock in your own name, rather than in the brokerage firm's name (street name), look in the financial section of your newspaper for the last trading day of the year (typically December 31). Only stocks with value are listed in the newspapers, so if yours no longer appears, it may have become worthless.

Instead of waiting for a stock to become totally worthless, try to sell the securities for a nominal value in order to fix the date and amount of the loss. Your brokerage firm may buy your almost-worthless securities, something that it does as a service to its customers.

---

### Extended Statute of Limitations

It is not always easy to fix the point that a security becomes worthless. In view of this, the tax law gives you more time to make a claim for a refund based on a worthless security. Generally, you have only three years from the due date of your return to submit a refund claim. For a claim based on a worthless security, you have seven years. A claim is made by filing Form 1040X, Amended U.S. Individual Income Tax Return.

If you are unsure in which year to claim the loss, it's generally a good idea to report it in the earliest year you suspect that the worthlessness occurred and then to renew your claim in each subsequent year if the earliest year proves to be incorrect. However, this strategy requires that you file an amended return to eliminate the loss from the earliest return and report it on a subsequent return.

## Penalty on Early Withdrawal of Savings

If you have money in a time deposit account or a certificate of deposit (CD), a savings vehicle that runs for a fixed term, and you need your money before the maturity date, you will pay a penalty to the bank (there's no tax penalty here). The penalty is usually a forfeiture of interest, but in some cases, it may include a forfeiture of some of the principal.

Fortunately, the penalty is tax deductible. It isn't a capital loss and it isn't used to offset capital gains. It is an ordinary loss that is fully deductible from gross income, whether or not you itemize your personal deductions.

### What to Do Now

To avoid having penalties, use multiple accounts or multiple CDs. Then stagger their maturities so you can continually have access to your money without incurring any penalty. Don't use the automatic renewal feature that typically accompanies these savings products, so you can control reinvestment according to your needs.

### Tax Reporting

The penalty (the forfeited interest and/or principal) is reported to you and to the IRS on:

- Form 1099-INT if the time deposit or CD was for one year or less.
- Form 1099-OID if the time deposit or CD was for more than one year.

You do not offset the interest for the year by the amount of the penalty and then report the net amount as income. Instead, you must report the full amount of interest for the year and then deduct the penalty amount from your gross income (you don't have to itemize deductions to take this write-off). However, it has the same effect as netting—your adjusted gross income reflects only the net amount.

### Early Redemption of U.S. Savings Bonds

You are not permitted to cash in Series EE and Series I savings bonds within the first 12 months of issuance (a six-month period had applied to bonds of issue dates of January 2003 and earlier). If you cash in these bonds within the first five years, you forfeit three months of interest. You don't deduct the loss for tax purposes. Instead, the Treasury reports only the interest that is actually paid to you (the interest minus the three-month penalty).

### Example

You hold a Series I savings bond that you cash in at the end of two years. You're due 24 months of interest, but you'll be paid only 21 months of interest (24 months of interest minus the three-month penalty). Form 1099-INT will be given to you showing 21 months of interest.

## Bank Deposit Losses

Banks sometimes fail, but the rate of such failures is very low. During the savings and loan crisis in the late 1980s, 206 banks went under and the U.S. economy weathered the storm. Currently the Federal Deposit Insurance Corporation (FDIC) is closely watching 76 troubled institutions; these have not failed yet.

It's rare but not unheard-of for someone to have a loss because a bank goes under and the deposits are not covered or not fully covered by FDIC insurance (see Chapter 3). For example, say a person has $300,000 in individual savings and checking accounts at one bank that fails in May 2009. Since only $250,000 is FDIC-insured, this person has a $50,000 loss. The tax law provides three ways in which to treat your loss:

1. Bad debt deduction
2. Casualty loss
3. Ordinary loss

You must choose which of the three options works best for your situation.

### Bad Debt

You can opt to treat your loss as a bad debt, which is classified for tax purposes as a short-term capital loss (regardless of how long your money was on deposit). This means you can deduct your loss against capital gains. If you do not have capital gains or if these losses are greater than your capital gains, you can only deduct up to $3,000 against your ordinary income. Any unused amount of the loss can be carried forward and used in a future year (see capital loss rules explained earlier in this chapter).

In order to treat the deposit loss as a bad debt, there must be no reasonable prospect of recovery from the insolvent or bankrupt bank. You must wait until the year in which your nonrecovery becomes clear.

### Casualty Loss

You can choose to treat your loss as a casualty loss, which means you must itemize deductions to claim the loss this way. The amount of your deposit loss is reduced by $100 right off the top—the $100 subtraction is a feature in the tax law for claiming a casualty loss deduction.

Casualty losses (after the $100 reduction) are deductible only to the extent they exceed 10 percent of your adjusted gross income (AGI), another condition in the tax law.

---

## What to Do Now

If you qualify to select any of the three deduction options, keep these factors in mind and run the numbers on each option to decide which one works best for you.

- Choose the bad debt deduction option if your loss can be fully used in the current year (you have capital gains to offset the loss or no more than $3,000 of bad debt in excess of your capital gains). If you suffered a deposit loss years ago but didn't know about it, it may be too late to claim an ordinary or casualty loss, but not too late for a bad debt deduction. Generally, you have seven years from the due date of your return for the year of the loss to amend it and report the bad debt deduction.

- Choose the ordinary loss option if your loss is under the dollar limit and you already have miscellaneous itemized deductions that offset the 2-percent-of-AGI floor and are *not* subject to the alternative minimum tax (AMT).
  Example: In 2008, you have an uninsured bank loss of $15,000. Your adjusted gross income is $60,000 and you also have $1,200 or more of other miscellaneous itemized deductions. You can fully deduct your $15,000 loss. But if you are subject to the AMT, selecting this option may increase your liability, because miscellaneous itemized deductions are not deductible for AMT purposes.

- Choose the casualty loss option if you already have casualty or theft losses for the year that offset the 10-percent-of-AGI floor.
  Example: In 2008, your car was damaged in an accident and you did not have collision insurance. Your loss on this incident was $6,000. You also have an uninsured loss on your bank deposit of $10,000. Assuming your adjusted gross income is $60,000 or less, you can then fully utilize the $10,000 bank deposit loss. But if the bank deposit loss was your only loss for the year, using the casualty loss method means you cannot benefit from the first $6,000 of your $10,000 loss because of the 10-percent-of-AGI floor.

Once you choose the option to treat your loss on bank deposits as a casualty loss, it's irrevocable and must be used for any additional losses you incur from the same financial institution.

You can use this option if you have an estimated loss. You don't have to wait until there is no reasonable prospect of recovery to claim a casualty loss deduction. If, for some reason, you eventually receive some or all of your money, you must report the recovery as income in the year you receive it to the extent your original deduction produced a tax benefit.

This option cannot be used by stockholders of the bank if they own more than a 1 percent interest. Similarly, this option cannot be used by the bank's officers or relatives of officers or stockholders.

## Ordinary Loss

You can decide to deduct up to $20,000 ($10,000 if you are married and file a separate return) as a miscellaneous itemized deduction, which is subject to the 2-percent-of-AGI floor. The dollar limit applies per institution, not per account. For example, if you have two accounts at the same insolvent bank, each for $15,000, your total deduction is limited to $20,000. But if you have those accounts at two separate insolvent banks, you could deduct a total of $30,000 ($15,000 for each account since this does not exceed the $20,000 per-bank limit) in the same year.

You can use the ordinary loss treatment only if none of your deposits were federally insured.

## Tax Reporting

Whichever option you use to report the loss, you must file Form 1040. If you treat the loss as a bad debt, you must file Schedule D to report the loss. In column (f) of Schedule D, enter the loss in parentheses to indicate that it is in fact a loss amount.

If you treat the loss as a casualty loss, file Form 4684, Casualties and Thefts, to report the loss. The loss is then entered on Schedule A.

If you claim the loss as an ordinary loss, file Schedule A to report the loss.

# CHAPTER 5

# Meeting Everyday Needs

A visit to the grocery store or a stop at the gas station is all you need to do these days to confirm that these are difficult economic times. The price of practically everything is up and paychecks aren't keeping pace. Many workers are jittery about their job security. Others are worried that their adjustable mortgage rates will reset at a level that makes it difficult or impossible to retain their homes. Doom and gloom are everywhere.

Acting like an ostrich and sticking your head in the sand to avoid unpleasantness won't reduce or eliminate your financial woes. The only smart course of action is to do something that can reduce your outlays and take some strain off your pocketbook. Two-thirds of American workers live paycheck to paycheck, so the need to find ways to cut costs cannot be minimized. Frugality isn't a dirty word and it doesn't make you cheap; it's a practical approach to economizing so you can have the things you need with the money you earn.

Looking ahead, economic times will surely improve; they always do. The strategies you use to see you through hard times will pay off even more when things get better. Developing good spending habits will create more wealth for you throughout your lifetime.

In this chapter you'll find out ways to create a budget that you can live with and learn creative ways to make your money go as far as possible. You'll see how to reduce the costs of health care, energy, and food—everyday essentials—and learn how to manage credit card debt more effectively. You'll also discover untapped personal resources that you can turn to in tough times to help you over a short-term financial slump. Topics covered in this chapter are:

- Stretching your dollars
- Reducing health care costs
- Saving energy costs
- Trimming the fat off food bills
- Handling credit card debt
- Owning a vehicle
- Tapping into personal resources as a last resort

## Stretching Your Dollars

It's simple mathematics: To make ends meet you either increase your income or decrease your expenses. There's no other way to match the money you have with the things you want or need to buy or pay for. Here are some ways to maximize your monthly cash so you can cover your bills and stay out of financial trouble.

### Make a Budget

A financial budget is a diet for your money. Like deciding whether to use your calories for a steak or ice cream, you also have to plan where your money will go each month. Sticking to a budget, like following a diet, will keep you from splurging on purchases that may feel good at the time but won't make you look good in the long run.

In order to make a budget, you need to track where your money goes. Experts suggest that you do this exercise: Write down every penny you spend for a month. Then you'll have a clearer idea of what you are actually spending your money on so you'll be able to craft a budget.

There are many ways to make a budget. You can use online budgeting tools, buy fancy software, or work with financial planners, alternatives that make sense if you can't do it on your own. But budgeting isn't all that difficult. All you need to be able to do is marshal key information about your income and expenses and then bring some common sense and honesty to the process.

- *List your monthly after-tax income.* This is the money you have left after withholding for income taxes, FICA (Social Security and Medicare taxes), and any other amount subtracted from your paycheck—for example, 401(k) contributions and flexible spending account (FSA) contributions.
- *List all of the fixed expenses you have each month.* Include your rent or mortgage payments, car payments, insurance premiums (divide any annual premium by 12 to get your monthly cost), phone bill, and alimony and child support where applicable. Some expenses, such as utility bills, dependent

care expenses, and transportation costs, may not be exactly the same each month, but you can average the annual costs over 12 months for purposes of your budget.

- *List all of the variable expenses each month.* These include amounts spent on clothing, recreation, personal care (haircuts, manicures), gifts, contributions to charity, and pocket money for you, your spouse, and your children. Build into your budget an amount for the unexpected, such as the need to replace a broken appliance or a dental bill not covered by insurance. Be realistic about this miscellaneous expense; look over your check register and credit card bills for the prior year to see what types of unexpected items you've had and what they cost.

- *List all the items you save for each month.* Build savings into your budget. Savings can include contributions to retirement plans, funding for your children's education, or saving for a specific goal (e.g., for a down payment on a home). Having short-term and long-term goals to work toward will help you stay on track with your budget.

After listing all of these items, compare the money you have (your after-tax income) with the money you need to spend (fixed expenses, variable expenses, and savings). Don't know how much you should be spending on a particular item? There's no fixed rule, but it may be helpful to know what the average consumer spends. The most recent Consumer Expenditure Survey from U.S. Bureau of Labor Statistics (Table 5.1) provides a breakdown.

If you find that the income you have won't cover your projected outlays, you must take action. To repeat what was said earlier, you have only two choices: increase your income or reduce your expenses.

### Increase Your Income

It is not uncommon for people to get second jobs to cover their families' expenses. Whether this is possible or practical for you depends on your situation. Here are

**TABLE 5.1** Annual Household Expenditures

| Item | Percentage of Household Spending |
| --- | --- |
| Housing | 32.7% |
| Transportation | 18.0% |
| Food | 12.8% |
| Personal insurance and retirement savings | 11.2% |
| Health care | 5.7% |
| Entertainment | 5.1% |
| Apparel and services | 4.1% |

*Source:* U.S. Bureau of Labor Statistics.

some other ways to find some extra cash:

- *Sell items online.* Amazon.com, eBay, and Craigslist are a few web sites to explore if you have items at home that you can sell. For instance, if your children have outgrown their crib, carriage, and baby toys, you can sell them. Whatever you receive is helpful. *Note:* You probably won't have any profit to report on these sales. If the money you get is less than what the item cost you, plus any selling expenses (e.g., eBay fees), you technically have a tax loss and don't have to report the sale.

**CAUTION**

Beware of home-based business opportunities such as envelope stuffing or piecework. Many of these are scams that charge you for materials or training but fail to deliver on the income promised.

- *Hold a garage/yard sale.* You don't have to move to clean out your basement, attic, and garage. Disposing of unwanted items may bring you only pennies on the dollar, but these pennies can add up to meaningful cash. The same tax treatment for online sales applies to these sales as well.

- *Obtain seasonal employment.* At holiday time, look for work at retailers. Also check for part-time opportunities at ski resorts in the winter and beachfronts in the summer if you are near any of these locations.

- *Offer personal services.* You may be able to advertise your services as a housecleaner, handyman, yard worker, or tutor.

### Ax the Extras

Assume that nothing in your budget is sacred and everything is fair game for the chopping block. Here's what you can eliminate:

- *Give up gourmet coffee.* Instead of expensive lattes, make your own. At work, drink what's available there or bring your own in a thermos.

- *Give up the second car.* If your family has two or more cars, see whether you can eliminate one. You can share rides or take public transportation. What you save on operational costs (gasoline, insurance, parking fees, etc.), will likely exceed any new costs for public transportation.

- *Give up bad habits.* Smoking and gambling are costly expenses month in and month out. If you smoke a pack of cigarettes a day, you can save by cutting back (and will probably save additional money in health care costs over your lifetime). In New York City, for example, with the hike in the state and city taxes on June 1, 2008, a single pack costs $9, so kicking the habit entirely would save over $3,200 annually.

- *Give up pay channels on cable TV.* Stick to basic service or change to satellite service if it is less costly.

- *Give up the health club membership.* Find no-cost and low-cost alternatives to get the exercise you want. Walking outside is free. Check out access to facilities at your local schools.

- *Give up tech and entertainment options.* Stop paying monthly service charges for Sirius Satellite Radio, Napster (music), OnStar, NetFlix, BlackBerry (if your cell phone is sufficient), and any other optional service that you can live without. The service may make your life a little better or easier, but they are costing you hundreds of dollars monthly, which adds up to thousands over the year.

### Save Money on What You Need

The fact that your children need new shoes or that you have to pay utility bills are just two examples of things that can't be eliminated from your budget. But you can find ways to reduce the cost of getting what you need. Each measure by itself doesn't seem significant, but when added together you can save hundreds or thousands of dollars annually. Here are nine commonsense ways to reduce your monthly outlays:

1. *Use online bill paying or have regular bills debited from your bank account to save on postage.* Postage keeps going up. The rate rose on May 12, 2008, to 42¢ for a first class stamp, and is set to adjust each May. If you usually pay five bills by mail each month, you'll save $25 in postage in a year by paying online; 10 bills will save you $50 (or more when the postal rates increase).

2. *Brown-bag it.* Instead of buying lunch at work, bring your lunch, along with a beverage if you don't have access to free beverages at work. Do the same for your children (who probably don't like the school lunch anyway).

3. *Visit the library.* Instead of buying books for casual reading that do not serve any reference purpose (you won't need to refer to them later on), check them out from the public library. Also use the library's free lending service for DVDs and other materials.

4. *Adopt good health practices.* Cut down on dental and doctor bills by being healthy. Flossing your teeth, eating healthful foods, regularly exercising, and getting enough sleep can help.

5. *Regift.* You can't avoid giving presents at birthdays, weddings, baby showers, and holidays, but you can be cost conscious about it. When you receive a present that you have no use for, save it and pass it on to someone who will appreciate it. You save on having to buy that person a present.

6. *Stay home.* You need recreation, but you don't have to spend an arm and a leg to get it. Instead of going out to the movies, turn on your TV or play

parlor games with friends and family. Instead of dining out, entertain at home.

7. *Comparison shop.* When buying anything over $100, be sure to check competitors' prices.

8. *Keep your car longer.* Instead of buying a new car, keep your current one in good repair. Investing in regular maintenance can keep the car in good operating order.

9. *Vacation closer to home.* Taking time off from work is important to your health and your relationships. But you don't have to go for an expensive adventure. Instead of paying for air travel or gas to drive the car to a distant location, along with lodging, meals, and activities, consider options closer to home. Vacation (called a "staycation") within your own city—many people never explore what's right under their noses. Or take day trips and return home each night.

### Stick to Your Budget

Creating a budget is a worthless exercise if you don't follow through.

- *Adhere to your spending allotments.* If you budget a certain amount for recreation, for example, you'll have to decline invitations from friends to engage in activities that will put you over your monthly allowance for this expenditure.

- *Review your budget.* It's a good idea to look over your line items at least every quarter, but certainly once a year. Also review your budget when there's a change in your circumstances (e.g., a new baby, a new job, or retirement). This will allow you to make necessary adjustments. Say you get a raise at work. This gives you more money to spend, so you can increase certain items, such as dining out or buying clothing.

## Reducing Health Care Costs

Today, there are an estimated 45.7 million Americans without health insurance. And even many of those who do have coverage through employers are being asked to pay an increasing share each year. If you're currently without coverage or fear you may find yourself in this boat, or you are shouldering a significant share of employer-paid coverage, look for ways to have the protection you need at an affordable price.

### Tax Deduction for Health Insurance

If you pay for coverage, the premiums are a deductible medical expense and help to reduce your after-tax cost for coverage. Deductible health insurance premiums include the cost of coverage for hospital, surgical, and other medical expenses (whether you pay it directly to the insurer or it is withheld from your wages under an employer plan); Medicare, consisting of Part A (hospital coverage, which is free only for persons covered by Social Security), Part B (for doctors and other nonhospital costs), and Part D (prescription drug coverage); and contact lens replacement coverage.

However, total medical expenses can be deducted as an itemized deduction on your federal income tax return only to the extent they exceed 7.5 percent of your adjusted gross income.

## Example

You paid premiums for yourself and your family during the year of $10,000 for private coverage. Your out-of-pocket costs (e.g., co-pays, deductibles, and noncovered expenses) amounted to $2,000 for the year, for a total outlay of $12,000. If your adjusted gross income is $85,000, you can deduct $5,625: 7.5 percent of $85,000 = $6,375; $12,000 − $6,375 = $5,625. The balance, or $6,375, is not deductible.

Self-employed individuals can deduct premiums for coverage for themselves and their family from gross income (they don't have to itemize deductions and can deduct *all* of the premiums). This rule also applies to S corporation shareholders owning more than 2 percent of their business.

Congress *may* change the rules to put self-employed individuals on a par with regular corporations. If the law is changed, premiums for self-employed individuals would become a deductible business expense. It would offset business income directly, effectively reducing net earnings on which self-employment tax is figured. If enacted, this change would effectively save self-employed individuals 15.3 percent of their premiums (the rate for self-employment tax).

## What to Do Now

Retain all receipts for medical procedures, medications, and devices. Some may be covered by insurance and therefore would not be deductible; others may not be covered by insurance, flexible spending accounts (FSAs), health reimbursement accounts, or health savings accounts (HSAs), and will be deductible if you itemize your medical expenses.

### Employer-Provided Coverage

If you work for a company that offers health coverage, this is an important money-saving fringe benefit. You may receive the coverage entirely tax free. If, as is common, you may pay a portion of your coverage, the part you pay is a deductible expense for you (as explained previously).

---

**What to Do Now**

To enjoy coverage without overspending, take these actions:

- If you and your spouse or domestic partner each have access to health coverage at work but must pay a share of the premiums, coordinate your choices. Decide who will take the coverage and who will not so you don't pay for duplicative services. In making your decision, evaluate both plans: review the extent of coverage, your co-pay requirements, and monthly cost to you.

- Follow your plan's rules for optimum coverage at the lowest price. For instance, stay in-network where possible, obtain referrals to specialists if necessary, and receive preapproval from your insurer for certain procedures when required.

- Stay alert to changes in coverage. New items may be covered; existing coverage may cost more, so look closely at notices that are sent to you from the insurer.

---

Learn about availability of COBRA coverage. This is coverage under your employer's group plan if you leave employment (regardless of whether you quit or are terminated). COBRA gives you the right to continue under the plan for 18 months (longer in certain cases). You pay the premiums, plus an administrative fee of no more than 2 percent. Access to COBRA coverage is a good thing because the cost to you is probably less than what you'd have to pay for coverage found on your own. Having COBRA coverage can carry you until you obtain a new job with its own medical coverage.

Under federal law, COBRA applies only to companies that regularly employee 20 or more workers annually, so if you work for a small employer you may not have COBRA availability. However, a number of states have "mini COBRA," which can apply to companies with as few as two employees, so check with your state insurance department if you have any questions.

### Flexible Spending Accounts

If you work for a company that offers flexible spending accounts (FSAs), consider taking advantage of them. These plans allow you to pay for your out-of-pocket medical costs on a pretax basis. You put a portion of your salary into the FSA—the amount depends on the limit fixed by the employer, what you think you can afford, and what you think you'll use within the year. If your contributions aren't used up within the year (or within an extended grace period that may be offered by an employer up to no later than March 15 of the following year), you lose this money forever.

## Example

Your annual salary is $45,000 and you contribute $2,500 to your FSA. On your W-2 form for the year, your taxable wages are $42,500 ($45,000 − $2,500). You don't pay income tax on the $2,500 contributed to the FSA, nor is this amount deductible. If you spend only $2,200 of the $2,500 in your FSA, you'll have lost $300 (it can't be carried over to the following FSA period). However, you might have lost that $300 anyway for income tax if the $2,500 had remained part of your taxable wages.

## What to Do Now

Learn the rules about your FSA—when you must sign up for the following year, whether you can change your contribution amount during the year, what you have to do to be reimbursed for out-of-pocket medical costs, and whether your plan has a grace period in which to use up your annual contribution.

### Health Savings Accounts

Health savings accounts (HSAs) are consumer-driven health care solutions designed to make you more discriminating about how you spend your health dollars. The concept combines a high-deductible (low-cost) health plan (HDHP) with a special savings account called a health savings account. You pay out of pocket for the first dollars of health care until you reach a dollar threshold fixed by the policy (the threshold is called a deductible, but has nothing to do with a tax deduction; it refers to what you must pay before the insurer starts to pay). Once you've paid out this amount, insurance covers the rest.

Health savings accounts can be an affordable way to obtain health coverage. While you bear many costs that are covered by traditional health insurance, you are assured that you have protection for serious and catastrophic illness or conditions. Increasingly, employers are offering HSAs as a health care option that is less costly for employees than traditional health insurance.

With an HSA, you can take withdrawals from the savings account at any time you want. If withdrawals are used to pay medical costs not covered by insurance, including over-the-counter medications, the money isn't taxed to you. If you use funds for nonmedical purposes, the money is income to you; you pay a tax on it, as well as a 15 percent penalty if you're under age 65.

The HDHP must meet minimum deductibles fixed by the tax law (see Table 5.2). The HDHP limits may be adjusted annually.

**TABLE 5.2** HDHP Limits for 2008

|  | Self-Only Coverage | Family Coverage |
|---|---|---|
| Annual minimum deductible | $1,100 | $ 2,200 |
| Maximum out-of-pocket expenses | $5,600 | $11,200 |

Once you have the necessary HDHP in place, you can fund your savings account. The tax law limits how much you can add to the account each year (see Table 5.3); HSA contribution limits are adjusted annually. You don't have to make the maximum contribution; you can add what you can afford. If you don't use up your contribution, the money, plus any earnings on it, carries forward indefinitely. In effect, you can stockpile a fund for medical expenses as long as you stay healthy or choose to pay medical costs with other money.

The costs of HSAs—both health insurance premiums and contributions to the savings account—are usually lower than traditional coverage. The costs are further reduced because you can claim two separate deductions for HSAs:

- The premiums for the high-deductible health plan are part of your itemized medical expenses (see previous discussion).

- Contributions to HSAs are deductible from gross income in the same manner as contributions to regular IRAs.

**TABLE 5.3** HSA Contribution Limits for 2008

|  | Self-Only Coverage | Family Coverage |
|---|---|---|
| Under age 55 | $2,900 | $5,800 |
| Age 55 or older | $3,800 | $6,700 |

## What to Do Now

If you don't have health coverage, using the HDHP/HSA combination may solve your coverage need. Determine whether it's suitable for your situation. If, for example, someone in your family under your policy has a serious health condition, this arrangement may not adequately address your financial exposure; you may need more traditional health coverage.

If you're interested in HSAs, resources to check out include:

- HSA Bank (www.hsabank.com)
- HSAfinder.com (www.hsafinder.com)
- HSA Insider (www.hsainsider.com)
- HSA Living (www.hsa.com)

If your employer offers an HSA, whether you are entitled to the deduction depends on who makes the contribution. If you do, then you claim it; if your employer adds money to your HSA, then your employer deducts it (you're not taxed on this contribution).

### Other Employer Health Plans

Companies may offer plans to help pay for health costs beyond traditional insurance, flexible spending accounts, and health savings accounts.

- *Health reimbursement accounts.* These are bookkeeping entries that companies make on behalf of employees up to dollar amounts they determine (e.g., $3,000 annually); employees can draw from these accounts to pay medical costs, and unused amounts are carried forward to be used in future years. When employees leave the company, any unused amounts are lost.
- *Archer medical savings accounts (MSAs).* Small employers can offer these health plans that combine insurance with a savings-type account; they are similar to Health Savings Accounts (discussed earlier). Self-employed individuals can use Archer MSAs too (the opportunity to set up new MSAs expired at the end of 2007 but Congress may extend them; existing MSAs can still be funded annually).

### What to Do Now

Talk to your company's human resources (HR) department or your supervisor to learn about your health care options so you can make full use of these payment plans.

### State Health Programs

States are beginning to initiate their own health solutions. For example, New York (www.ins.state.ny.us and click on "Healthy NY") offers health care programs for individuals and small business owners (including sole proprietors) within the state. Most important, there is a special program (Child Health Plus) for children, so even parents who forgo their own health coverage can obtain coverage for their children (dependent children up to age 19, or 23 for full-time students). Students who graduate and are no longer covered by a parent's policy may also be eligible for this coverage.

You can learn more about insurance options in your state by visiting Insure U (www.insureuonline.org), a site from the National Association of Insurance Commissioners.

## Saving Energy Costs

The price of a barrel of oil in May 2000 was about $25 and in May 2007 it was about $65; in May 2008 it topped $125 (in July $145), and some economists are predicting $200 a barrel within two years. The high price of oil isn't reflected just in the cost of driving your car. It shows up in heating your home. And other energy costs—natural gas and electricity—have also risen dramatically. All of this means you're paying more every day for things you need. You can't bring down these prices on your own, but you can make changes in your lifestyle and habits that will reduce your consumption and save you money. Here are some strategies to explore.

### Use Alternative Forms of Transportation

Instead of driving a gas-guzzler, look at other options:

- *Use your own power.* Walk or bicycle where possible. Not only will this save you money, but it will also contribute to physical fitness. *Alert:* Congress has added a new tax break for cyclists starting in 2009. Employers can reimburse employees who cycle to work for their bikes and maintenance; up to $20 per month is tax free.

- *Use public transportation.* While this may not be a practical choice in some locations, certainly those in most metropolitan areas can use buses, subways, and trains—at least some of the time. *Tax break:* Employees who receive employer-paid transit passes are not taxed if the monthly amount does not exceed a set amount ($115 in 2008). If you pay for the passes through a salary reduction at work, you aren't taxed on this amount up to the monthly limit.

- *Buy an alternative-fuel vehicle.* A gas-electric hybrid vehicle uses less gasoline. *Bonus:* You will be helping the environment and may be eligible for a federal tax credit (go to www.irs.gov/newsroom/article/0,,id=157557,00.html for a list of vehicles certified by the IRS as eligible for a tax credit). There may also be state tax breaks, including exemption from sales tax and/or income tax write-offs (go to http://go.ucsusa.org/hybridcenter/incentives.cfm to view tax breaks in your state).

### Save at the Gas Pump

With the price of gasoline at record highs, any and all ways you can use to reduce your consumption are money savers. Here are some common sense ways to consider:

- *Keep your car in good working order.* A well-tuned car will consume less gas than one needing service.

- *Keep tires properly inflated.* A car uses more gas when tires don't have enough air.

- *Avoid idling.* One hour of idling can waste a gallon of gas. If you're going to be at a standstill for more than a minute or two, it pays to shut down the engine.

- *Don't exceed the speed limit.* You'll lower your gas usage by 15 percent if you drive at 62 rather than 70 miles per hour.

- *Don't use the air conditioner in city driving.* Only use it sparsely when you must, and then keep the temperature at 75 degrees or higher. (It may not matter whether you use the air conditioner in highway driving; leaving the windows open creates drag that is also a gas-waster.)

- *Map your route.* Don't drive needlessly; spend some time before each trip deciding where you need to go and the best ways to get there and back.

- *Buy gas from wholesale clubs.* Gas from BJ's Wholesale Club, Sam's Club, and other wholesale clubs runs significantly lower in price than at regular gas stations (typically 12¢ or more). In most states, you don't have to be a member to buy gas from a club.

- *Use a gas card.* Enjoy discounts (typically 1 percent to 5 percent) when you use a gas-branded credit card, such as one from Shell or ExxonMobil. Or obtain a 5 percent rebate by using an AAA-sponsored Visa card.

- *Shop around for lower gas prices.* Go to www.gasbuddy.com and www.gaspricewatch.com to comparison shop in your area.

- *Check fuel economy when buying a new car.* Compare your choices at www.fueleconomy.com.

For reducing home heating, cooling, and electricity costs, see Chapter 2.

## Trimming the Fat off Food Bills

The price of just about every food item is up dramatically from a year ago. Food costs rose by 4 percent in 2007, and the U.S. Department of Agriculture predicts they'll rise by as much as 4.5 percent during 2008. Some items have gone up even more—milk is up 17 percent, and eggs are up 25 percent.

For some, the cost of food has become prohibitive. About 1.3 million more people, for a total of 27.7 million, are now receiving food stamps.

Here are 25 ways to reduce the cost of food (you may have heard them before or used them in the past, but now may be the time to revisit them):

1. *Be an organized shopper.* Make a list and stick to it to avoid impulse purchases. Keep track of what things cost so you'll recognize a good sale. Know what you already have at home in your refrigerator or pantry so you don't duplicate (and waste) items.

2. *Eat in, not out.* Preparing meals at home versus dining out (even in fast-food restaurants) is significantly less costly. Typically, consumers

report that 80 percent of meals are eaten at home while 20 percent are eaten out. In today's economy, however, 55 percent of consumers say they're preparing more meals at home. This can be viewed as a positive thing: Families can eat together and share their experiences from the day. Meals can more nutritious, contributing to less weight gain and better health.

3. *Buy in bulk.* When items you need (that won't go bad) are on sale, stock up.

4. *Grow your own.* You don't need a farm or a lot of acreage to grow your own produce. A little plot of land is all you need to grow a few tomatoes or other items that will help trim your grocery bill. Even a window-box garden for herbs can provide savings.

5. *Plan meals better.* Waste is not something you can easily afford today. Better meal planning can ensure that the ingredients you buy will be used up before they spoil.

6. *Become coupon conscious.* Coupons from stores and manufacturers can dramatically reduce the amount of dollars spent at the grocery. A study by Prospectiv shows coupon usage up 72 percent in August 2008 compared with six months earlier.

7. *Shop at discounters.* Buying at Wal-Mart, Sam's Club, Costco, and other discounters can save you money, especially if you can buy items in large sizes.

8. *Avoid prepared foods.* Instead of buying a packaged salad, buy the ingredients for a salad you make yourself. Weigh the benefit of saving time using prepared foods against the dollars saved by doing it yourself.

9. *Reduce consumption of junk food.* Cookies, chips, soda, and other no-nutrition snacks are costly and not good for your hips or your health. Buy raw popcorn (which is less costly than packaged products) and pop it yourself.

10. *Comparison shop.* Don't rely on the same store to meet all your needs. Check the circulars to see which stores in your area are offering the best buys each week.

11. *Check labels carefully.* Look at unit prices and prices per ounce to find the best deals—the largest sizes of an item aren't necessarily the lowest cost per ounce.

12. *Shop when you're full.* Shopping on an empty stomach may prompt you to buy items because you're hungry, not because you need them.

13. *Buy nonfood items in places other than the grocery.* Cosmetics, toiletries, paper goods, and other nonfood items are usually more costly in grocery stores than in discount stores such as Wal-Mart, Kmart, or even some chain pharmacies.

14. *Check for freshness.* Don't waste money on items that have purchase dates that have expired or are about to expire (before you can use them). Don't buy items in damaged packages or cans; this may indicate problems inside.

15. *Use proper storage procedures.* Put food away promptly upon returning from the store so items don't spoil too quickly. Wrap items well or use vacuum sealers to preserve freshness.

16. *Use powdered milk in recipes.* While the taste may be hard to swallow by the glassful, using powdered milk in cakes or other recipes will cut costs significantly, given the high cost of a gallon of milk today.

17. *Buy day-old bread and baked goods.* If you plan to freeze these items, you won't notice any difference from just baked when you defrost them.

18. *Buy generic.* Some store brands are less costly but just as tasty as national brands (you're paying for their advertising). Good choices are condiments and paper goods.

19. *Shop by yourself or with another adult.* Leave the kids at home to avoid requests for costly and unhealthy items.

20. *Share twofers with a friend.* Often promotions let you buy two items at a reduced price. If you can't use both, get a shopping buddy to share the items and the savings.

21. *Brown-bag your lunch and make your coffee.* Don't eat out or buy at costly salad bars. Only use company cafeterias if they are subsidized; otherwise prepare your own lunch at home. Cut back or eliminate costly coffee purchases out; brew your own at home and take it with you.

22. *Keep your coins out of the vending machine.* If you need a late-afternoon snack or a bottle or can of something to drink, bring your own (e.g., keep an energy bar and a bottle of water with you).

23. *Use your tap.* The quality of water in most places in the United States is very high and costs pennies or nothing. Use bottled water for special situations, like in the car or at the gym, not as your mainstay. If you don't like the taste of your home's water, try a water filter.

24. *Buy from growers.* Regional or local farmers markets provide fresh items at lower cost than stores.

25. *Fish and hunt.* Catch your own fish and game. Use some now and freeze the rest.

## Handling Credit Card Debt

One of the biggest drains on your pocketbook may be the interest you pay each month on your credit cards. The Federal Reserve reported in May 2008 that Americans' credit card debt in the first quarter of 2008 totaled $957.2 billion. The average household in 2007 had $8,500 in credit card debt.

Credit cards offer a big convenience—you don't have to carry cash with you and can buy things now that you'll pay for later on. The problem is that you'll end up paying more for things than if you'd paid cash because of the cost of financing if you don't pay your monthly credit card bill in full and on time. If you pay only the minimum monthly amount, it will take you years to pay off your debt. Instead, create a plan to pay down debt more quickly and then try to live debt free.

- *Ask for cancellation of credit card debt.* If the credit card company agrees to reduce your outstanding balance or cancel it altogether, you are better off from a debt perspective. However, you may have an unexpected tax bill to deal with and wish you'd had access to that credit.

  Generally, the cancellation of personal debt is taxable income to you because you have been relieved of a debt you owed. The debt forgiveness is excludable from your income only if the cancellation occurred while you were in bankruptcy or if you were insolvent immediately before the cancellation (insolvency means that your debts exceed your assets).

- *Budget for repayment.* Build into your monthly budget the money you need to pay off your debt in as short a time as possible. Apply any extra funds (e.g., a tax refund, a bonus, a lottery winning) to pay down this debt. If you had budgeted for savings, it may make sense to apply this to debt repayment. You're probably paying a higher interest rate on the debt than you could earn on the savings.

- *Increase monthly payments.* The more you pay off each month, the more quickly you'll reduce your debt and the more you'll save in interest payments you no longer have to make. According to Bankrate.com, if you pay only the $60 per month minimum on a $3,000 credit card balance, it would take eight years to eliminate and cost you $2,780 in interest. If you increase your monthly payment by $50, you'd wipe out the debt in three years and save $1,800 in interest charges. To see what effect adding money to your payment each month will do to the time it takes to pay off the debt and the interest you'll save, visit Bankrate.com's credit card calculator at www.bankrate.com/brm/calc/MinPayment.asp.

- *Pay off high-interest-rate cards first.* If you're paying down debt on more than one card, apply the greater share of your monthly money for this purpose to the card, or cards, with the higher interest rates.

- *Ditch your cards.* Live without plastic. Cut up your cards or put them away for emergency use only. Save up for purchases you expect to make. For example, create a holiday savings fund (you set the total). Then when holiday time approaches, you'll have the cash on hand to buy your holiday gifts instead of continuing to pay for them long after the holiday season is over if you had charged your purchases.

- *Use a credit counselor.* If you can't get a handle on your debt, consider working with a professional. To find a reputable credit counselor, go to the National Foundation for Credit Counseling at www.nfcc.org (you can search by zip code).

# Owning a Vehicle

To many Americans, owning a car is almost a constitutional right. Two- and three-car garages are common in communities across the country.

With soaring gas prices at the pump, along with the other costs of ownership (car payments, insurance, maintenance, etc.), car ownership can be called into question. Determine whether it makes fiscal sense to own a car, or a second car, or whether you and your family can get by without a vehicle, especially in an urban area. You can raise cash and avoid high gas prices by selling an extra car now.

---

**What to Do Now**

Don't be too quick to sell a large SUV. It may be difficult, if not impossible, to find a buyer. And the price you receive may not be sufficient to satisfy any remaining car loan. Instead, limit usage of a gas-guzzling SUV; use another family car or public transportation whenever possible.

---

### Tax Incentives for Certain Vehicle Ownership

If you want to own a less costly vehicle, consider those that run on alternative fuel. There may be federal and state tax incentives for buying a hybrid or other alternative fuel vehicle. The tax break is designed to offset somewhat the added cost of the alternative-fuel feature. For example, there is a federal tax credit for purchasing a certified vehicle (you can review the IRS list at www.irs.gov/newsroom/article/0,,id=161076,00.html).

### Repossession

If you purchased your car on credit and can't make the payments, the car may be repossessed (taken away from you and sold to pay off your outstanding debt). The repossession may extinguish the debt still owed on the car loan.

Taxwise, a repossession of your personal car can result in a taxable gain or a nondeductible personal loss. Figure your gain (or loss) as if you'd sold the vehicle rather than having had it repossessed. Gain (or loss) is the difference between your adjusted basis (usually what you paid for the vehicle) and the amount realized (the smaller of the outstanding debt for which you are personally liable or the fair market value of the vehicle).

**TABLE 5.4** Worksheet for Repossession of a Vehicle

| Gain (or Loss) on Repossession | |
|---|---|
| 1. Enter the vehicle's basis (usually cost) | _____ |
| 2. Enter the smaller of the outstanding debt or the vehicle's fair market value | _____ |
| 3. Gain (or loss)—subtract line 2 from line 1 | _____ |
| **Ordinary Income on Debt Cancellation** | |
| 1. Enter the outstanding debt before repossession | _____ |
| 2. Enter the fair market value of the vehicle | _____ |
| 3. Ordinary income—subtract line 2 from line 1 | _____ |

### Example

You bought a new car for $15,000, putting $2,000 down and financing the balance with a loan for which you are personally liable. Later, the credit company repossesses the car when the loan has been reduced to $10,000 and the car is worth $9,000. Your nondeductible loss in this situation is $6,000—the difference between the car's basis of $15,000 and the amount realized of $9,000 (which is smaller than the outstanding debt of $10,000). You also have $1,000 of ordinary income from debt cancellation (the difference between the outstanding debt and the value of the repossessed car).

If your lender also canceled all or part of your outstanding car loan, the debt cancellation usually is ordinary income to you. You can exclude the income from the debt forgiveness only if the cancellation occurred while you were in bankruptcy or if you were insolvent immediately before the cancellation (insolvency means that your debts exceed your assets).

Use the worksheet in Table 5.4 to figure either your gain or your loss from a car's repossession, as well as ordinary income from the debt cancellation.

## Tapping into Personal Resources as a Last Resort

If you need money but can't get it through conventional sources, such as a bank loan or even credit card borrowing (maybe you're already tapped out there), then consider some other ways to come up with the cash you need. These alternative personal resources should be used only when all else fails and should not be looked upon as easy money.

- *Taking out a home equity loan.* If you have equity in your home (the proceeds you would pocket if you sold your home today and paid off any existing mortgage), you can arrange for a line of credit. Today, lenders are wary of giving these loans, as declines in home values have eroded considerable equity for some homeowners. Details about home equity loans are explained in Chapter 2.

- *Borrowing from your 401(k) plan.* Your plan may allow you to borrow from your account. The tax law limits this amount to no more than 50 percent of your account balance up to $50,000. The interest rate charged by the plan is usually very modest, but you must make repayment in level amounts over no more than five years (the term can be longer only if you borrow to buy a home). *Downside:* You eat into your potential retirement savings. And if you leave employment, you must repay all of the outstanding balance or you are taxed on it as if you'd taken a distribution.

- *Taking a hardship distribution from your 401(k) plan.* Generally, retirement plans are restricted for retirement and don't allow you to take withdrawals before leaving employment. However, the plan may allow you to take hardship distributions if you have tapped out your other financial resources and need the money for certain approved reasons:

  - To purchase a principal residence.
  - To prevent eviction from, or foreclosure on, a principal residence.
  - To pay medical expenses for you, your spouse, or a dependent.
  - To pay certain educational expenses for you, your spouse, or a dependent.
  - To pay funeral costs for you, your spouse, or a dependent. *Downside:* Hardship distributions are fully taxable, so the amount you take from the plan is depleted to a degree by the taxes you owe on the money. Hardship distributions may also be subject to a 10 percent early distribution penalty unless you meet an exception to the penalty rule. The exceptions include your being at least 59½ years old, being disabled, or using the funds to pay for deductible medical costs.

---

**What to Do Now**

If you need to use your 401(k) money to pay one of the allowable expenses, contact the plan administrator. Be prepared to fill out paperwork showing that you have no other source of financing to pay these expenses.

---

- *Borrowing from your life insurance policy.* If you have permanent life insurance (a whole life or universal life policy) and have built up cash value in the policy, you can borrow against it. The interest rate charged on this loan is modest. There is no set repayment requirement, but interest continues to accrue. *Downside:* If you don't repay what you borrowed before you die, your beneficiary will receive only a net amount, the policy's face value less what you owed (including interest). This could leave your beneficiary in a financial crunch of his or her own.

- *Borrowing against your brokerage portfolio.* If you have personal savings in stocks and bonds held at a brokerage firm, you can take a margin loan. This means borrowing against the value of your securities. The limit: 50 percent (90 percent in the case of Treasuries). The interest rate is usually modest, but changes monthly. There is no fixed repayment requirement; you pay back the money when and to the extent you choose. **Downside:** If the value of your portfolio declines, you may have to sell securities to pay down your margin loan.

- *Borrowing from family and friends.* If you need money and can't get it through your own financial resources, you may turn to those you know for help. LendingCircle (www.lendingcircle.com) can help to structure the loan.

### Tax Rules for Deducting Interest

Whether or not the interest you pay is tax deductible depends on the source of the borrowing and the reason for the loan. As a general rule, you can't deduct interest on personal debt. There are two exceptions: You can deduct interest on home equity borrowing (there's a $100,000 limit on the qualified debt) and on student loans up to $2,500 of interest each year (there's an income limit, so if you are over this limit, the interest isn't deductible).

For all other borrowing, deductibility depends on the reason for the loan (not the source of the loan). For instance, if you borrow from your brokerage account and use the funds to go on vacation, the interest isn't deductible. If you take that money and buy 100 shares of X stock, the interest is treated as investment interest. It is deductible (with no dollar limit) to the extent of your investment income for the year; excess interest can be carried forward and becomes deductible as an offset to investment income in succeeding years.

If you borrow for business purposes, then all of the interest is deductible as a business expense.

### Example

If you borrow $2,500 from your life insurance policy to apply to your daughter's wedding, the interest on this loan isn't deductible. If you use the money to buy a taxable bond, then the interest is deductible if you have investment income at least equal to this interest. If you use the money to start a sole proprietorship, the interest is fully deductible as business interest.

# CHAPTER 6

# Handling Education Costs

Education is the key to success today in almost every field. The U.S. Bureau of Labor Statistics (BLS) found in 2002 that those with a college degree earned 1.8 times more than those with only a high school diploma and those with an advanced degree earned 2.6 times more. BLS reported in October 2007 that 67.2 percent of high school graduates from the class of 2007 were enrolled in colleges or universities.

Unfortunately, the cost of pursuing a higher education isn't always easy to manage. These costs continually escalate at more than the normal rate of inflation. The College Board reported in October 2007 that the average cost of tuition and fees at a four-year public university rose by 6.6 percent to $6,185. At a private university, the increase was 6.3 percent to $23,712. When you add on the cost of room and board, books, travel to and from home, and miscellaneous expenses, the total bill is out of the reach of most families' pocketbooks. A bachelor degree can easily exceed $100,000. What can you do to secure a diploma for your children or yourself?

There are ways to reduce costs or obtain financial assistance to swing the bill. You need to plan ahead to have the widest range of options. Education planning falls into two main categories: saving up and paying. The first category should begin when a child is born, giving you roughly 18 years to save up. The second category begins once a child enters college and runs for the balance of the child's education (which may even entail graduate school). In this chapter you will learn about:

- Saving up for higher education
- Paying for college: no-cost and low-cost alternatives
- Scholarships, fellowships, and grants
- Leveraging tax breaks
- Student loans
- Strategies for financial aid
- Using home equity
- Borrowing from IRAs
- Employer assistance
- Help for military personnel

## Saving Up for Higher Education

In today's tough economy, it is challenging for many families to squirrel money into education savings vehicles. Concerns about paying bills and meeting current expenses may be paramount.

For those who have *some* extra money and who want to apply it to college savings, there is a wide array of savings vehicles to choose from.

### What to Do Now

In saving for higher education, consider the impact that some of these savings vehicles can have on qualifying for financial aid. Determining the impact can, of course, be difficult to do because you can't know now (when you're saving) what the cost of higher education and your financial situation will be in the future. Keep in mind that under the federal financial aid formula, only 5.64 percent of a parent's assets are considered available to pay for education, whereas 20 percent of a student's assets are taken into account. This fact should be used to decide how best to save for education.

### Custodial Accounts

You can set up bank or brokerage accounts under your child's Social Security number. You or some other adult acts as custodian, deciding how to invest the money and when to use it for the child's benefit. Once the child reaches the age of majority in his or her state (typically 18), the child gains control over the funds; there's no guarantee that the child will use the money for college.

In the past, custodial accounts were a sound savings vehicle. There is no cost to setting them up with a bank, brokerage firm, or mutual fund. They can be used for modest savings; there are no minimums required. However, tax law changes in recent years make custodial accounts less attractive savings vehicles. Under the so-called kiddie tax, the child's earnings over a set amount are taxed to the child at the parent's highest tax rate. Applicability of the kiddie tax used to end when a child attained age 14. That age increased to 17. Starting in 2008, the kiddie tax continues to apply to a child under 18, as well as to those under 24 who are full-time students and are not self-supporting. In effect, at the very time when funds are needed to pay for college, a young person's investment earnings may be taxed at higher rates than if there were no kiddie tax.

Of course, withdrawals from a custodial account are not taxed, because the funds have already been taxed. For instance, say a grandparent adds $1,000 to a custodial account and the account earns 5 percent interest. That interest is taxed to the grandchild under the kiddie tax rules. When $1,050 is withdrawn, none of the withdrawal is taxable.

Custodial accounts may still be useful if earnings fall below the kiddie tax threshold. In 2008, the first $900 of a child's earnings is tax free. The second $900 in income is taxed to the child at the child's rate (say 10 percent). Only investment income over $1,800 in 2008 is subject to the kiddie tax (i.e., taxed to the child at the parent's highest rate, which could be as great as 35 percent). To have earnings of $1,800, the custodial account would have to hold $36,000 earning 5 percent. Thus, custodial accounts in modest amounts may still be useful savings vehicles.

## Trusts

A trust is an arrangement in which property is held for one person by another. Money or assets are placed in a trust for the benefit of someone (called a beneficiary), with an adult (or trust department of a bank) acting as trustee. The trustee manages the money and acts in accordance with the terms of the trust regarding use of the funds for the beneficiary. Wealthy individuals who can afford to part with substantial funds may set up a trust for the benefit of a child.

*Advantage.* Using a trust gives you great control over how the money is invested and how it is spent. The terms of the trust can restrict the use of the money to such purposes as paying for college and thus can avoid having the money frittered away by the beneficiary.

*Disadvantages.* There are usually costs to setting up the trust (up to several thousand dollars) and annual costs for running it. The same kiddie tax problem for custodial accounts applies to trusts as well.

**What to Do Now**

Trust rules are highly complex, so the use of a trust should not be undertaken before you consult with a tax adviser.

### 529 Plans

Families can save substantial funds in state-sponsored programs or through a private plan. Named after the section of the Tax Code that governs the plans, there are two types of 529 plans: tuition plans and savings plans.

- *Tuition plans allow you to prepay the cost of tuition and fees.* There are state tuition plans and a private plan (www.independent529plan.org) in which more than 250 private institutions participate. Using a tuition plan guarantees that you'll have the money to cover the tuition, regardless of increases over the years, if you contribute a set amount.
- *Savings plans let you invest your contributions.* The money available from the plan to pay college costs depends on how well the investments perform. Investments are made by professional fund managers, although you may choose from certain investment options. There are no guarantees, and some plans have lost money.

*Advantages*. The main benefit to 529 plans is that money grows on a tax-deferred basis and becomes tax free if withdrawals are taken only for qualified education expenses. There are no income limits on contributors as there are with other tax-advantaged savings vehicles (contributions can even be made through UPromise at www.upromise.com where rewards from making certain everyday purchases can be swept into 529 plans). You can retain control over the account, changing the beneficiary, for example, if the original beneficiary doesn't go to college. Contribution limits are fixed by the plan (over $300,000 per beneficiary in some states).

Funds in 529 plans are *not* counted as a student's assets for financial aid purposes, even if the account is in the student's name.

While there is no federal income tax deduction for contributions, there may be tax breaks at the state level. For instance, New York allows a deduction for contributions of up to $5,000 per person ($10,000 per couple). You usually aren't limited to savings through the plan offered by your state, but you may forfeit the tax breaks if you use an out-of-state plan.

**What to Do Now**

Determine which 529 plan works best for you. To link to 529 plans in each state, go to SavingForCollege.com (www.savingforcollege.com). Consider the investment options of each plan, who is managing the plan, and what costs are associated with your choices.

### Coverdell Education Savings Accounts

Coverdell education savings accounts (ESAs) offer the opportunity for modest savings; there is an annual cap on contributions, which is currently $2,000. Like a regular IRA, funds in an ESA grow tax deferred. However, unlike an IRA, withdrawals for qualified education expenses are never taxed.

This savings vehicle can only be used for a child under age 18. The money can stay in the account, but once the child turns 30, the funds are automatically taxed to the child and subject to a 10 percent penalty. However, this tax result can be avoided by rolling the funds over to an ESA for another family member, such as a younger sibling.

Contributions are *not* tax deductible and the maximum contribution of $2,000 can be made only if the contributor's modified adjusted gross income (MAGI) does not exceed $95,000 for singles or $190,000 for joint filers (the allowable contribution amount phases out when MAGI exceeds $95,000/$190,000, and disappears completely when MAGI is $110,000 for singles or $220,000 for joint filers). The contributor need *not* be closely related to the child. For instance, an aunt or uncle can contribute to the child's ESA if the MAGI limit is met. However, total contributions on behalf of a child for the year can't exceed the annual cap (currently $2,000). (Military death benefits for someone who died after June 17, 2008, can be contributed to an ESA without regard to the income and contribution limits.)

> **CAUTION**
>
> Coverdell ESAs currently can be used to pay for any education above preschool. However, the current rules, including the $2,000 contribution amount, are set to expire at the end of 2010. After that time, the contribution limit will be only $500, and tax-free distributions will be limited to qualified higher education costs.

The number of financial institutions offering ESAs is small, probably because of the limited contributions that can be made to the account. Check with banks in your area and also consider the College Savings Bank CollegeSure certificate of deposit (CD) (www.collegesavings.com/csb/esa.asp), State Farm (www.statefarm.com/learning/life_stages/college_fund/coverdel.asp), and E*Trade Financial (https://us.etrade.com/e/t/plan/educationsavings/covesa). When selecting a financial institution for the ESA, look closely at the fees, charges, and expenses for maintaining the account.

## Paying for College: No-Cost and Low-Cost Alternatives

When you think about no-cost and low-cost alternatives for paying for college, you may be thinking only in terms of scholarships that cover expenses. This is not necessarily the full picture (scholarships are discussed later in the chapter). Consider the strategies that follow, and work closely with your child's guidance counselor and school financial aid officers to put together a payment package suited to your unique situation.

### No-Tuition Schools

There are a handful of top-notch schools that don't charge any tuition. Competition for entry is fierce because of the schools' quality. *Examples:* All four of the military institutions (although there is a service requirement), Cooper Union, Berea College, and the Curtis Institute of Music.

A growing number of Ivy League (e.g., Princeton University and the University of Pennsylvania) and state universities offer free tuition for students from low-income families. These schools no longer impose any loan requirement for low-income students, effectively making tuition free.

### Accelerated Programs

Today, the U.S. Department of Education's National Center for Education Statistics (NCES) says that only about 40 percent of students graduate from college in four years. Many take five or six years to complete their education. The added time means added cost.

Consider the savings for the family if a student can get a diploma in three years! Most schools do not charge extra for carrying a heavier course load each semester. Just one extra course each semester can reduce the time to graduation by six months or more. There may be an added fee for attending a midyear or summer session, but the cost will be lower than it will be later on when tuition rises. Completing college in less than four years can be done.

In deciding whether to do accelerated study, balance the student's attendance year-round or taking an extra course load against the need or desire to work. It's not practical in most cases for a student to do both.

### Cooperative Programs

The flip side to getting out of college in a shorter time is spending a longer time there while combining education with work experience. A number of schools offer cooperative programs that extend the time to completing a college degree to five years. Drexel University in Philadelphia has one of the largest cooperative programs in the United States, but there about 500 other cooperative programs.

In a cooperative program, the curriculum includes the work; the work is not merely a supplemental way to make money. In a work-study program, which is often confused with a cooperative program, students do work on their own time as a way to help finance their education.

During the work period in a cooperative program (typically two or three full semesters), the student gains work experience for which he or she usually is paid. This can help defray the cost of college.

To find cooperative programs, look at the Directory of College Cooperative Education Programs at www.greenwood.com and the National Commission for Cooperative Education at www.co-op.edu.

### Junior College First

The annual tuition at state junior or community colleges is usually lower than the annual tuition cost of a four-year school. What's more, the student attending a junior or community college often lives at home. This saves the family outside room and board and some tuition. Then, upon completion of an associate degree, the student can transfer to a four-year institution to complete a bachelor degree. The total cost for this college experience will be lower than having attended the four-year institution for the full four years.

In terms of credentials, the transfer student holds the same diploma from the four-year college as a student who attended the school for all four years.

### State Schools for In-State Students

The price of tuition at these institutions is still a bargain when compared with private school prices. Going out of state means higher tuition, but even this may be lower than comparable private colleges.

### Stay Local

Although many people believe that part of the college experience is being away from home, there is a cost factor to this choice. Living at home while attending college locally ensures that a child receives a college education at a substantially reduced price.

### Military Programs

Educational programs for military personnel are discussed later in this chapter.

## Scholarships, Fellowships, and Grants

The availability and range of "free money" are vast. An estimated 20 million scholarships worth more than $1 trillion are up for grabs each year. Some scholarships are dependent on financial need. Others can be awarded because of athletic or musical talent or for some other special characteristic.

Three important grant programs include:

1. *Pell Grants*—needs-based grants for undergraduates. Pell Grant amounts are listed in Table 6.1.
2. *Academic Competitive Grants*—for those with a grade point average (GPA) of 3.0 or better. The Academic Competitive Grant is $750 for the first year and $1,300 for the second year. This grant can be paid in addition to the Pell Grant.
3. *National SMART Grants*—for third- and fourth-year students pursuing undergraduate studies in physical, life, or computer sciences; mathematics, technology, or engineering; or certain foreign languages critical to national security. The grant is up to $4,000 and can be paid in addition to the Pell Grant.

**TABLE 6.1** Pell Grants

| Academic Year | Amount of Grant |
| --- | --- |
| 2008–2009 | $4,800 |
| 2009–2010 | $4,800 |
| 2010–2011 | $5,000 |
| 2011–2012 | $5,000 |
| 2012–2013 | $5,400 |

Scholarships are tax free if granted to study in a degree program. There is no dollar limit on how much you can receive tax free. However, the tax-free portion is limited to tuition, course-related fees, books, supplies, and equipment. Any portion of the scholarship for room and board or incidentals is taxable. Also, certain awards that may appear like scholarships are still taxable (e.g., a Fulbright award is taxable unless the foreign earned income exclusion applies).

## What to Do Now

The starting point for finding scholarships is the college office or guidance counselor at the student's high school. The next step is to check options at the college of choice.

Online resources for finding scholarships include:

- CollegeBoard.com (www.collegeboard.com)
- FastWeb (www.fastweb.com)
- Hispanic College Fund (http://site.hispanicfund.org/scholarships.php)
- School Soup (www.schoolsoup.com/scholarships)
- University Sports Scholarships and National Collegiate Athletic Association (NCAA) Clearinghouse (www.collegesportsscholarships.com/ncaaclearinghouse.htm) for athletic scholarships

## Leveraging Tax Breaks

The tax law helps defray some of the cost of paying for higher education by allowing you to claim a deduction or credit for certain expenses. In most cases, the tax breaks won't fully compensate you for your outlays, but they do help. The breaks apply whether you get the money from your savings or borrow it. Each special tax break has its own rules on eligibility, the types of expenses that qualify, and other particulars.

The various breaks are not of equal value in terms of tax savings. They include:

- *An income exclusion.* You do not have to count certain income as taxable, effectively saving you the taxes that would otherwise have been due on the income. The value of the exclusion to you depends on your tax bracket (and whether the income that is excluded would push you into a higher bracket if it were reported).
- *A tax deduction.* The value of the tax deduction depends on your tax bracket. The higher your bracket, the greater the value of the deduction to you. For instance, if you are in the 15 percent tax bracket, a $1,000 deduction saves you $150. Those in the 35 percent tax bracket save $350 from the same $1,000 deduction.
- *A tax credit.* A credit is a dollar-for-dollar reduction of your tax bill. A $1,000 credit saves you $1,000 in taxes.

**CAUTION**

There are some unscrupulous businesses that purport, for a fee, to find scholarships; they take your money and provide you with no more information than you could find on your own for free. Before engaging any help in your scholarship search, check out the company with the Better Business Bureau and your child's college guidance office.

## What to Do Now

When you qualify for multiple benefits related to the same expense, determine which break will provide you with the greatest tax savings. You cannot double dip for tax breaks with respect to the same college costs. For example, if you claim a tax credit for your tuition, you can't deduct the tuition as well. Usually, the credit will be better than a deduction, but you need to crunch the numbers to be sure.

### Hope Credit

In 2005 (the most recent year for statistics), more than 5 percent of all returns claimed an education credit—either the Hope credit or the Lifetime Learning credit (discussed in the next section). These credits totaled $6.119 million.

You can take a Hope tax credit for tuition and fees for the first two years of higher education in a course of study leading to a degree. The credit applies for each eligible person who is a freshman or sophomore.

The credit amount is 100 percent of the first fixed cost and 50 percent of the next fixed cost. Fixed costs can be adjusted for inflation. In 2008, that fixed cost is $1,200, so the top credit per eligible student is $1,800 (100 percent of $1,200, plus 50 percent of $1,200).

TABLE 6.2 2008 MAGI Phaseout Range for Education Credits

| Filing Status | MAGI |
| --- | --- |
| Married filing jointly | $96,000–$116,000 |
| Other filing status* | $48,000–$58,000 |

*No credit can be claimed for married filing separately.

This tax break can be claimed only if your modified adjusted gross income (MAGI) does not exceed a set threshold (see Table 6.2). If your MAGI is below the phaseout range, you get a full credit amount; if it's above the range, you can't claim any credit. If you're within the range, you take a partial credit. For this purpose MAGI means your adjusted gross income increased by the foreign earned income exclusion and certain other foreign items if applicable. Your MAGI can be adjusted annually for inflation.

Usually, the credit relates only to expenses paid within the year. However, you can claim a credit if you prepay for an academic period that begins within the first three months of the following year.

## Example

Your child's semester begins in February 2009. In December 2008 you pay tuition for the February semester. You can claim the credit on your 2008 return (if you meet the MAGI limit).

No credit can be claimed for a student who has a felony drug conviction on his or her record.

### Lifetime Learning Credit

You can claim a tax credit for tuition and fees for any higher education, including graduate school. The top credit is $2,000. The credit applies per taxpayer, so if you have three students in college and/or graduate school at the same time, your top credit is still $2,000.

The credit applies whether you are studying for a degree or simply taking a course in a nondegree program.

The same MAGI phaseout ranges as for the Hope credit apply to the Lifetime Learning credit.

### Tuition and Fees Deduction

You may be able to take an above-the-line deduction (no itemizing required) for tuition and fees for higher education for yourself, your spouse, or a dependent. The tuition and fees deduction is limited to $4,000 ($2,000 for those with higher income), no matter how many qualified people are in attendance. In 2005 (the most recent year for statistics), nearly five million returns claimed total deductions for tuition and fees of nearly $11 million.

**TABLE 6.3** MAGI Limits for the Tuition Deduction

| Filing Status | MAGI Limit for $4,000 Deduction | MAGI Limit for $2,000 Deduction |
|---|---|---|
| Married filing jointly | Not more than $130,000 | More than $130,000 but not more than $160,000 |
| All other taxpayers | Not more than $65,000 | More than $65,000 but not more than $80,000 |

The tax break can be claimed only if your modified adjusted gross income (MAGI) does not exceed a set threshold (see Table 6.3). For this purpose MAGI means your adjusted gross income increased by the foreign earned income exclusion and certain other foreign items.

The deduction can't be claimed if you are someone else's dependent. For instance, a student claimed as a dependent by the parent can't take the deduction; only the parent can if the parent's MAGI is below the limit. A married person filing a separate return is barred from claiming the deduction.

> **CAUTION**
> This deduction applies only through 2009 unless Congress extends it.

The deduction is limited to payments for tuition and fees. Student activity fees and books can qualify if the cost is paid to the eligible institution. It does not apply to room and board or other expenses.

### Tax-Free Savings Bond Interest

U.S. savings bonds have always been known as a safe investment. They can also be a good way to pay for college on a tax-advantaged basis. The interest that would otherwise be taxable when you redeem the bonds can be tax free if the redemption amount is used to pay higher education costs.

To qualify for tax-free interest, the bonds must have been issued after 1989 to someone who is at least 24 years old. A child who receives a gift of an EE or I bond at birth or for special events and cashes them in at college time can't claim the interest exclusion because he or she wasn't at least 24 years old when the bond was acquired.

The bond must be redeemed to pay tuition and fees for higher education. The bond can also be redeemed if the proceeds are then used to fund a 529 plan or a Coverdell ESA.

The bond owner must redeem the bond to pay for higher education costs for bond owner, spouse, or dependent child. Thus, a grandmother can't redeem her bonds to pay for a grandchild's college tuition.

There is no limit on the amount of bonds that can be redeemed as long as it doesn't exceed tuition and fees. The bond owner's MAGI can't exceed set limits (see Table 6.4). The limits can be adjusted annually for inflation.

TABLE 6.4 Phaseout Ranges for Savings Bond Interest
Exclusion

| Filing Status | MAGI |
| --- | --- |
| Married filing jointly | $100,650–$130,650 |
| Other filing status* | $67,100–$82,100 |

*No exclusion can be claimed for married filing separately.

# Student Loans

According to the National Postsecondary Student Aid Study (NPSAS) released
in 2006, more than 35 percent of students must borrow money to cover the
cost of higher education. Few students can pay in full out of pocket or secure
scholarships to cover the entire bill.

**What to Do Now**

Usually, it's best to exhaust all federal student loan options before looking into
alternative loan sources. For general information about government loans, go
to Sallie Mae at www.salliemae.com. For information about all types of
student loans, go to FinAid at www.finaid.org.

## *Federal Student Loans*

These are the greatest source of college financing. There are a number of
different federal student loan programs:

- Federal Stafford loans are fixed-rate, low-interest loans available to students attending accredited schools at least half-time. The interest rate is
  currently 6.8 percent, but can change for future borrowing. The annual cap
  on borrowing under this loan program depends on the year of study: $3,500
  for freshmen, $4,500 for sophomores, and $5,500 for juniors and seniors
  (higher limits apply to emancipated students, such as $20,500 for graduate
  students). Lifetime caps on borrowing under this program also apply.

- Federal Perkins loans are low-interest loans for undergraduate and graduate students with exceptional financial need. The rate is currently
  5 percent.

- Federal ParentsPlus loans are low-interest student loans for parents of
  dependent undergraduate students.

Eligibility for federal loans depends on completion of the Free Application for Federal Student Aid (FAFSA), a loan application. Completing it is
free, but requires extensive financial information. You can apply online at

www.fafsa.ed.gov; the process should take an hour or two. The form must be submitted by the deadline. The federal deadline for the 2009–2010 school year (July 1, 2009, to June 30, 2010) is June 30, 2009. The deadline for state student financial aid is usually much earlier (to see your state's deadline, go to www.fafsa.ed.gov/before003a.htm).

The government encourages families to pursue federal loan programs before looking at other types of loans. For details, go to www.federalstudentaid.ed.gov.

### Commercial Loans

To supplement federal loan programs, there are many private (alternative) loan programs that can help you pay for college, including:

- Signature Student Loan
- Tuition Answer Loan
- Signature Student Loan for Community Colleges
- Continuing Education Loan
- Career Training Loan

It's usually wise to use these loans only after exhausting available scholarships, federal student loans, work-study, and a school's financial aid package. Private loan programs usually bear higher interest rates than federal loan programs.

### Private Noncommercial Student Loans

In the wake of the credit crunch and the tightening of credit by traditional lenders, such as Sallie Mae and large commercial banks, students and their families may have to look to new sources—family, friends, and private lenders (called peer-to-peer lending). There are several online resources that facilitate these loans by figuring out payment schedules and formalizing loan agreements.

- **Fynanz** (www.fynanz.com). This site guarantees repayment of loans (50 percent to 100 percent, depending on the borrower's creditworthiness). Borrowers must have a co-signer (which reduces the risk for the guarantor). Interest rates vary, but can be cut by 1 percent when 10 percent of the loan has been repaid. There's an up-front fee for borrowers. Currently available in seven states, it is set to go nationwide in 2009.
- **GreenNote** (www.greennote.com). Students can tap into their social network to find their own lenders, such as school alumni. The fixed-rate loan is comparable to the rate under the Stafford program. Borrowers pay a fee (the greater of $49 or 2 percent of the loan). Repayment can be postponed until graduation.

- **Prosper** (www.prosper.com). This site structures three-year loans by private lenders who can check the credit rating of borrowers and verify that the student is enrolled in college. The site assigns the borrower a risk factor that is used to set the interest rate. Borrowers pay an up-front fee (1 percent to 3 percent). Repayment begins immediately (not deferred until after graduation).

- **Virgin Money USA** (www.virginmoney.com, click on Personal Loans and then on Student Payback). This site enables you to formalize your loan agreement. For instance, it can be used by parents who pay for their child's education to get a payback promise in writing from the child. There are up-front fees and a $9 per payment fee.

- **Zopa** (www.zopa.com). This site combines investments with loans—family and friends of borrowers purchase certificates of deposit (CDs), and a portion of the interest is used to repay the loan. Loans are limited to $25,000 and must be repaid over five years. Interest varies, depending on the borrower's credit rating.

### Cancellation of Student Loans

Although the cancellation of debt usually is taxable income, there is a special exception for student loans. There is no income from the cancellation of a student loan if:

- The loan is made by the federal government, a state or local government or agency, or an educational institution, and

- The loan is canceled because you work for a certain period of time in certain professions in certain locations (usually in teaching, medicine, law, or other specific fields).

Education loan repayment assistance from the National Health Service Corps Loan Repayment Program or a state education loan repayment program eligible for funds under the Public Health Service Act are not taxed to you if you provide primary health services in areas short of health professionals.

## Strategies for Financial Aid

According to the National Postsecondary Student Aid Study (NPSAS) released in 2006, more than 63 percent of all undergraduates must rely on some form of financial aid to see them through. To qualify for financial aid, be sure to complete all necessary forms and applications and submit them by the applicable deadline. A school's unique deadline may be before receiving an acceptance or rejection letter.

Don't assume that you won't qualify for financial aid; federal and school financial aid formulas may allow you to qualify despite you or your parents having a good income. For example, Harvard University provides financial aid to families with income below $180,000 by reducing the tuition to no more than 10 percent of that income (e.g., $18,000 for a family with $180,000 of income, rather than the usual $30,000 tuition bill).

The FAFSA form for 2008–2009 is based on 2007 income tax information. Going forward, be sure to factor in your current income decisions that could affect future financial aid for you or your child. For instance, if your child is still in high school, selling stocks in 2008 for capital gains may be a good strategy. This allows you to lock in gains and avoid including this income on the 2009–2010 FAFSA form.

### Appealing Financial Aid Offers

If, after you completed and submitted the FAFSA form, a school proposed a financial aid package, you may accept it. But if the package falls short of your expectations, you can appeal if you have sufficient grounds. You can't appeal merely because you don't like what was offered; you need a good reason:

- You have a complex personal and financial situation that you don't believe was adequately factored into the package.

- Another school has interpreted your family's financial situation differently, but the student prefers this school.

### Change in Circumstances

What happens if you apply for financial aid based on the prior year's income, but your financial circumstances are dramatically different now? Most financial aid offices will take the following into account:

- Divorce.
- Death or disability of wage earner.
- Loss of employment of a wage earner.
- Loss of other income or benefits, such as child support, by the borrower, spouse, or parents.

Contact the financial aid office immediately to bring this information to its attention. Put your reasons for requesting additional aid in writing. Be prepared to provide documentation, such as W-2 forms or wage statements.

## Using Home Equity

Despite declines in home values in the past year or so, many homeowners still have considerable equity in their homes (equity is what you could pocket if you sold your home and paid off any outstanding mortgages) (see Chapter 12). Some may want to use this financial resource to help pay for college.

*Advantages*. A home equity loan or a home equity line of credit (HELOC) is easy to arrange. Such a loan usually bears an interest rate that is lower than what the rate would be for a personal loan. Taxwise, interest on a home equity loan is deductible if the balance does not exceed $100,000 and you itemize your deductions (i.e., you don't claim the standard deduction).

*Disadvantage*. When you borrow against the equity in your home, you put your home at risk. If you can't repay the loan, the bank can foreclose on the mortgage and you can lose your home.

---

### What to Do Now

Determine the extent of your potential home equity borrowing. Consider putting a HELOC in place. You pay interest only when and to the extent you tap into your HELOC. For example, if you have a $50,000 HELOC, you don't pay any interest until you draw on some of this line of credit.

---

## Borrowing from Individual Retirement Accounts

An IRA is designed for retirement savings. To the extent you use money for nonretirement purposes, such as paying for a child's education, the less money you'll have for the IRA's intended purpose of your retirement security.

However, you are allowed to access your money at any time for any purpose. Withdrawals are taxable (as they are in retirement). In addition, withdrawals may be subject to a 10 percent penalty if taken before age 59½.

The tax law lets you make withdrawals to pay for the higher education costs of yourself, your spouse, or a dependent without any penalty (regular income tax still applies).

What can you use the money for? Penalty-free withdrawals are restricted to qualified expenses. These include tuition, fees, books, and supplies and equipment that are required for enrollment or attendance. Room and board are qualified expenses only if the student is attending college at least half-time. Buying a computer is *not* a qualified expense if the school does not require its use for any course and there is access to a computer at the school library or in other school locations.

Watch the timing of withdrawals carefully. Only withdrawals made in the same year in which the qualified expenses are paid can be penalty free.

---

### Example

The 10 percent penalty applies if you withdraw funds from your IRA in December 2008 to pay a tuition bill in January 2009. The penalty also applies if you withdraw funds in January 2009 to cover a tuition payment you charged to your credit card in 2008.

---

**What to Do Now**

Tapping into your IRA to pay for higher education costs should be your last resort. Look to other ways to meet this obligation and keep your retirement savings intact for your future.

---

## Employer Assistance

When it comes to finding ways to pay for higher education, leave no stone unturned. One way to get "free money" is through an employer's education assistance program. Not every company offers help with learning, but many (particularly larger) companies do. Some options:

- *Help from an educational assistance plan.* Courses, whether leading to a degree or just interesting and helpful to you, may be paid with assistance from your company. Up to $5,250 of such help each year is tax free. The courses need not be job-related. The company's plan may cover spouses and dependents, providing broad financial help for your family's educational aspirations.

- *Work-related education.* If your company pays for job-related courses, *all* of the company's payments on your behalf are tax free. Usually, you must obtain a certain grade (e.g., a B or higher) in order to secure this fringe benefit.

- *Tuition assistance.* Those who work for colleges and universities may be eligible for free or discounted education at their employer's facilities. Some institutions may offer reciprocal learning opportunities, so you can take courses at neighboring schools while enjoying the same free or discounted cost. Some employers may extend this break to employees' children.

## Help for Military Personnel

Since the GI Bill was created at the end of World War II, those pursuing a military career, and veterans, as well as their dependents, can enjoy considerable financial assistance for higher education. There are several different types of programs; some are for those on active duty while others apply to veterans:

- Montgomery GI Bill for active duty.
- Montgomery GI Bill for reservists.
- Reserve Educational Assistance Program.
- Veterans Educational Assistance Program.

- Survivors and Dependents Educational Assistance Program.
- National Call to Service Program.

For details, go to www.gibill.va.gov/GI_Bill_Info/benefits.htm.

### New GI Bill

Certain military personnel can now obtain greater financial assistance in pursuing an education. The breaks include:

- Paid upfront tuition (capped at more expensive schools)
- Annual stipend of $1,000 to cover books and supplies
- Monthly living stipend based on the Department of Defense Basic Housing Allowance for the region in which the person attends school

The benefits must be used within 15 years of the completion of military duty. For details on the new GI bill, go to www.gibill.va.gov.

# CHAPTER 7

# Mishaps, Disasters, and Catastrophes

Things happen. Tornadoes, fires, floods, accidents, and other unexpected events can change your life in the blink of an eye. The impact of these events on your personal and financial life can be devastating. You can lose property, financial records, and, in extreme cases, be forced to relocate to a new home.

Technically, a catastrophe is defined as an event in which there is $25 million or more in insured property losses and the event affects a significant number of people. The biggest catastrophes in recent years include the World Trade Center attack on 9/11, Hurricanes Katrina, Rita, and Wilma, the 2008 Midwest floods and Hurricane Ike. Total catastrophe losses in 2007 exceeded $6.7 billion.

But you do need not be touched by a major catastrophe to have a catastrophe of your own. You can suffer your own disastrous event—a fire, a prolonged electrical outage, or a storm—that seriously impacts you and your property.

You can't control the weather and other acts of God or be assured of good health. You can't prevent lawsuits or accidents. You can't be sure you won't lose your job or that your business won't go under. You can, however, be prepared for just about any unexpected and traumatic event from a financial perspective.

And you can use tax breaks to ease the impact of your financial losses and help you recover from the experience. In this chapter you will learn about:

- Insuring against property losses
- Deducting property losses
- Condemnations
- Thefts
- Seeking and obtaining damages
- Long-term care
- Asset protection
- Identity theft
- Bankruptcy

## Insuring against Property Losses

The first line of defense against property losses is having adequate insurance to cover potential events. Here are some of the types of policies you need to consider:

- *Homeowners insurance.* This policy insures the home and its contents from damage or destruction. It also protects you from liability claims of third parties. For example, if someone is injured in your home and sues you, personal damages may be covered up to the policy's limit.

- *Renters insurance.* This policy insures the contents of the residence as well as providing liability protection.

- *Flood insurance.* Don't assume your homeowners insurance policy protects you from loss if your home is damaged or destroyed by water from a storm. Depending on where your home is located, you may need federal flood insurance. Check the rules with the Federal Emergency Management Agency (FEMA) at www.fema.gov/business/nfip.

- *Vehicle insurance.* If you own a car, truck, motorcycle, boat, or other vehicle, be sure to carry adequate insurance to protect the vehicle as well as to provide liability coverage.

- *Umbrella policy.* The amount of coverage you have in your basic policies, such as a homeowners policy or car insurance, may not be enough in today's terms with legal awards spiraling ever higher. You can use an umbrella policy to supplement your existing liability coverage. This policy works in tandem with your other policies to pick up where they leave off. You can add $1 million, $5 million, or more to your existing coverage.

You can deduct personal insurance premiums, such as those for your home or car, for tax purposes. If, however, you have a deductible home office, then the portion of your premiums related to the home office space becomes part of your home office deduction.

---

## What to Do Now

Work with a knowledgeable insurance agent to assess your exposure and determine what type and amount of insurance you need to carry.

"Going bare" (not carrying coverage) puts everything at risk and is something you should not do. If you are in a financial crunch and are having difficulty paying premiums, work with the insurance company or an agent to find ways to reduce premiums. For instance, you may want to increase the deductible (your share of financial responsibility for any loss) to reduce the premiums.

Make sure your coverage keeps up with a changing economy. If, for example, the cost of rebuilding your home rises because of higher material costs, be sure that your homeowners insurance policy will provide adequate coverage. If you have replacement value coverage, you're assured that you do; if you don't have replacement value coverage, you'll need to adjust the policy benefit (and the premium). Don't assume that the insurance company will do this automatically or make adjustments that reflect your reality.

---

### Having a Disaster Plan

Living in a post-9/11 and post-Katrina world should make you conscious that anything can happen. Are you prepared to get through a disaster and recover from it? It helps to have a plan.

### Safeguarding Your Family

The first concern, above all else, is the safety of your family and yourself. Make arrangements for communicating with each other and finding safety during storms or other serious events. Online resources to help you craft a plan for your family include:

- American Red Cross (www.redcross.org/flash/brr/English-flash/default.asp)
- Department of Homeland Security (www.ready.gov/america/makeaplan/index.html)
- Insurance Information Institute (www.iii.org/prepare/home)

## Safeguarding Your Financial and Tax Data

If your home were hit by a fire or flood, what would happen to your tax receipts, records of your stock purchases, and other critical data, not to mention your family photos and other irreplaceable things? Or you could simply mistakenly erase important data in your computer (43 percent of people do this annually) or your hard drive could crash (it happens to 13 percent of hard drives each year). What if your laptop is lost or stolen? (Only three of 100 missing laptops are ever recovered.)

To protect yourself, organize your financial information and store it safely. Besides making it easier for you to retrieve at any time, it can help you recover money and cut taxes if disaster strikes.

### BACK UP FINANCIAL DATA

If you keep your financial records on your computer, you must back up the data regularly to protect it from loss.

- *Use online backup services.* These automate the backup process; just leave your computer connected to the Internet and the backup is done at the time you specify (e.g., every night at 1:00 AM). The cost for this service usually depends on the amount of information you back up. *Examples:* Data Deposit Box (www.datadepositbox.com) charges $2 per gigabyte (GB) each month; Xdrive (www.xdrive.com), an America Online (AOL) service, is free; Carbonite (www.carbonite.com) charges a flat $49.95 per year.

- *Back up to disk.* Back up your data to disk and store it in a safe place (a fireproof safe at home or, preferably, in a remote location that would not be impacted by a disaster in your area).

### SAFEGUARD IMPORTANT PAPERS

Store papers in the appropriate location:

- *Safe-deposit box.* Store items that are irreplaceable (or extremely difficult to replace). Keep copies of these papers at home. *Examples:* Adoption papers, marriage license, divorce decrees, military records, passport, Social Security card, burial lot deed, property records (deeds, titles to vehicles), and an inventory of the contents of your home. *Caution:* Don't keep your will in the box; keep a copy there with instructions on where the original can be found (e.g., with the attorney who prepared it).

- *Home safe.* Store at home those items that are replaceable (even if inconvenient or somewhat difficult to do). Consider getting a fireproof box or safe for at-home storage. *Examples:* Insurance policies, credit card numbers, account numbers of banks and brokerage accounts, and copies of tax returns, wills, living wills, and durable powers of attorney.

**What to Do Now**

When storing any papers, it's wise to stash irreplaceable documents in a ziplock plastic bag to prevent water damage.

With your papers, keep a list of your important contact information, such as the phone numbers of your insurance agent, accountant, and attorney. These individuals usually have copies of your important papers or can help you obtain them if they are lost.

## Deducting Property Losses

If your property is damaged or destroyed in a casualty event, such as a fire, storm, or flood, you hope your insurance will cover all or most of your loss. However, if your insurance falls short, you may receive some financial break by claiming a tax loss for the damage. There is no dollar limit on how much you can deduct, but you must itemize deductions (in lieu of the standard deduction) to write off personal casualty losses.

What's your loss? The tax rules are cold and strict; your loss is limited to the decrease in the value of the property from the casualty or its adjusted basis (usually your cost), whichever amount is smaller. If property is damaged or destroyed, follow these rules of thumb:

- For property that had appreciated from the time you acquired it to just prior to the event, your loss is based on adjusted basis.
- For property that had declined in value from the time you acquired it to just prior to the event, your loss is based on fair market value.

**Example**

You bought a painting for $20,000 that is completely destroyed by a fire. Immediately before the fire, the painting's value was $100,000. Your homeowners insurance policy does not cover this item and you do not have a separate policy to cover fine arts. Your tax loss is based on your adjusted basis of $20,000, which is less than the painting's value of $100,000.

Your car is totaled in an accident and you don't have collision coverage on it. You paid $20,000 for the car, and it was worth $8,000 before the accident and just $1,500 scrap value after the accident. Your tax loss is based on the decrease in the value, or $6,500 ($8,000 − $1,500); this is less than the car's adjusted basis of $20,000.

### Factors Reducing Your Deduction

Even if you have a loss, this doesn't guarantee that it will be deductible. There are two tax law reductions of personal casualty losses:

- You must reduce each casualty loss by $100. This applies per casualty, not per item in the casualty event. If you have the misfortune to suffer two casualties in the same year, say a fire and a car accident, then you have two $100 subtractions.

- You must reduce your deductible loss by 10 percent of your adjusted gross income (AGI). This factor will substantially reduce your deduction and may prevent you from claiming any write-off.

### Example

A hurricane damages your home and your uninsured losses, after reducing them by $100, are $7,600. If your adjusted gross income is $76,000 or more, you cannot take any casualty loss deduction. If your AGI is, say, $50,000, your deduction is limited to $2,600 ($7,600 − $5,000).

Unfortunately, you can't recover losses that are sentimental or of personal value. The family photo album that's lost in a tornado won't give you any tax break; it may have tremendous personal value but no value for tax purposes. Storing photos online is one way to protect these irreplaceable items from loss.

### What to Do Now

Obtain an appraisal to determine the value of property before and after a casualty. Online resources for finding a qualified appraiser:

- American Society of Appraisers (www.appraisers.org)
- Foundation of Real Estate Appraisers (www.frea.org)
- International Society of Appraisers (www.isa-appraisers.org).

Use the cost of repairs as a measure of your loss. Restoration costs are viewed as the amount of your loss if you make only necessary repairs to bring the property back to its precasualty condition.

### When to Deduct the Loss

Usually, you take the deduction in the year in which the casualty occurs. However, if the casualty is a disaster event, where your local area is designated by the U.S. president as qualifying for federal disaster relief, you can choose instead to deduct the loss in the prior year. This can create a tax refund for the prior year, giving you immediate cash to use for rebuilding.

Whether it's a good idea to claim the disaster loss in the prior year depends on your personal tax situation. You'll get the most tax mileage for the deduction in the year in which your adjusted gross income is lower (because of the 10-percent-of-AGI threshold explained earlier).

### Disaster Relief Payments

If you are the victim of a disaster, you may receive assistance from the government or from nonprofit organizations. These payments to you are tax free, regardless of amount. Examples of tax-free disaster relief payments made because of a federally declared disaster:

- Personal, family, living, or funeral expenses.
- Expenses for the repair or rehabilitation of a personal residence, whether you own or rent the home.
- Expenses for the repair or replacement of the contents of a home.

### Gain on Your Casualty Loss?

Having property damage because of a casualty event doesn't mean you have a tax loss. You may even have a tax *gain*. This results when the insurance proceeds and other recoveries you receive are greater than the adjusted basis of the property. For instance, in the example discussed previously, if you had insured the painting for $100,000, its value, you'd have an $80,000 gain as a result of the fire ($100,000 less $20,000 adjusted basis). The tax law calls this an involuntary conversion.

Fortunately, if you have an involuntary conversion that gives you a tax gain, you don't necessarily have to pay tax on this gain now. You can postpone the tax by reinvesting the proceeds into replacement property within set time limits:

- Two years for losses to personal property (other than a home's contents). The two-year period starts on the date of the damage or destruction and ends two years after the end of the first year in which any part of your gain is realized.
- Three years for business or investment real estate (not including inventory).
- Four years in the case of casualty to your home and its contents.
- Five years in special circumstances. For instance, the government extended the replacement period for victims of 9/11, Hurricane Katrina, Greensburg, Kansas tornado, 2008 Midwest floods, and Hurricane Ike.

The replacement property doesn't have to be an exact match to what was destroyed. However, it must be similar or related in service or use. One residence must be replaced by another, although one could be a single-family home and the other a condominium. Replacing a residence with vacant land won't qualify for postponing tax on gain.

### Involuntary Conversion of a Principal Residence

Instead of postponing gain by buying a replacement home, you can exclude gain under the home sale exclusion rules. Assuming you owned and used the home as your principal residence for at least two years prior to the casualty event and the home is considered destroyed, then gain can be excluded up to $250,000 ($500,000 on a joint return).

Destruction need not be total, but it must be so substantial that it is viewed as a full destruction. The IRS says that only a full destruction (not a partial one) qualifies for the home sale exclusion. A "full destruction" means that the home is damaged to such an extent that the remaining structure can't be used to advantage in restoring the home to its precasualty condition. Another measure of full destruction is having the cost of repairs substantially exceed the fair market value of the home prior to the casualty.

If the gain from the involuntary conversion exceeds the home sale exclusion, you can postpone tax on the excess gain by obtaining a replacement home within the four-year time limit explained earlier.

---

### What to Do Now

If you are the victim of a disaster, check with FEMA (www.fema.gov) and local agencies to see whether you are entitled to any grants, relief payments, or other benefits.

---

### Other Tax Breaks for Disaster Victims

In addition to having a choice of when to deduct your loss, other federal tax breaks may be yours:

- Extended due dates for filing returns and making IRA contributions.
- Abatement of interest and penalties on underpayment of income tax for the length of any postponement of tax deadlines.

If there are any special tax breaks for your casualty event, the IRS will publicize them as news items on its web site (www.irs.gov).

## Condemnations

You may lose your home to a government action, called condemnation. This occurs when your property is deemed unsafe, a condition that can result after a casualty event. Or it can occur when the government takes your property for a public purpose, such as expanding a road or building a school, in a legal process called eminent domain. The U.S. Supreme Court in recent years has taken a liberal view of what constitutes a public purpose, allowing seizure to enable developers to construct better buildings that enhance the government's tax rolls.

If your home or part of your property is condemned, you may wind up with a tax gain as a result of a condemnation even though you've really lost something. The insurance proceeds or government settlement may exceed your home's adjusted basis. When this occurs, you have a tax gain even though it doesn't feel like you've gained anything. Like an involuntary conversion, you can postpone tax on this gain by reinvesting the proceeds in a new home.

If you receive an award, this starts the clock running on the replacement period (two years for a residence), even if you contest the amount of the award.

## Thefts

If your property is stolen and your loss isn't covered by insurance, you may be able to deduct your loss. The theft generally must be something illegal under state law in order for your loss to be deductible. The same tax rules for casualty losses apply to theft losses as well.

---

### What to Do Now

Check your homeowners and automobile insurance policies for terms and conditions of your property coverage. For instance, if you lose your expensive watch while away from home or your personal laptop is stolen from your car, is the loss covered? Are your children's items covered by your policy when they are away at school? You may be able to add coverage at a nominal amount for items away from home (usually this additional coverage is called a rider to your basic homeowners policy).

If there are limits, such as how much jewelry, silver, and art is covered, consider increasing these limits if you can afford to do so or obtaining a separate policy.

---

## Seeking and Obtaining Damages

If you're wronged, you may seek legal redress by filing an action in court. These actions can arise because of personal injury, damage to property, discrimination, employment actions, or for any number of other reasons. The United States is the most litigious society in the world. Each year there are 3.3 tort actions (malpractice and other personal wrongs) filed for each 1,000 people—80 to 90 million lawsuits annually. Over 70 percent of the world's lawyers are in the United States.

Recovering damages is a process designed to make you whole. If you are injured or wronged in some way, legal action may be the best resource. Legal actions related to your job are covered in Chapter 8.

The tax law may or may not penalize you for recovering damages. It all depends on the nature of the case. If you recover damages for physical personal injury, compensatory damages are not taxed. In all other cases, however, damages, whether awarded by a court or received because of a settlement out of court, are fully taxable. These include punitive damages, damages for breach of contract, and damages for being discriminated against.

### Structured Settlements

**CAUTION**

There are a number of shady companies that will pay you only pennies on the dollar; they take advantage of those in distress. Only work with a legitimate company that pays you a fair amount for your award. When in doubt, talk with a financial adviser about a lump-sum payment.

If you are awarded money that is to be paid out over time through a structured settlement, you are assured to have the money on hand when needed to pay medical bills or other expenses. However, you may want money now. You can accelerate receipt of the money by selling to a third party your rights to future payments. There are companies that will pay you a lump sum for a portion of your award now, discounted for the time value of money (you'll effectively receive less in total than if you'd waited to receive payments over time); they then have the right to receive all your payments.

### Attorney's Fees

These can be substantial and may be based on an hourly rate or a percentage of the award. Before engaging an attorney to represent you, be sure you fully understand how payment works.

There is a tax trap when it comes to attorney's fees. You can't deduct fees if they relate to obtaining tax-free income. For instance, if one parent sues the other for child support (which is not taxable), the cost of the attorney can't be deducted. The same is true for tax-free personal injury awards.

If the award is taxable, then the attorney's fees can be deducted as a miscellaneous itemized deduction. However, miscellaneous itemized deductions up to the first 2 percent of adjusted gross income are lost; only amounts in excess of 2 percent are deductible. Individuals subject to the alternative minimum tax (AMT) effectively lose any benefit from deducting attorney's fees because miscellaneous itemized deductions are not allowed for the AMT. Fees related to certain discriminations are deductible, whether or not you itemize other deductions.

# Long-Term Care

If you get an acute disease, such as cancer or a heart attack, traditional medical insurance, Medicare, and supplemental (Medigap) policies will pay for most treatment. If, however, you suffer from a chronic condition, such as Alzheimer's or merely old age, these medical policies won't pay for your personal care. Family members can and often do help as long as they can. But often, a person requires professional care in-home or in a nursing home. The cost of such care can be tremendous. According to the Genworth Financial 2008 Cost of Care Survey, the average cost of a private room in a nursing home in the United States per day is $209 (or $76,285 annually). The average hourly rate for in-home personal care from a non-Medicare-certified, licensed agency is $18 (or $432 for round-the-clock care).

Who can afford such care? Only the very wealthy can pay for long-term care out of pocket. The poor can rely on Medicaid, a needs-based federal-state program that pays for long-term care if a person's assets and income are below certain amounts.

## Long-Term Care Insurance

Those of moderate means who want to protect their assets from the devastation of long-term care may want to carry long-term care insurance. This product is expensive and may never be needed, but can pay some or all of the cost of long-term care if it becomes necessary. The policy pays a fixed dollar amount (e.g., $200 per day) if you become incapacitated and require long-term care (as defined in your policy).

The cost of carrying this protection is lessened to some degree by a tax write-off. The tax law lets you deduct a portion of long-term care premiums as part of your itemized medical deduction. The deductible amount of the premium depends on your age at the end of the year (see Table 7.1). The deduction limit can be adjusted by the IRS annually for inflation.

**TABLE 7.1** Deduction for Long-Term Care Premiums for 2008

| Age | Deduction Limit |
| --- | --- |
| Age 40 or younger | $310 |
| Age 41–50 | $580 |
| Age 51–60 | $1,150 |
| Age 61–70 | $3,080 |
| Age 71 or older | $3,850 |

*Source:* IRS.

### Actions to Take

In shopping for long-term care insurance, use caution. Even though premiums are supposed to be fixed for the life of the policy based on your age when you first buy it, some carriers have been forced to increase premiums dramatically. They miscalculated their claims and are making up their losses with policyholders.

Determine whether you want certain features of a long-term care policy. If you are younger than 70, you might want to include an inflation adjustment; you'll pay for this feature but will receive greater benefits if needed. Also decide on the term of the benefit—lifetime or for a limited number of years. For instance, the benefit plan must give you or your family adequate time to transfer your assets so that Medicaid can take over the cost of your care without using up all of those assets (see Medicare planning, discussed in a following section).

### Accelerated Death Benefits

If you have a life insurance policy on yourself, you may be able to receive some of the death benefits while you're alive. The money can be paid to you directly from the insurance company as an advance on what is owed under the policy. Or the money can be raised by using a viatical settlement where you sell the policy to a company that is in the business of buying such policies.

Taxwise, the receipt of accelerated death benefits can be tax free, just like they would be tax free to your beneficiaries if payable on death. To be tax free, you must be terminally ill (i.e., have a condition or illness that a doctor certifies is expected to result in death within 24 months). You can use the money for any purpose, including paying for long-term care.

You can also tap into benefits from a life insurance policy if you have a chronic condition that makes you unable to care for yourself. Only the amount of benefits used for long-term care is tax free. If you receive a per diem amount, only the sum up to an amount fixed by law ($270 in 2008) is tax free. A licensed health care practitioner must certify that you have a condition that makes you unable to perform for a period of 90 days or more at least two of the following activities:

- Bathing
- Continence
- Dressing
- Eating
- Toileting
- Transferring (getting in and out of bed)

A person can also qualify as having a chronic condition if it is certified that the individual requires supervision for his or her own safety because of a cognitive impairment, such as Alzheimer's disease.

### Medicaid Planning

If a person's income and assets are below amounts fixed by law, the cost of long-term care can be paid by the government. In effect, a person must impoverish himself to qualify for Medicaid. This can be done by paying for long-term care until personal assets are exhausted. Often, however, this means transferring assets to family members to preserve the family's wealth while becoming eligible for Medicaid.

Early planning for transfers is necessary because the law creates a look-back period that can prevent eligibility. Assets transferred within five years of applying for Medicaid that are not for adequate consideration (e.g., they are gifts to family members) are taken into account in determining eligibility; only transfers made more than five years before applying can escape scrutiny.

---

**What to Do Now**

Work with an elder law attorney *before* making any transfers or taking any other actions if you or a relative is concerned about long-term care planning. You can find an elder law attorney through the National Academy of Elder Law Attorneys (NAELA at www.naela.org).

---

## Asset Protection

Today, at the drop of a hat, someone commences a lawsuit. You face a one-in-four chance of being sued sometime in your life. If you're the one being sued, your hard-earned wealth can be in jeopardy. Assets can also be at risk for a variety of other reasons, such as divorce or serious health issues. What can you do to protect yourself?

### Using Business Entities

If you're self-employed, any business creditor, or any person injured by your business who wins a legal action against you, can reach your personal assets for satisfaction. In contrast, if your business is set up as a certain type of entity, business creditors can only reach assets owned by the business; your personal assets are protected. Consider using legal entities that provide personal liability protection:

**CAUTION**

Even if you have an LLC or a corporation, you remain liable for any loans you've personally guaranteed if the business can't make good on its obligations. You are also fully liable to the federal government for any income tax and Social Security and Medicare taxes that you've withheld from your employees' wages but have not turned over to the U.S. Treasury.

- Limited liability companies (LLCs).
- Corporations. Both C (regular) and S corporations give you the same legal protection for your personal assets.

> ### What to Do Now
>
> You can incorporate or form an LLC yourself or use an online business formation company; the cost is modest compared with the legal protection you gain. However, it's a good idea to discuss your plans with an attorney before taking any legal steps.

### Trusts

Can you shield assets from creditors' claims by placing them in a trust you create? It depends. If someone else creates a trust for your benefit (e.g., your parent creates a trust for your benefit), then assets can be fully protected. For instance, the trust can include a spendthrift clause that prevents the beneficiary from wasting assets or allowing his or her creditors to reach trust assets. If you set up a trust for your own benefit, protection may be limited.

- *Domestic trusts.* Certain states, including Alaska, Delaware, Nevada, Rhode Island, and Utah, allow you to create a trust for yourself that provides protection for your assets. You can control the trust. The point is to keep your creditors from getting the assets held by the trust. These domestic trusts are relatively new, so it's not yet clear how well they'll protect assets.

- *Foreign trusts.* Offshore trusts set up in certain countries make it more difficult, if not impossible, for creditors to reach your assets. Of course, U.S. citizens and residents remain taxable on their worldwide income, so there is no tax advantage for going overseas.

> ### What to Do Now
>
> The cost of setting up and managing these trusts can be substantial, so don't consider them unless you have sizable assets. If you decide you want to explore them, talk to a knowledgeable attorney (don't try to do it yourself).

### Prenuptial and Postnuptial Agreements

For some, one of the most financially and personally devastating events is the dissolution of a marriage. Matters can be settled in advance, when the parties are on good terms, by using legal contracts, called prenuptial agreements if signed before the marriage, or postnuptial agreements if signed after the marriage. The agreement can stipulate which spouse is entitled to what benefits, such as property and/or alimony. The agreement can also cover nonfinancial matters, such as custody of children.

These agreements are not only for the rich; they can be used by anyone who wants to protect assets if the worst should happen. They are commonly used in second marriages, especially when there are children from prior marriages to protect. They can run for the term of the marriage, or expire at a fixed time, say after five or 10 years of marriage.

> **CAUTION**
> If you want an agreement to waive a spouse's right to qualified retirement plan benefits, the waiver must be made after the marriage; it can't be waived by a fiancé.

## Identity Theft

Identity theft has been called the fastest-growing crime in the United States. Identity theft occurs when someone uses another person's Social Security number and other personal information to get credit or do other fraudulent acts under the person's name. According to the Privacy Rights Clearinghouse, there were 8.9 million victims of identity theft in 2007. The average loss per person from the fraud itself as well as legal fees and lost wages was $5,720. It took an average of 25 hours to resolve the problem and reclaim identity.

While there's no absolute protection from becoming a victim, you can take steps both to minimize the likelihood that someone will obtain your identity and to get help and money to reclaim your identity if you do fall victim to identity thieves.

### Smart Credit Practices

Be vigilant about your personal identity. Don't give out personal information to any unsolicited caller or respond to any unsolicited e-mail. These may be fraudulent measures to obtain your identity.

Guard your Social Security number, credit card numbers, and bank account numbers. Don't let people look over your shoulder to view this information.

Monitor your bank account and credit card statements carefully. Make sure there are no unauthorized transactions.

Order a free copy of your credit report each year from AnnualCreditReport (www.annualcreditreport.com), a web site sponsored by the three major personal credit reporting services, Equifax (www.equifax.com), Experian (www.experian.com), and TransUnion (www.transunion.com).

### Credit Monitoring Services

Keep a close watch on credit activity under your name. You can do this by paying for a service that checks your credit activity and reports to you if there are any suspicious changes. This allows you to respond promptly if you detect any problems.

### Insurance against Loss

Check whether your homeowners insurance policy provides identity theft protection. You may be able to add coverage for a nominal amount.

Consider carrying a separate insurance policy for identity theft protection. The cost can be very modest—$15 to $30 per year for coverage up to $15,000, with a $100 deductible. The following carriers offer coverage (but it may not be available in every state):

- Allstate Insurance (www.allstate.com)
- American International Group (www.aig.com)
- Chubb Group of Insurance Companies (www.chubb.com)
- Encompass Insurance (www.encompassinsurance.com)
- Erie Insurance (www.erieinsurance.com)
- Farmers Group, Inc. (www.farmers.com)
- Fireman's Fund (www.firemansfund.com)
- Liberty Mutual (www.libertymutual.com)
- Nationwide (www.nationwide.com)
- Travelers Insurance (www.travelers.com)
- West Bend Mutual (www.westbendmutual.com)

## Bankruptcy

Bankruptcy, which is a court-supervised legal action, is a last resort to dig your way out of financial ruin. If your debts exceed your assets and you see no way to pay off your creditors, even after working with a professional credit counseling service, you might want to seek bankruptcy protection. In this down market, the number of personal bankruptcy filings has increased by 40 percent in 2007 when compared with 2006, according to the National Bankruptcy Research Center. This means that about 1.4 percent of all households filed for bankruptcy. Data for 2008 is unavailable, but it's a good guess that filings have not slowed down.

*Advantages*. Filing for bankruptcy stops creditors from hounding you for payment. You can restore order to your life. Depending on which type of bankruptcy action you use, you'll pay off your creditors over time or emerge from bankruptcy free from debt and ready to start anew.

*Disadvantages*. You seriously damage your credit rating, impairing your ability to borrow money to buy a home or a car or obtain a credit card for years to come. A bankruptcy stays on your credit report for 10 years.

### Types of Bankruptcy

There are two types of bankruptcy options for individuals:

- *Chapter* 7. This is a liquidation of your assets, giving you a fresh start. Your assets, other than exempt assets (discussed in the next section), are amassed and sold, and the proceeds are then distributed to your creditors.

- *Chapter* 13. This is a repayment plan. It's *mandatory* for those with income above their state's median who can pay at least $6,000 over five years (you can't use the fresh start option). In effect, if you have a decent salary, you won't be able to use the fresh start option and will have to work out a repayment plan. (Chapter 12 is a repayment plan for family farmers.)

### Exempt Assets

If you can use bankruptcy, it doesn't mean you'll lose everything you own. Under federal bankruptcy law, certain assets are exempt; you can retain them even though you go through bankruptcy. These include:

- *Homestead.* No more than $125,000 can be protected unless the homeowner resided in the state at least 40 months prior to filing for bankruptcy. Thus, Florida allows *full* homestead protection, but if someone files for bankruptcy after moving into a home and doesn't meet the 40-month rule, only $125,000 of the home's equity is protected.

- *Retirement plan benefits.* All benefits in a qualified retirement plan are fully exempt. So, too, are all assets in an IRA rollover. Funds in a contributory IRA or Roth IRA are exempt only up to $1 million.

- *Education savings.* Funds in 529 plans and Coverdell education savings accounts (ESAs) are exempt if they have been in the plan for more than two years prior to filing for bankruptcy. Contributions to these plans between 365 and 720 days prior to filing are exempt only up to $5,000 per beneficiary. There is no exemption for contributions to these plans made within one year of filing for bankruptcy.

### Nondischargeable Debts

Even if you successfully complete the bankruptcy process, not all of your debts can be extinguished. You continue to owe:

- *Alimony and child support.* Property settlements, however, need no longer be paid.

- *Bills for luxury items.* You can't run up a big credit card bill and then escape payment by filing for bankruptcy.

- *Debts related to certain intentional actions.* If you commit fraud or drive drunk, debts arising from these actions are not dischargeable.
- *Federal and state income taxes.* Some taxes are dischargeable; others are not.
- *Secured loans.* The collateral pledged for the loans must be used for the intended purpose.
- *Student loans.*

# CHAPTER 8

# Problems with Your Job

The unemployment rate in September 2008 was about 6.1 percent, which is not considered alarming. However, some experts were predicting that the rate would top 6.5 percent by the end of 2008; this would be viewed as a rate of considerable concern. Although rates are currently well below the highs of the early 1980s when the rate approached 10 percent, if you or someone in your family is part of the statistic, you may be hurting.

Job layoffs have become common events today. Some industries, such as the financial sector and the automobile industry, are especially hard hit. If you or someone in your family has lost a job or is concerned about job security, what can you do to make the best of a bad situation? Plenty.

If you've lost a job, you may be eligible to collect unemployment benefits. While these benefits may not cover all your expenses and won't last forever, they can help in the short run. If your company is experiencing layoffs, you may be offered early retirement or given a severance package as a way to make your leaving a little easier. How do you evaluate an early retirement offer? What does a severance package mean to you, and what choices can you make to optimize your benefits?

If you've lost a job, think of this as an opportunity. You can look for a new job as soon as possible. The tax law underwrites to some extent the cost of looking for a new job. Or you may want to start your own business. Or you may be able, depending on your overall financial position, to enjoy your unexpected retirement.

Even if you don't lose your job, you can encounter problems. You may experience discrimination, sexual harassment, or other personal violations that you'd like to contest. If you have financial issues, your wages may be subject to garnishment. These legal and financial issues can impact your job.

In this chapter, you will learn about:

- Job layoffs
- Early retirement
- Severance packages
- Unemployment benefits
- Job-seeking expenses
- Relocating
- Suing your employer
- Garnishment

## Job Layoffs

When the economy is down, companies may be forced to lay off workers in order to stay afloat. Some industries hardest hit because of the economy are the airlines, financial services, and automobile manufacturers. Some major corporate layoffs announced in June 2008 include General Motors, 30,000 (over three years); Bear Stearns, 7,000; Citigroup, 3,000; Continental Airlines, 3,000; United Airlines, 1,500; American Airlines, thousands. Big corporations aren't the only companies laying off workers; smaller firms facing rising fuel prices and other cost challenges are eliminating jobs to stay afloat. Unfortunately, there is usually nothing you can do about this.

### Wrongful Termination

In some cases, you may suspect that you've been terminated for unlawful reasons, such as age discrimination. If you believe you've been unfairly terminated, consult with an employment law attorney.

A company is allowed to ask you to waive any legal rights as a condition of accepting an early retirement package or severance package. Don't sign any agreement before determining your rights under the law.

### Decisions about Retirement Plans

You may be given an opportunity to take your retirement plan benefits with you or leave them with your employer's plan (they still belong to you). This opportunity usually is open only for a limited period (say 60 days). If you don't take your benefits as a distribution or roll them over to an individual retirement account (IRA) or retirement plan with a new employer, you may not be able to reach them until you attain the plan's normal retirement age (say 65).

Should you take your benefits or leave them in the plan? It depends. You gain the most flexibility over your money if you roll the benefits into an IRA. This allows you to control the investments and your future distributions.

However, you may prefer the investment options in the company's plan or you just don't want to be bothered; in this case, you can leave the money where it is.

If your funds in the plan are under $5,000, you may have no choice. Your employer may opt to distribute them to you (or allow you to make a rollover), even if you preferred to leave them in the plan.

### Paying Off Outstanding Plan Loans

If you've borrowed from your 401(k) plan, you must repay the funds at this time, even though the term of the loan may run for several more years. If you don't or can't repay the money, the outstanding balance is treated as a distribution and is taxable to you. If you are under age $59^1/_2$, you may also be subject to a 10 percent early distribution penalty. The penalty does not apply if you separate from service after age 55.

---

**What to Do Now**

Find out about any benefits to which you may be entitled (severance packages are discussed later in the chapter).

Develop a game plan for your future. Decide whether you want to:

- Find another job. Job hunting is a challenging undertaking, especially in bad economic times. Find job-hunting tips from Monster.com (www.monster.com) and CareerBlazers (www.careerblazers.com).

- Start your own business. Losing a job may be an opportunity to go in a new direction by starting your own business. While becoming an entrepreneur is never an easy task, it may be the best avenue to pursue; middle-aged and older workers who had earned substantial salaries may have a hard time replacing those earnings with a new job. Learn about starting a business from the Small Business Administration (www.sba.gov).

- Go back to school for retraining or to obtain a new career direction.

---

### Tax Credit for Health Coverage

If your job layoff is the casualty of a trade agreement or changing economic conditions that shift jobs offshore, you may be able to claim a special tax credit for health coverage. If you qualify, the government pays 65 percent of your health insurance premiums under the Consolidated Omnibus Budget Reconciliation Act (COBRA) continuation coverage or insurance through a state-run program. You pay the balance of the premiums (35 percent) from your own pocket.

### ELIGIBILITY

The government determines your eligibility and sends you Form 8887, Health Insurance Credit Eligibility Certificate. It specifies your classification:

- Eligible TAA—someone who is eligible to receive a trade adjustment allowance (TAA).
- Alternative TAA—someone who is eligible for an alternative trade adjustment allowance (who would have received a TAA but has not exhausted unemployment benefits).
- PBGC pension recipient—a retiree age 55 or older who is receiving benefits from the Pension Benefit Guaranty Corporation. For 2008, you must have been born before 1953 to qualify.

### QUALIFYING INSURANCE

You must be covered under specific types of insurance, including:

- Certain state-sponsored health insurance (the state must elect to have it be qualified for this purpose).
- COBRA.
- Coverage under a group plan available through your spouse's employer.
- Coverage under your individual policy, provided you were covered during the entire 30-day period that ends on the date you separated from the employment that makes you an eligible individual.

Certain coverage is nonqualifying. Examples include:

- Any coverage of which at least 50 percent is paid by your (or your spouse's) employer.
- Federal Employees Health Benefits Plan (FEHBP).
- Medicaid.
- Medicare.
- Medicare supplemental (medigap) insurance.
- State Children's Health Insurance Program (S-CHIP).
- Tricare (for certain military personnel and their families) or supplemental Tricare.
- Workers' compensation.

### CLAIMING THE CREDIT

The tax credit is claimed on your return by completing Form 8885, Health Coverage Tax Credit. The credit is refundable, so if it brings your tax liability below zero, you can receive a tax refund.

You can also obtain the credit on an advanced basis. Your state workforce agency or the PBGC can give you instructions for enrolling in the advanced tax credit plan. Once enrolled, you pay only 35 percent of the health care cost; the government pays the rest to the insurer. If you receive the credit on an advanced basis, then you can't claim the tax credit on your return.

## Early Retirement

Maybe you had planned to continue on the job until you reached full retirement age for Social Security. Unfortunately, your employer may have other plans. Some companies, in an effort to trim the payroll, may offer inducements to workers to get workers to accept early retirement. If you find yourself in this situation, weigh carefully the choices before you.

Consider the impact on you personally. You may prefer to be in a work environment so you can interact with other people and feel productive. Or you may prefer having the time to do other things, such as athletics or volunteering for charity (if you can afford not to work). If you are married, your spouse may have an opinion on your work status.

Also consider the true meaning of the early retirement offer. You may not have any real choice; accept the offer or expect to be laid off (if not immediately, then sometime soon). Or the job buyout may present a real choice for you.

### Advantages of Early Retirement

If you leave your current employer, there's nothing to stop you from looking for a new job, starting a business, or simply kicking back and enjoying retirement. In other words, early retirement gives you many options for your future.

There are monetary considerations to retiring early. *Not* working saves you:

- Social Security and Medicare taxes you'd otherwise owe on earnings.
- Commuting costs for getting to and from work.
- Work-related expenses, such as clothing and eating out.

### Disadvantages of Early Retirement

There are financial drawbacks to not working:

- You no longer have a paycheck (unless you get a new job or start a business). You may be able to begin taking retirement benefits. If you are at least 62 years old, you can start receiving Social Security benefits. However, starting benefits at age 62 means a permanent reduction in benefits for rest of your life. Benefits that start at age 62 are reduced by a set percentage compared with those that commence at your normal retirement age (between 65 and 67, depending on your year of birth). For example, those born between 1943 and 1954 who retire at age 62 will have their benefits reduced by 25 percent. To see what Social Security benefits you would be entitled to, use the "Quick Calculator" from the Social Security Administration web site (www.ssa.gov/planners/calculators.htm).

- You can't contribute to a retirement plan. Unless you have already amassed a sizable retirement fund, taking early retirement may mean having a smaller income during your retirement years.
- You may not have health coverage. Unless you can continue coverage under your employer's plan or you are at least 65 years old and covered by Medicare, you'll have to obtain health coverage on your own. This can be an expensive endeavor.

If you believe that you have a real choice of either continuing on the job or accepting an early retirement package, then use Table 8.1 to help you make a decision about whether to accept the offer. Compare your income before to what it would be after taking early retirement. Some points in completing the table:

- Factor in your retirement income in light of any early retirement inducements you may receive (see severance packages discussion later in the chapter).

**TABLE 8.1** Working versus Early Retirement

| Income and Expenses | Remaining on the Job | Retiring |
|---|---|---|
| Income | | |
| Salary/wages | | |
| Severance payment | | |
| Social Security benefits | | |
| Pension income | | |
| Income from 401(k)s and IRAs | | |
| Expenses | | |
| Federal income taxes* | | |
| FICA | | |
| Medical insurance | | |
| Commuting/job-related expenses | | |
| Life insurance | | |
| Annual after-tax income | | |

*There may also be state and local income taxes.

- FICA (to pay for Social Security and Medicare taxes) is 7.65 percent of your salary/wages up to a limit ($102,000 in 2008) and 1.45 percent on amounts above the limit.
- Figure your job-related expenses at 5 percent to 10 percent of your wages.

## Example

Take this hypothetical example of someone earning $90,000 who is offered an early retirement package at age 63. He also receives a severance payment of $30,000 ($10,000 for each year prior to his full retirement age of 66 for Social Security purposes). Assume he's in the 25 percent tax bracket. Taking Social Security benefits at age 63 would mean a monthly payment of $1,500. Assume that his pension income is $24,000 per year and he can draw out $10,000 from his IRA without depleting it too greatly. He can continue medical coverage under COBRA for 18 months at a cost of $750; thereafter personal coverage for the next six months (until Medicare eligibility) is $1,200 per month.

Working versus Early Retirement—Year One

| Income and Expenses | Remaining on the Job | Retiring |
|---|---|---|
| **Income** | | |
| Salary/wages | $90,000 | |
| Severance payment | | $30,000 |
| Social Security benefits | | $18,000 |
| Pension income | | $24,000 |
| Income from 401(k)s and IRAs | | $10,000 |
| *Total income* | $90,000 | $82,000 |
| **Expenses** | | |
| Federal income taxes* | $22,500 | $20,500 |
| FICA | $ 6,885 | |
| Medical insurance | | $ 9,000 |
| Commuting/job-related expenses | $ 4,000 | |
| Life insurance | | $ 1,000 |
| *Total expenses* | $33,385 | $30,500 |
| Annual after-tax income | $56,615 | $51,500 |

*There may also be state and local income taxes.

The difference in working versus retirement, $5,115, works out to less than $3 per hour (based on working 1,750 hours per year).

*(continued)*

*(Continued)*

In year two, there is no additional severance payment, and medical insurance costs go up for the last six months of the year.

Working versus Early Retirement—Year Two

| Income and Expenses | Remaining on the Job | Retiring |
| --- | --- | --- |
| **Income** | | |
| Salary/wages | $90,000 | |
| Severance payment | | |
| Social Security benefits | | $18,000 |
| Pension income | | $24,000 |
| Income from 401(k)s and IRAs | | $10,000 |
| *Total income* | $90,000 | $52,000 |
| **Expenses** | | |
| Federal income taxes* | $22,500 | $13,000 |
| FICA | $ 6,885 | |
| Medical insurance | | $11,700 |
| Commuting/job-related expenses | $ 4,000 | |
| Life insurance | | $ 1,000 |
| *Total expenses* | $33,385 | $25,700 |
| Annual after-tax income | $56,615 | $26,300 |

*There may also be state and local income taxes.

The difference between working and early retirement in year two becomes more dramatic because of the greatly reduced income (no additional severance payment).

It's not easy to compare what your after-tax income would be following early retirement. There are so many variables. If you stay on the job, you might receive a raise in year two. Your Social Security benefits in year two will be adjusted for inflation; pension benefits are fixed in most cases and do not adjust for inflation. You might be able to take greater distributions from an IRA or a 401(k) plan if investments in the account perform well.

If you are offered a lump-sum buyout and view this money as cash to live on, determine how long the buyout will last. You might, for example, use the lump-sum buyout to purchase a commercial annuity that will pay you an income for life. You can see what the lump sum will buy you in monthly annuity payments for life (or for a certain term, such as 5, 10, 15, or 20 years), depending on your current age, gender, and whether you want a joint annuity with your spouse, by using the immediate annuity calculator at Annuity Shopper.com (www.annuityshopper.com).

---

### What to Do Now

By law, you must be given at least 21 days to decide whether to accept the offer. Don't be too hasty. Factor in both personal and financial considerations before making a decision on an early retirement offer. Work with a lawyer or financial adviser to decide whether to accept a company's early retirement package (if you believe there is a real choice and rejecting the offer won't mean you'll lose your job anyway).

---

## Severance Packages

What are the key components of a severance package? There are no firm rules; the law does not require an employer to give a severance package, though most do to a greater or lesser extent. Typical features of a severance package include:

- *Severance pay.* You may receive a lump sum, often reflecting your length of service with the company (the longer you're there, the greater the severance pay). Alternatively, some companies continue to pay your wages for a set period (usually up to several months).

- *Health and accident benefits.* If the company has been paying all or some of the cost of your health coverage, it may continue to do so for a certain period (usually up to several months). If the company regularly employs 20 or more workers, then you are entitled to continue paying for group health coverage under the employer's plan through COBRA for 18 months in most cases. However, state law may provide "mini COBRA," entitling you to continue health coverage for some lesser period even though the employer is not subject to federal COBRA rules. With COBRA, you pay the full cost, plus up to a 2 percent administrative fee.

- *Pension credits.* The company may give you some additional credit toward your retirement benefits as if you'd continued on the job. Alternatively, the company may give you the option of taking either additional pension credits or a severance payment. Which option is better? Compare the severance payment with the additional pension credit multiplied by 100; then choose the larger alternative.

## Example

Your company terminates you and offers you a severance payment of $25,000. Alternatively, you can take pension credits that amount to an extra $300 per month in pension payments. In this case, the pension credit is greater ($300 × 100 = $30,000). If the pension credit had been only $250 a month or less, then the severance payment would have been better. However, you may want the cash now if you need it to live on or, perhaps, to start up a business of your own.

- *Fringe benefit continuation.* You may be able to take over certain insurance coverage that your employer had been paying. This can apply to disability insurance, life insurance, and long-term care insurance. Doing this allows you to continue your coverage, usually at lower cost than you could obtain on your own.

- *Supplemental unemployment benefits.* In addition to benefits you can collect from state unemployment, you may be entitled to additional unemployment benefits through a union or other association.

- *Outplacement services.* Your employer may provide help for you to find a new job. This can include providing you with office space from which to search for employment, guidance counseling, and even retraining assistance.

### Tax Treatment

Each component of the severance package has its own unique tax treatment:

- *Severance pay.* Not only is severance pay fully taxable, but it is also subject to Social Security and Medicare taxes.

- *Health and accident benefits.* Benefits paid by your former employer continue to be tax free. Once you begin to pay for your own coverage, you can deduct the premiums as an itemized medical expense if your total medical expenses exceed 7.5 percent of your adjusted gross income *and* you opt to itemize personal deductions.

- *Pension credits.* You aren't taxed when you receive the additional credits; you'll pay taxes when and to the extent you receive retirement benefits from the plan. If, however, you opt for an additional severance payment in lieu of pension credits, the cash is fully taxable, as explained earlier.

- *Supplemental unemployment benefits.* Like state unemployment benefits, supplemental unemployment benefits are taxable to you *except* to the extent of any contributions you made to the fund. However, supplemental benefits are not subject to Social Security and Medicare taxes.

- *Outplacement services.* The value of this benefit usually is not taxed to you.

---

## What to Do Now

If you are terminated, meet with your company's human resources (HR) person to determine the extent of your severance package, if any. Find out what you must do with respect to various benefits (e.g., medical coverage or continuing your life insurance policy). You may need to take action within a set time limit or lose out on the benefit. For instance, you typically have up to two months following termination to decide whether to take COBRA coverage if it is available to you. This means signing forms and paying the premium within the time limit.

If you are not sure how to access your options, work with your own financial adviser before accepting any company offers.

---

## Unemployment Benefits

If you are or have been laid off through no fault of your own, you may be eligible for weekly benefits through a federal-state program called unemployment insurance (UI). The program is administered by each state, and the rules vary somewhat from state to state.

### Eligibility

You must work for a minimum number of weeks to be eligible for state unemployment benefits. If you worked part-time, you may be entitled to partial benefits. If you're self-employed, you are not entitled to UI benefits, even though your business may now be defunct.

Usually, after applying for benefits, it takes a couple of weeks before checks will begin. Some states may have a waiting period of one week (no check will be issued for the first week of unemployment).

To continue receiving your checks, you must demonstrate continued eligibility. This means filing for benefits each week (or every other week if that is your state's rule), usually by telephone or online. You must show:

- You are still unemployed.
- You have been actively seeking work. Some states have special programs to encourage self-employment under which you can continue UI benefits while starting up your own business.
- You have not turned down a work opportunity.

You must report any earnings you receive for any work performed.

For more details, contact your state unemployment insurance agency (www.servicelocator.org/OWSLinks.asp).

### Amount of Benefits

The amount of benefits you receive each week is based on your earnings during the past 52 weeks. The amount of benefits can't exceed your state's maximum benefit. In New York, for example, the current maximum benefit is $405 per week; in Texas, it's $378 per week; in Hawaii, it's $523; in Alabama, it's $235 per week.

Benefits usually are paid for up to 26 weeks in most states. From time to time during periods of high unemployment, benefits may be paid during an extended period of 13 weeks or even 26 weeks. (At the time this book was prepared, Congress was considering some extension of unemployment benefits.) Some states have special programs to extend the benefit period for seven weeks at a time (up to a maximum of 20 additional weeks).

### What to Do Now

Consider using voluntary income tax withholding on your unemployment benefits. The withholding rate on unemployment benefits is 10 percent (file IRS Form W-4V, Voluntary Withholding Request, with your state unemployment office). Depending on your overall income, using withholding can avoid the need to pay quarterly estimated taxes.

Consider using direct deposit to receive your weekly check if your state offers this option. This ensures that you automatically receive your payment on time.

## Job-Seeking Expenses

When you fall off a horse, the best advice is to get back on as quickly as you can. The same is true for losing a job during this economic downturn. Fortunately, the tax law lets you deduct the cost of looking for a new job in the same line of work if you itemize deductions. The cost is treated as a miscellaneous itemized deduction; it is deductible only to the extent it exceeds 2 percent of your adjusted gross income.

### Example

In 2008, you are laid off from your job as a human resources professional in a financial services company. You look for another position doing the same type of work. Your adjusted gross income in 2008 is $45,000 and you have no other miscellaneous deductions besides your job-hunting costs. Only job-hunting expenses in excess of $900 (2 percent of $45,000) are deductible. For instance, if your costs are $1,200, you can deduct $300 ($1,200 – $900).

Deductible job-hunting expenses include:

- Job agency fee that you pay. If your new employer reimburses you for this fee, it may be taxable to you.
- Resumes.
- Postage.
- Travel expenses.

## Relocating

Some parts of the country may be better than others to find work or start a business. For instance, in April 2008, the unemployment rate in Wyoming was 2.6 percent, the lowest in the country, and in Idaho, Nebraska, North Dakota, and Utah the rate was 3.1 percent, compared with 6.9 percent in Michigan, the highest in the country, and 6.7 percent in Alaska, 6.2 percent in California, and 6.1 percent in Rhode Island.

Certainly, some parts of the country are less costly to live in than others. Just look at what it costs for a gallon of gas in different locations. The AAA reported that over the Memorial Day weekend 2008, the price of a gallon of gas at the pump topped $5 in some places in Alaska, while it was only $3.50 in Arizona.

You may want make a change in where you live even before finding a new position, or you may want to wait until you've secured a new job or opened your own business. Either way, use an online calculator from Bankrate.com (www.bankrate.com/brm/movecalc.asp) to see the impact of the cost of living in different areas. If you're thinking about starting your own business, check how business-friendly your proposed new location is for entrepreneurs by viewing data from the Small Business & Entrepreneurship Council (www.sbecouncil.org and click on "Small Business Survival Index").

### Moving Your Home

You may be forced to move because you cannot afford your current home, you find a new job in a different city, or you are seeking work in a location with a better economy. Or you may be moving purely out of choice; you want a different lifestyle, better weather, or to be closer to family. Whatever your reason for moving, recognize that moving can be costly.

You can get a rough idea of what it will cost you to move within the continental United States by using an online calculator from Move (http://moving.

move.com/move/Tools/MovingCalc.asp) and MoverMax (www.movermax.com/moving_guides/before_the_move/quick_moving_cost_estimates.asp).

If you find a new job that requires you to relocate, the cost of the move may be tax deductible. (The same is true if you relocate because of self-employment elsewhere.) A deduction for moving your household items and family is a deduction from gross income (you don't have to itemize to take it). There is no dollar limit on how much you can deduct.

However, the move must be far enough and the new job must last long enough to qualify for the deduction. You must meet two tests:

1. *Distance test.* The distance between your new job location and your former home must be at least 50 miles more than the distance between your old job location and your former home. The location of your new residence is irrelevant for the distance test. If you move across country, it's a given that you meet this test; if you move across town, measure the distance.

2. *Time test.* You must work full-time in your new location for a certain number of weeks (39 weeks for employees; 78 weeks for self-employed individuals). If you file jointly, either spouse can meet the time test.

Usually, the move must take place within a year of finding a new job. However, if you postpone moving your family because of a child's schooling or for another good reason, this one-year rule won't prevent you from taking the deduction.

You can deduct the actual costs of moving your family, your pets, and your household items. If you drive to a new location, you can use an IRS-fixed standard mileage rate (19¢ per mile for the first half of 2008 and 27¢ per mile for the second half of 2008).

**CAUTION**
The cost of moving for your first job or when you retire is not tax deductible.

If your new employer pays the relocation costs or reimburses you for them, the costs are not taxable to you as long as the employer believes you would have been entitled to deduct them if you hadn't received reimbursement (i.e., you meet the time and distance tests). Of course, you can't also claim a deduction for the costs; you already are getting a tax-free fringe benefit.

## Suing Your Employer

Things can happen on the job that may be uncomfortable, injurious, or illegal. Examples of injuries you may experience on the job include:

- A physical injury because of an accident or otherwise.
- Discrimination in hiring, advancement, firing, job assignment, or pay on the basis of age, sex, race, religion, or national origin.
- Sexual harassment.

- Retaliation for whistle-blowing.
- Nonaccommodation for a disability.

What can you do? The course of action you should take depends on the type of injury you experience.

### Reporting to the Company

If you experience any type of injury—physical or otherwise—be sure to follow company procedures on reporting it. The employee manual usually details the course of action (e.g., telling a superior or reporting to HR).

In some cases, taking this first step is critical to your ability to take matters further. For instance, a workers' compensation claim can be denied if you did not first report it to the company when the injury occurred.

### Reporting to the Government

Certain types of actions (or inactions) require you to report them to the government; government agencies will then seek to correct the problem. For example, hourly employees who believe they are not being paid overtime in accordance with federal and/or state law should bring this to the attention of the U.S. Department of Labor (www.dol.gov) and/or their state labor department. The government can recover back wages on behalf of employees.

### Working with an Attorney

If you have questions about your rights or want to take legal action beyond what may already have taken place, contact a knowledgeable attorney. Be sure the professional you engage has expertise in the area you are concerned with. For instance, if you have questions about workers' compensation, look for an attorney with experience in this highly specialized area. If you believe you've been retaliated against for blowing the whistle on a fellow worker or on the company itself, find a lawyer who knows this legal specialty.

## Garnishment

Your creditors, including a spouse or former spouse to whom you owe alimony and/or child support, can seek court action to receive the money they are owed by getting a regular share of your paycheck. This is called garnishment. (If you owe federal taxes, the IRS can garnish wages without obtaining a court order.)

The amount that can be taken from your pay to satisfy creditor claims can't exceed the lesser of 25 percent of your disposable earnings or the amount by which your disposable earnings exceed 30 times the current minimum hourly wage (currently $6.55 for the federal minimum wage; $7.25 starting July 23,

2009). In effect, 75 percent of your wages are exempt from withholding. If your state provides greater protection of your wages for you, then state law overrides federal law in this case. Find your state's law on garnishment through BCSalliance.com at www.bcsalliance.com/y_debt_statelaws_garnishments.html.

You can't be terminated from your job merely because you are subject to garnishment.

# CHAPTER 9

# Handling Business Losses

If you own a business, a bad economy is sure to impact you in some way. Your costs for fuel and other items are going up. Access to capital may be difficult. Customers may take longer to pay you, and there may be more who default on their obligations.

Knowing that an economic downturn is part of the natural economic cycle and that eventually conditions will improve may be little comfort now. However, you can weather this economic storm by using sound strategies to see you through.

Some businesses, though, may be on the ropes or may even be forced to go under. Again, tax and legal rules can help you get out from under your business burden.

In this chapter you will learn about:

- Finding money to weather the storm
- Better collection efforts
- Reducing overhead
- Adjusting prices
- Using down time productively
- Net operating losses
- Tax limitations on business losses

- Special breaks for farmers
- Aborted business ventures
- Winding up a business
- Bankruptcy

## Finding Money to Weather the Storm

Capital is king when it comes to starting, growing, and sustaining a business. Having cash on hand enables you to pay your bills when they come due so you can maintain a good credit rating. This allows you to have access to capital in the future.

In today's economy, money is tight. This means lenders are using more stringent standards for making loans; only business owners and companies with the best credit have access to most commercial loans. The good news, however, is that if you can get a loan, the rate you pay is relatively low. As the Federal Reserve has repeatedly cut interest rates used by banks to borrow money over the past two years or so, this has brought down the cost of borrowing money for business owners as well.

### Bank Loans

Mark Twain said, "A banker is a fellow who lends you his umbrella when the sun is shining, but wants it back the minute it begins to rain." Well, the storm is here—do you have access to money? It may not be too late to act so that you'll have the funds waiting for you if you need them.

If your credit is good, apply for a line of credit through a bank or a business credit card. A line of credit gives you access to the money you need; you pay interest on only the amount you use. For example, if you obtain a $20,000 line of credit and use $5,000, you'll pay interest on $5,000. When you repay the part you borrowed, your line returns to the full limit. Typically, a line of credit lasts for just a few years, after which time you must renew the line to keep it in operation. As long as you have a good repayment history, renewing the line probably won't be a problem.

You may want a fixed loan for certain purposes, such as to buy a building or equipment. You can learn about various financing options through the Small Business Administration (SBA at www.sba.gov/services/financialassistance/index.html).

Today, many of the major lenders may no longer be viable lending sources. They have tightened their lending rules to very strict limits. However, smaller, local banks still have money to lend (that's what they're in business to do) and may have less stringent lending standards.

> ### What to Do Now
>
> Improve your chances of qualifying for a loan by developing relationships with local lending officers. Find out who the decision makers are (the teller behind the window usually can't help you get a loan).
>
> Determine from them what they require from you in order to borrow money. For instance, depending on the amount you want to borrow, you may need to create a formal business plan or you may only need to provide various financial statements, including a profit and loss statement, balance sheet, and tax returns for the past several years.

## Credit Unions

Many people think of credit unions as rinky-dink banks that offer savings and checking accounts just to those who work for companies that participate in the credit unions. Today, credit unions are allowed to offer commercial financing, and many do.

For example, America First Credit Union (www.americafirst.com/business_services/business_lending/) offers lines of credit, equipment loans, commercial real estate loans, and loans to buy a business or a franchise. Pentagon Federal Credit Union (www.penfed.org/productsandrates/loans/smallbusinessloans/overview.asp) has partnered with the National Cooperative Bank to be able to offer SBA loans.

## Angel Investors

Angel investors are private individuals or groups that function like venture capitalists but do much smaller deals. For instance, the average size of an investment per round by a group of angels in 2007 was about $265,000. The Angel Capital Association (ACA), in its *Angel Group Confidence Report* in February 2008, said it remained optimistic about investment in 2008 despite the state of the economy. The group said it expected to see an increase in the number and amounts of investments.

What does it take to win the interest of angels?

- *Being in a hot sector.* Current favorites include: software, information technology (IT) services, energy, medical devices and equipment, and business products and services.

- *Having a great business plan.* Angels are bombarded with requests for capital (over half receive between 11 to 30 investment opportunities annually) and make their initial decision on whether a business's concept, as explained in the plan, grabs them.

### Peer-to-Peer Lending

This relatively new option, also called people-to-people lending, for obtaining capital has been facilitated by the Internet. Join an online site, create a listing for your loan request (you must share information about your income and allow potential lenders to view your credit report), and then potential lenders bid to lend you money (as they bid, the interest rate declines). The proceeds—loans typically range from $8,000 to $20,000—are deposited into your bank account and monthly payments are debited to your account. Some resources are:

- Prosper.com (www.prosper.com) allows you to obtain a personal loan (you can then use the proceeds for your business).
- Zopa (https://us.zopa.com) is a worldwide social finance company (people-to-people lending) that gives loans up to $25,000 at about half the interest rate charged by major lenders. Zopa has partnered with half a dozen credit unions, including Forum Credit Union and Provident Credit Union, to make these loans available to members.

### Nonprofits

There are numerous regional nonprofit organizations—economic development groups—willing to lend money to businesses that create jobs in an area. If you can meet certain mandatory job creation benchmarks (e.g., 25 new positions over three years), you can gain access to this funding source.

### Factors

If you sell products on credit, you can turn your receivables into cash. Sell your receivables to a factor; the factor pays a discount off the face of the receivable (the amount of the discount depends on the creditworthiness of the debtor and other factors). Cash received from the factor can be used to purchase more inventory to boost sales. To find a reputable factor, check these organizations:

- Factors Chain International (FCI at www.factors-chain.com)—a global network of leading factoring companies.
- International Factors Group (IFG at www.ifgroup.com/ifg-presentation .asp)—a global factoring association.

### Other Financing Sources

If you have exhausted the traditional sources of capital explained here, don't give up; you can find the money you need. Consider a tried and true method: borrowing from family or friends. Another option is using merchant cash advances. This form of financing is based on your sales via credit cards and not on your credit rating or collateral. The interest rate on this type of borrowing is very steep, so caution is advised. Some options:

- AdvanceMe (www.advanceme.com).
- Merchant Cash Advance (MCA) (www.merchantcashadvance.com).
- Rapid Advance (www.rapidadvance.com).

## Better Collection Efforts

Cash flow, which is essentially the cycle of money coming into your business through sales and money going out to pay expenses, is vital to all businesses. Without adequate cash flow, you can get into serious financial trouble and may even lose your business. The National Federation of Independent Business recently reported that 30 percent of the 65.7 percent of businesses with cash flow concerns say that difficulty collecting money owed is the main reason. What can you do to keep from finding yourself in the uncomfortable position of being a bill collector or, even worse, failing to get paid the money that's owed to you?

### Limit Credit to Customers

Most businesses do not have to let customers buy on credit. They can accept payment through credit and debit cards, essentially letting customers obtain their own financing. Of course, in some businesses, it's industry practice to complete work before getting paid or to extend credit to customers. If you have been waiting for payment, consider a change in your credit policy.

---

### What to Do Now

You can modify your credit policy:

- *Require some or all payment up front.* If you provide services, be sure that you are paid as the work is completed so you're not waiting for a lump sum after you've done all the work. This will help your cash flow and avoid the possibility of being stiffed for the entire amount.

- *End sales on credit.* Require customers to arrange their own credit, by charging purchases to a credit card or arranging their own bank loans.

- *Restrict credit to only good customers.* Check the credit ratings of customers to whom you want to give credit. (Obtain permission from customers to do this.) Then, for consumer customers, contact one of the three main credit-reporting companies: Equifax (www.equifax.com), Experian (www.experian.com), or TransUnion (www.transunion.com). For business customers, check with Dun & Bradstreet (www.dnb.com) or another business credit–reporting company.

---

### *Improve Collection Practices*

If you do sell on credit, because it is industry practice or just because you believe the customer will pay you, make sure that you take steps to help collections. You don't want to become a banker for your customers or be short of cash when you need it.

---

## What to Do Now

Be proactive:

- *Bill promptly.* Don't wait until the end of the month to send out bills for work completed or goods sold during the month.

- *Stay on top of receivables.* Make sure you know what is owed to you at all times. You can use online solutions, such as Bill.com (www.bill.com) and MyBizHomepage (www.mybizhomepage.com) to easily monitor your receivables.

- *Use follow-up policies.* Reinvoice as soon as the payment date has passed without receiving payment. For example, if your invoice required payment within 14 days of the invoice date, resend the invoice on the 15th day. Generate a personal call if reinvoicing fails to produce immediate results. Offer to work out payment terms (e.g., part now and the rest next month).

- *Turn to professionals.* Once an account receivable has aged, you may be helpless to collect anything yourself. Use a collection agency or an attorney for this purpose. Using a professional means you'll never receive all that is due you (part will go to pay the professional, even if the full amount of the invoice is collected). But half a loaf (or whatever share is yours) is better than none.

- *Contact the attorney general in the customer's state.* When a deadbeat customer is a business and this business is out of state (making it too costly to pursue action in small claims court), consider filing a complaint with the attorney general in the customer's state. Often, the attorney general's office will prod firms to pay up.

---

## Reducing Overhead

In tough economic times, sales may lag. If you can't boost sales to maintain profit margins, take the complementary approach and reduce overhead. This may be easier said than done in today's economy, with inflation adding to prices on just about everything.

### Cut Discretionary Spending

There are many fixed costs that you can't do anything about. But most businesses have some items that vary from month to month, and these expenditures can be scaled back in this economy.

---

**What to Do Now**

Cut back or eliminate spending on such costs as business travel and entertaining. If you must do these activities, opt for low-cost alternatives (e.g., economy air travel instead of business class; less costly restaurants).

Also look at subscriptions and memberships when they come up for renewal. Do not renew anything that is not essential to your business at this time.

Minimize employee raises and bonuses. But, to avoid hard feelings, explain the company's fiscal situation. In today's economy, job security is paramount, so a smaller-than-expected raise probably won't drive an employee away.

---

### Conserve on Fuel

Employ conservation measures to save on fuel. A little savings here and a savings there can add up to big savings for the year. Even more, you not only save money, but you're also helping the environment.

---

**What to Do Now**

In the winter, keep thermostats a little lower; in the summer, follow the reverse strategy.

Change to energy-saving lightbulbs to reduce electricity usage.

Restrict business driving where possible to cut gas costs. For instance, instead of meeting face to face, try teleconferencing or videoconferencing where appropriate. The cost for these alternatives may be little or nothing, saving you both gas costs and travel time.

---

## Adjusting Prices

After paring down your overhead, you may still be challenged to stay in the black. Another way to maintain profitability and avoid losses is to raise your prices. You can do this across the board, by upping prices to reflect your higher costs. For instance, some bakeries have posted higher prices because of the hike in the price of flour (about four times higher than nine months previously). You might consider adding a surcharge, which is a temporary price increase to account for your higher fuel costs or other increased expenses. For instance, some delivery companies are adding a fuel surcharge to reflect just the higher cost of gasoline.

---

**What to Do Now**

Fire your unprofitable customers—those that take up a great deal of your time or create a lot of headaches but don't help your margins. Your revenue may dip, but your margins will rise, and you'll have more time to devote to more profitable customers and to finding new ones.

---

## Using Down Time Productively

If customers aren't banging down your door, use the slow time to help your business.

### Strategic Planning

Use the time you have now to review your business model and your marketing plan. Think about where you want your business to be a year from now and five years from now—and what it will take to get you to your goal.

### Marketing

Slow times may mean more time for you to network with other business owners. This will help you build relationships now that can translate into more business in the future.

If your current customer base isn't bringing in satisfactory revenue, expand your horizons. For example, if you have a bricks-and-mortar store, consider adding an online presence to capture customers nationwide and market to them.

Diversification is key. You may need to expand your lines to attract a wider audience for your business. If sales are slow, you'll have more time to devote to new guerrilla marketing efforts.

## Net Operating Losses

If your losses from business, deductions from your work as an employee, and any casualty and theft losses exceed your business income, you may have a net operating loss (NOL). While losses aren't a good thing and represent actual economic outlays on your part, there is an upside. You can use an NOL as an offset to income in certain prior years. This reduces the taxes owed for those years, giving you an immediate tax refund. The tax refund is cash that you can use to keep your business going in these tough times.

Net operating losses can be claimed by individuals or regular (C) corporations. If your business is set up as a multimember limited liability company (LLC), partnership, or S corporation, the owners claim NOLs on their personal tax returns. Losses from the business pass through to owners; NOLs are created by the owner's share of the business's operating losses.

## Figuring NOLs

The fact that you show a business loss on your tax return doesn't automatically mean you have a net operating loss. First see if you have a potential NOL by determining whether you show a negative figure:

- *Individuals.* Your adjusted gross income, reduced by itemized deductions or the standard deduction (but before personal exemptions) is less than zero.
- *C corporations.* Taxable income is less than zero.

Once you see there's a potential NOL, then you have to make certain adjustments to arrive at a tax-deductible NOL.

### INDIVIDUALS

Adjust your taxable income by adding back certain items. Add back:

- Personal exemptions.
- Net capital losses.
- Nonbusiness losses.
- Nonbusiness deductions (e.g., deductions for IRA contributions, alimony payments, itemized deductions).

**CAUTION**

If a corporation's ownership changes hands, special limits apply to prevent one corporation from effectively buying tax losses from another. These rules are highly complex and require the assistance of a tax professional.

You do not have to add back moving expenses, loss on rental property, loss on the sale of accounts receivable if you are on the accrual method of accounting, or loss on the sale or exchange of stock in a small business company or small business investment company if the loss is treated as an ordinary loss (see Chapter 4 for an explanation of Section 1244 stock).

The computation is made on Schedule A of Form 1045 (see Figure 9.1).

### C CORPORATIONS

These entities figure their NOLs by first reducing gross income by deductions. Then the tentative NOL is adjusted by a full dividends-received deduction. Instead of applying the 70 percent or 80 percent limit, a full deduction is used.

Form 1045 (2008)                                                                                           Page **2**

**Schedule A—NOL** (see page 6 of the instructions)

| | | |
|---|---|---|
| 1 | Enter the amount from your 2008 Form 1040, line 41, or Form 1040NR, line 38. Estates and trusts, enter taxable income increased by the total of the charitable deduction, income distribution deduction, and exemption amount | **1** |
| 2 | Nonbusiness capital losses before limitation. Enter as a positive number | **2** |
| 3 | Nonbusiness capital gains (without regard to any section 1202 exclusion) | **3** |
| 4 | If line 2 is more than line 3, enter the difference; otherwise, enter -0- | **4** |
| 5 | If line 3 is more than line 2, enter the difference; otherwise, enter -0- | **5** |
| 6 | Nonbusiness deductions (see page 6 of the instructions) | **6** |
| 7 | Nonbusiness income other than capital gains (see page 6 of the instructions) | **7** |
| 8 | Add lines 5 and 7 | **8** |
| 9 | If line 6 is more than line 8, enter the difference; otherwise, enter -0- | **9** |
| 10 | If line 8 is more than line 6, enter the difference; otherwise, enter -0-. **But do not enter more than line 5** | **10** |
| 11 | Business capital losses before limitation. Enter as a positive number | **11** |
| 12 | Business capital gains (without regard to any section 1202 exclusion) | **12** |
| 13 | Add lines 10 and 12 | **13** |
| 14 | Subtract line 13 from line 11. If zero or less, enter -0- | **14** |
| 15 | Add lines 4 and 14 | **15** |
| 16 | Enter the loss, if any, from line 16 of Schedule D (Form 1040). (Estates and trusts, enter the loss, if any, from line 15, column (3), of Schedule D (Form 1041).) Enter as a positive number. If you do not have a loss on that line (and do not have a section 1202 exclusion), skip lines 16 through 21 and enter on line 22 the amount from line 15 | **16** |
| 17 | Section 1202 exclusion. Enter as a positive number | **17** |
| 18 | Subtract line 17 from line 16. If zero or less, enter -0- | **18** |
| 19 | Enter the loss, if any, from line 21 of Schedule D (Form 1040). (Estates and trusts, enter the loss, if any, from line 16 of Schedule D (Form 1041).) Enter as a positive number | **19** |
| 20 | If line 18 is more than line 19, enter the difference; otherwise, enter -0- | **20** |
| 21 | If line 19 is more than line 18, enter the difference; otherwise, enter -0- | **21** |
| 22 | Subtract line 20 from line 15. If zero or less, enter -0- | **22** |
| 23 | Domestic production activities deduction from Form 1040, line 35, or Form 1040NR, line 33 (or included on Form 1041, line 15a) | **23** |
| 24 | NOL deduction for losses from other years. Enter as a positive number | **24** |
| 25 | **NOL.** Combine lines 1, 9, 17, and 21 through 24. If the result is less than zero, enter it here and on page 1, line 1a. If the result is zero or more, you **do not** have an NOL | **25** |

Form **1045** (2008)

**FIGURE 9.1** Form 1045 (Schedule A), Figuring NOLs for Individuals

Net operating losses from other years are ignored for purposes of figuring the current year's NOL.

Losses that are subject to the passive activity rules are not taken into account in figuring the NOL.

### *Carrybacks and Carryovers*

You have flexibility when it comes to using your net operating losses. You can carry an NOL back for a set number of years, explained next, or opt to carry it forward for up to 20 years.

The carryback period generally is two years. However, there are certain special carryback periods that may apply to you:

- Three years for small businesses (those with average annual gross receipts of $5 million or less during a three-year period) for NOLs arising from a government-declared disaster.

- Five years for farmers and ranchers, and for businesses affected by Hurricanes Katrina, Rita, and Wilma, the tornado in Greensburg, Kansas, 2008 Midwest floods, and Hurricane Ike.
- Ten years for NOLs arising from product liability.

If you carry back the NOL, you must carry it back to the earliest year first. For instance, if you have a regular NOL in 2008 (subject to a two-year carryback), you must carry it back to 2006. If it isn't used up in that year, you then carry the remainder to 2007. If the NOL is not fully depleted in these two years, you can then carry it forward to 2009 and succeeding years until you use it up (but for no more than 20 years).

If your marital status in the carryback or carryover years differs from your status in the NOL year, only the spouse who has the NOL can claim it. If you file a joint return, the NOL deduction is limited to the income of the spouse who had the NOL. Special rules apply for carrybacks to a year involving a different marital status than the status in the year the NOL arises.

If you want to forgo the NOL carryback (e.g., because you were in a low tax bracket then but expect to be in a higher bracket in the future or because you don't want to call attention to an earlier return), you can elect to waive the NOL carryback. Make the election by attaching your own statement to your tax return for the year in which the NOL arises (C corporations merely check a special box on their tax returns to waive the NOL carryback). The waiver applies for both regular tax and alternative minimum tax (AMT) purposes.

---

### What to Do Now

Keep track of your carrybacks and carryforwards, especially when you have NOLs arising in different years. This will enable you to apply them in the correct order.

---

## How to Claim an NOL

There are two ways to claim an NOL carryback.

1. File Form 1045, Application for a Tentative Refund, to obtain the refund quickly. The IRS generally acts on the refund request within 90 days of the filing of the form. When you carry back the NOL, you have to refigure certain deductions, credits, and other items in the carryback years. These are items figured with respect to your adjusted gross income (AGI). For example, the NOL will lower your AGI, which may increase your itemized deduction for medical expenses, miscellaneous itemized deductions, and

personal casualty or theft losses. You also have to refigure the alternative minimum tax if applicable to you.

2. File an amended tax return for the carryback year. The carryback does *not* affect self-employment tax for the carryback years.

---

### Note

C corporations can expedite their NOL carryback refund by filing Form 1139, Corporation Application for Tentative Refund. Or, if they expect to have an NOL in the current year, they can extend the time for paying taxes for the immediately preceding year by filing Form 1138, Extension of Time for the Payment of Taxes by a Corporation Expecting a Net Operating Loss Carryback. This form is filed after the start of the year in which the NOL is expected, but before the tax for the preceding year is required to be paid (i.e., before March 15 for calendar-year corporations).

---

## Tax Limitations on Business Losses

Just because your business has suffered financial losses doesn't mean you can write them all off. Certain rules in the tax law apply to business losses to limit deductions for the losses.

### Basis

If you are an owner of partnership, limited liability company (LLC), or S corporation (a pass-through entity), business losses claimed on your personal return cannot exceed your tax basis in the company. Losses in excess of basis can be carried forward and used in future years to the extent of basis at that time. There is no time limit on these carryforwards.

#### PARTNERSHIPS AND LLCs

Basis is determined, in part, by the way in which an owner acquires his or her interest in the company. If the interest is acquired by contributing directly to the entity (typically in the start-up of the company), basis is the cash and an owner's basis of the property contributed to the company. If the interest is purchased from a previous owner, basis is the cash and the value of the property paid. If the interest is acquired by performing services for the company, basis is the amount of compensation reported. However, an interest only in the profits of the company, and not a capital interest, is not taxable under certain conditions and, thus, does not give rise to any basis. If the interest is inherited from a deceased owner, basis is the value of the interest for estate tax purposes (generally its value on the date of death).

Once you know your starting basis, adjust it annually—up or down—by the following items. Increase basis by:

- The owner's distributive share of the company's income.
- The owner's share of tax-exempt income, such as life insurance proceeds.
- Excess of depletion deductions over the basis of depletable property.
- Additional capital contributions.
- Share of new partnership liabilities (limited partners in limited partnerships do not increase their basis by a share of liabilities assumed by the general partners).

Decrease basis by:

- The owner's distributive share of company losses (including capital losses).
- The owner's share of expenses that are not deductible in figuring the company's income.
- Distributions to the owner by the company.
- The owner's share in any decrease in partnership liabilities.

## S CORPORATIONS

Basis for purposes of deducting pass-through losses means your basis in your S corporation stock (essentially what you contributed to the corporation to acquire your shares), plus any money you lent to the corporation. If you acquired the shares by inheritance, the basis generally is the shares' value on the date of death, reduced by the portion of the value attributable to income in respect of a decedent (earnings accrued before death but paid out after death).

Guaranteeing a third party's loan to the corporation does not, in and of itself, increase your basis. Only when the corporation defaults and you are required to make good on your guarantee can you add the payments to your basis. You cannot increase your basis by your share of corporate liabilities.

Once you know your starting basis, adjust it annually—up or down—by the following items. Increase basis by:

- The owner's share of the corporation's ordinary income.
- The owner's share of separately stated items reported on Schedule K-1 (other than tax-exempt income).
- Excess of depletion deductions over the basis of depletable property.
- Additional capital contributions.

Decrease basis by:

- The owner's share of the corporation's losses.
- The owner's share of expenses that are not deductible in figuring the company's income.
- Noncapital and nondeductible corporate expenses reported on Schedule K-1, such as 50 percent of meals and entertainment costs and nondeductible penalties.
- Distributions not includible in the shareholder's income, such as dividends in excess of basis.

## Hobby Losses

If your business has losses this year, that may not be a unique situation and the losses are probably deductible according to the rules discussed in this chapter. But if you suffer losses year after year, you may not be permitted to deduct losses in excess of business income unless you can show that you have undertaken the business in order to make a profit. This limitation on losses is called the *hobby loss rule.* It is designed to prevent people who collect coins and stamps, breed dogs and cats for fun, or engage in other hobby activities from deducting what the law views as personal expenses. Any activity done mainly for recreation, sport, or other personal enjoyment is suspect, but the hobby loss rule can apply to *any* activity.

### IMPACT OF HOBBY CLASSIFICATION

If you can't prove that you have a profit motive, then any year in which you make money must be fully reported, but any year you have losses (expenses in excess of revenue), you cannot deduct them. These losses are lost forever (you can't carry them forward).

### PROVING PROFIT MOTIVE

There is no bright line that you can rely on to show you have a profit motive; it's a matter of the facts and circumstances of your situation. Some factors that help demonstrate a profit motive:

- You carry on the activity in a businesslike manner (e.g., you keep good books and records, have a separate business bank account, and have a written business plan).
- You spend considerable time and effort on the activity.
- You depend on the activity for income.
- You change your methods of operation from those that don't work to those that do.
- You have been profitable in some years.

- You turn to advisers to help make you profitable.
- You expect to make a profit from the appreciation of assets in the business.

### PRESUMPTION OF PROFIT MOTIVE

You can delay an IRS examination of your business if you choose to rely on a presumption: If you are profitable in three out of five years (two out of seven years for horse-related activities) from the time you start up, you're presumed to be engaged in the activity for profit. (You use the presumption by filing Form 5213, Election to Postpone Determination as to Whether the Presumption Applies That an Activity Is Engaged in for Profit, within three years of the due date of the return for the year in which you first carry on the activity.) But opting to use this presumption virtually guarantees that the IRS will look closely at your business, so most tax experts don't advise using the presumption.

## Passive Activity Losses

Owners of rental real estate may be hit hard in this economy; units may be vacant for some time while the cost of operations keeps rising. So too are many other investors in businesses that have been floundering under tight credit and escalating prices. These owners need to pay special attention to the passive activity loss (PAL) rules to see how the rules apply to them and whether and to what extent they can take losses to ease their financial burden.

If you work full-time in the day-to-day activities of your business, then the PAL rules probably don't apply to you. But if you do not materially participate in a business activity you own, or that activity is rental real estate (regardless of material participation, explained later), the PAL rules may limit the amount of losses you can deduct each year.

Material participation means you satisfy one of seven tests in the tax law. The basic test requires a minimum of 500 hours of participation during the year (which works out to a mere 10 hours a week for 50 weeks). Material participation can be met with as few as 100 hours during the year if no other owner in the activity participates more.

### IMPACT OF THE PAL RULES

Losses (deductions in excess of income) from passive activities (business you don't materially participate in and rental real estate activities) cannot be deducted in excess of passive activity income for the year. Excess passive losses can be carried forward and used in future years to the extent of passive activity income in those years (called suspended losses).

You can claim all suspended losses in the year you dispose of your entire interest in the activity. A disposition means a sale to an unrelated party, abandonment of the business, or a business becoming completely worthless.

---

**Example**

You are a silent partner in a restaurant that is struggling. Your share of the loss for this year is $10,000 (assume you have no other passive activities). You can't deduct the loss this year, because you do not have any passive activity income to offset it. You can carry the loss forward, though. Say the business goes under next year. You can deduct the $10,000, plus any loss for next year, on next year's return.

---

Similar rules apply to tax credits related to passive activities. For instance, an owner of a certified historic building may be eligible for a credit for rehabilitation of the structure, but the credit would be limited by the PAL rules.

Passive activity losses are figured on Form 8582, Passive Activity Loss Limitations; passive activity credits are figured on Form 8582-CR, Passive Activity Credit Limitations. Closely held C corporations are subject to special PAL rules, and they figure their losses on Form 8810, Corporate Passive Activity Loss and Credit Limitations.

### EXCEPTIONS TO THE PAL RULES

You can deduct losses beyond the PAL limits in two key situations:

1. If you own rental real estate and you actively participate in the activity (e.g., you set rents, screen tenants, and review expenses), you can deduct excess losses up to $25,000 each year if your adjusted gross income (AGI) does not exceed $100,000. The $25,000 limit is reduced as AGI rises to $150,000; no excess loss is allowed once AGI tops $150,000. These dollar amounts are halved for married persons filing separate returns.

---

**Example**

You own a multifamily rental property. Rental income for the year is $40,000; rental expenses for the year (including depreciation on the building) are $70,000. Even though you use a management agent to collect the rents, you actively participate in the activity by setting the rents and screening tenants. Your adjusted gross income for the year is $95,000. Of your $30,000 loss ($70,000 − $40,000), you can deduct $25,000 this year; the $5,000 excess loss is a suspended loss that is carried forward.

---

2. You are a real estate professional who can deduct all of your losses. To qualify as a real estate professional, you must work in construction, conversion, management, brokerage activities, or rental real estate, and you must devote a certain amount of time (fixed by law) to the real estate activities.

### At-Risk Rules

In the heady days of tax shelters, it was not uncommon for someone to invest in a business by contributing only a small sum of cash and a large note on which there was no personal liability (but which was used to create basis against which to claim losses). These investments threw off losses that investors took to offset their income from other sources. The risk to the investor was small; if the business failed, only the small cash investment was lost. Congress closed this loophole by creating the at-risk rules.

The at-risk rules prevent you from deducting losses in excess of amounts that you have at stake in a venture. At-risk amounts include cash contributions, the basis of property you contribute, and notes for which you are personally liable (your economic stake in the venture).

#### IMPACT OF THE AT-RISK RULES

If you are subject to the at-risk rules, losses in excess of your at-risk basis (cash, the basis of property you contributed, and notes for which you are personally liable) cannot be deducted currently. They can be carried forward and used in a future year if your at-risk basis increases. There is no cap on the carryforward period.

When the activity is sold, gain is treated as income from the activity, so you can then offset the gain by the amount of your carried-forward losses.

The at-risk rules are figured on Form 6198, At-Risk Limitations. The at-risk rules are applied before the PAL rules are applied.

#### REAL ESTATE FINANCING

Nonrecourse financing from commercial lenders or government agencies is treated as being at risk if the loan is secured by the real estate and the property is owned by a partnership, limited liability company, or S corporation in which you have an interest.

## Special Breaks for Farmers

Farmers, like other business owners, have ups and downs. However, farmers face unique situations; they are at the mercy of weather and other conditions that can create boom or bust. The tax law recognizes their unique plight and provides a number of special tax breaks to help make tax reporting a little kinder to this important sector of the nation's economy.

There are many special tax rules for farmers. These can be found in IRS Publication 225, Farmer's Tax Guide, at www.irs.gov. The following are some key provisions.

### Sales of Livestock Caused by Drought, Flood, or Other Weather Conditions

While these sales generally are reported in the current year, you can opt to report them in the follow year (i.e., postpone reporting the sale by one year). To use this option, you have to show that you would not have sold them this year but for the weather conditions and you are eligible for federal assistance because of weather conditions. You must file a separate election with your tax return for the year of the weather conditions for each class of animals (e.g., sheep, cattle).

There is another option: You can continue deferral of reporting the sale indefinitely if proceeds are reinvested in similar livestock until the end of the first year ending after the first drought-free year (assuming the drought-free year ends in or after the last year of a four-year replacement period).

### Income Averaging

Farmers' income usually fluctuates from year to year. During this poor economy, many farmers are experiencing record revenues because of high commodity prices. The tax law recognizes these income fluctuations and provides a method of relief, called income averaging. You can choose to figure the tax on your farming income (called elected farm income) by averaging it over the past three years. If you make this election, it will lower the tax on this year's income if income was substantially lower in the three prior years.

However, averaging does not always save taxes; figure your taxes with and without it to determine whether to make the election.

The income averaging option also applies to commercial fishermen.

### Limit on Farm Losses

Some farm owners use losses from farming activities to offset income they earn from other sources. The Heartland, Habitat, Harvest, and Horticulture Act of 2008 closes what Congress has viewed as a loophole. For tax years beginning after December 31, 2009, there is a new anti-tax-shelter rule that limits the amount of farming losses that can be used to offset nonfarming business income. The limit on losses reported on Schedule F is the greater of $300,000 ($150,000 for a married person filing separately) or the net farm income received over the past five years. The loss limit for partnerships and S corporations is applied at the owner level (the loss limit doesn't apply to C corporations).

This loss limit applies to farmers receiving certain subsidies (direct or countercyclical payments under Title I of the Food, Conservation, and Energy Act of 2008, or Commodity Credit Corporation loans).

The unused losses can be carried forward and used in subsequent years.

## Aborted Business Ventures

What if you started to investigate the purchase of a business but, because of the poor economy or other reasons, didn't follow through? You may have paid for professional fees and other costs even though the business never got off the ground.

Fortunately, the tax law lets you deduct these costs if you can show that you went beyond a general search and actually focused on a particular business. The costs related to initial investigation are not deductible.

### Example

You travel to look at various business opportunities. You select one business and have your lawyer start to draw up contracts for its purchase. You can't get financing and the deal falls through. You can't deduct your initial travel costs during your investigatory phase; you can deduct the legal fees related to the aborted business venture, because you had focused on a specific business.

## Winding Up a Business

If you want out and can't sell your business, you can wind up your affairs and shut your doors. You can deduct certain expenses related to winding up a business:

- *Unamortized costs.* If, for example, you formed the company in 2003 and had been amortizing your start-up costs, you can now deduct any remaining start-up costs on the final return for the business.

- *Other expenses.* You may incur additional legal and accounting fees to close up your business. You may owe state filing fees to terminate the business. These costs are deductible on the final return for the business.

## Bankruptcy

A business may be so strapped that its creditors force it to go under or the business has to ask a court for help to stay afloat. This is collectively called the process of bankruptcy, and it is a drastic and serious step. There are a number of variations on how to proceed. You choices depend on how your business is organized (entity type) and whether you want to stay in business if possible.

- *Sole proprietors.* Owners are treated like other individuals. They can get a fresh start under Chapter 7 of the bankruptcy law, but most are forced to use a payment plan under Chapter 13 (personal bankruptcy is discussed in Chapter 7).

- *Family farmers.* Farmers can use a simplified reorganization plan under Chapter 12 of the bankruptcy law if debts fall within a certain limit.
- *Other business entities.* The entities can be liquidated with proceeds distributed to creditors under Chapter 7, or can be reorganized under court supervision to continue operations under Chapter 11. *Caution:* General partners can be sued by the trustee in bankruptcy if partnership assets fall short of partnership debts.

### Types of Bankruptcy

Which type of bankruptcy solution is best for a business? It depends on the facts and circumstances. Sole proprietors may have no choice but to use the repayment plan, whether or not they continue the business operations.

Other entities may prefer to liquidate if they see the business as a failure (they have no heart for continuing the business); if the market is such that even if economic conditions recover, the business wouldn't be viable; or if the debts are so overwhelming that restructuring doesn't make economic sense.

### Bankruptcy Alternatives

If you want to continue your business, you can work with a credit professional to help restructure the company's debts. This lets you work your way out of debt in a manageable manner and avoid bankruptcy. For example, Corporate Turnaround (www.corporateturnaround.com) negotiates on your behalf with vendors, lessors, credit card companies, and other business creditors to set up a repayment plan that you can handle.

When seeking a company to help restructure your debt, look for members of the Turnaround Management Association (www.turnaround.org/Membership/Browse.aspx), an international nonprofit association dedicated to corporate renewal and turnaround management. Members sign a code of ethics to provide professional, competent assistance.

# CHAPTER 10

# Serious Medical Issues

**S**erious medical issues arising from disease, injuries, congenital conditions, or chronic conditions can be devastating in so many ways. Besides the personal concerns about pain, mortality, relationships, and the ability to have a good quality of life, there are many financial issues as well. There is the cost of paying for the illness or condition itself, which can be staggeringly high. And there is the cost of living with long-term conditions or disabilities, which can also be very costly for the individual and his or her family.

There are a number of government programs designed to provide financial safety nets for individuals affected by serious medical issues and their families. These programs provide payments to help with medical and other living expenses. They usually aren't sufficient to pay the full costs of treatment and family expenses.

The tax law provides some relief, too, by providing some tax breaks related to medical costs and disability payments. In this chapter, you'll learn about:

- Deducting medical costs
- Living with disability
- Paying for the cost of disability
- Disability insurance
- Workers' compensation

- Social Security disability benefits
- Other government disability programs
- Medicaid
- Retirement plan distributions

## Deducting Medical Costs

You don't have to be reminded about the high cost of medical care, including ever-rising premiums for insurance. And even if you have insurance, it usually doesn't cover everything. For instance, even if you have a medical policy, you still owe co-payments for doctor's visits, medication, and other covered expenses. Also, medical insurance may not cover the cost of experimental treatments that you undertake in the hope that they will be medically helpful.

If you, your spouse, or a dependent has medical costs that are not covered by your insurance, or if you have no insurance, you can deduct the payments on your tax return. A deduction for medical expenses is limited to amounts that, in total, exceed 7.5 percent of your adjusted gross income (AGI). The deduction is allowed only if you choose to itemize your personal deductions rather than take the standard deduction.

### Example

Your family's medical expenses for the year that were not covered by insurance total $8,800. Your adjusted gross income is $76,000. You can deduct $3,100 ($8,800 − 7.5 percent of $76,000). If your AGI had been $117,400 or more, no medical deduction would have been allowed.

### *Deductible Medical Costs*

If insurance, your employer, or someone else doesn't pick up the tab, you can write off a wide array of unreimbursed medical expenses. These include:

- Fees for professional services. You can also deduct the cost of an attendant's services for in-home care (even though the attendant is not a licensed health care professional) if medical services are provided. Medical services include bathing, dressing, and giving medication.
- Hospital services.
- Medical equipment and supplies.
- Medical treatments.
- Medicines and drugs.
- Premiums for medical insurance policies (including Medicare Part B and Part D).

- Schooling for physically or mentally disabled individuals (e.g., learning Braille, training for dyslexia). The cost of meals and lodging is counted as a deductible medical expense if boarding at the school is required.

Although cosmetic surgery usually isn't deductible, the cost becomes deductible if it is done to improve a disfigurement related to a congenital abnormality, disfiguring disease, or accidental injury.

In addition to medical expenses for you, your spouse, and dependents, you can also add in any medical costs you pay for your children or other relatives you support but can't claim as dependents because their gross income exceeds the annual limit ($3,500 in 2008). For instance, if you're contributing more than half of your mother's support by paying her medical costs but you can't take a dependency exemption for her because her gross income is over the annual limit, you can still count your medical payments for her as part of your deductible medical costs.

---

### What to Do Now

If you're contributing to your parent's support, make sure your payments go toward the parent's medical expenses, rather than to other living expenses. For instance, say your mother needs $10,000 a year from you, but she also has income of $8,000. Arrange to pay your mother's out-of-pocket medical costs rather than letting her use her money for this purpose, so you can deduct that much of your support payment as part of your medical deduction.

---

### Personal Injury Settlements

If you receive a lump-sum payment for a personal injury action (e.g., you were injured in a car accident), the payment to you is tax free. Only punitive damages are taxable to you.

You don't have to reduce your medical expense deduction by the lump-sum settlement, even if you use part of the money to pay your medical bills. However, if the settlement specifically earmarks some of the payment for medical costs, then you must reduce your medical deduction accordingly.

If the settlement earmarks some of the payment for future medical costs, then you'll have to reduce those future medical payments by the allocated settlement payments in figuring your medical costs. Once you've used up the settlement on medical costs related to the injury for which the settlement was made, then all future medical costs are fully deductible.

### Tapping Individual Retirement Accounts

If you lack the funds to pay your medical bills, the tax law lets you use your individual retirement account (IRA) funds for this purpose without penalty, even if you're younger than age $59^1/2$. To use this penalty exception, your medical costs must exceed 7.5 percent of your adjusted gross income, whether or not you itemize your deductions.

However, you'll still owe regular income tax on the IRA withdrawals, even though you use the money to pay your medical bills. Thus, using IRA money to pay these bills should only be a last resort after exhausting your other options.

## Living with Disability

Over 51 million Americans are classified as being disabled. Living with a disability can be very challenging for the disabled person and his or her family. The family often bears some or all of the cost of care, which can be very expensive.

Disability may be permanent and irreversible, such as the loss of a limb or blindness. Disability may be temporary or reversible, such as being out of commission due to substance abuse. Either way, the cost of medical treatment and care can be a deductible medical expense. The deduction for medical-related costs is covered earlier in this chapter.

### Modifying Homes

If you, or someone in your family, have a condition or disability, you may need to make structural changes or additions to your home. Doing this may entitle you to a tax deduction.

- *Costs of improvements to cope with a disability.* The full cost is a deductible medical expense. *Examples:* Railings, ramps, support bars, relocating outlets and fixtures, widening doorways and halls for wheelchair access. Stair and wheelchair lifts, but not elevators, also fall within this category.

- *Costs of improvements for other conditions.* Only the portion of the cost that does not increase the value of the home is a deductible medical expense.

## Example

You install an air-cleaning system to make it easier for your asthmatic child to breathe. The system does not add anything to the value of your home, so its cost is fully deductible. But if you install a swimming pool to help your child recover from a combat-related injury, and the swimming pool, which costs $20,000, adds $15,000 to the value of your home, only $5,000 (the excess cost that does not add to the home's value) is a deductible medical expense.

### Living in Special Facilities

Unfortunately, because of a disability, living at home may not be the best arrangement for the disabled individual; special facilities may offer needed round-the-clock supervision and support. The special facilities may be called a nursing home, a continuing care facility, a group home, or something else.

The cost of the special facilities, including lodging, meals, and medical attention, is a deductible medical expense if you can show that the placement is due to a disability or condition and a doctor advised the placement. (You can't take a deduction if government programs pay for the cost of your disabled relative living in a group home or special facility.)

### Prepaying for Special Facilities

If you are caring for a disabled child and arrange for the child's lifetime care in a special facility when you die, you may be able to deduct up-front payments. If you make a nonrefundable advance payment to a private facility for the lifetime care and treatment of your physically or mentally disabled dependent, you can treat the up-front payment as a current deductible medical expense.

## Paying for the Cost of Disability

The National Safety Council reports that a disabling injury occurs every two seconds in the United States, and, according to the U.S. Census Bureau, over 51 million Americans are classified as disabled. These are stark statistics.

For many people, disability can cause not only pain and loss of personal freedom, but also financial hardship. Disability is the cause of more than half of all mortgage foreclosures (only 2 percent of foreclosures are the result of death). Unexpected disability causes about 350,000 personal bankruptcies each year.

The onset of a disability may mean that income previously relied upon for personal living expenses is no longer available. There is also the added cost of care, including medical treatment and personal care. And family members may be limited in their ability to work if they are needed to provide care for the disabled person.

Some income replacements for the disabled person, which are covered in this chapter, include:

- Payments from disability insurance
- Life payments of life insurance benefits
- Workers' compensation
- Social Security disability income (SSDI)
- Supplemental Security Income (SSI)

- Other government disability programs
- Retirement plan distributions

## Disability Insurance

Most Americans do not have private disability insurance, even though three out of 10 working people become disabled for some period between the ages of 35 and 65, and one in five people are disabled for five years or longer before they reach age 65. The Social Security Administration says 70 percent of workers don't have long-term disability insurance.

---

### What to Do Now

If you currently have a disability policy from your employer and you leave the job, determine whether you can continue this coverage by paying the premiums (usually, a disability policy is portable).

If you don't have a disability policy, consider purchasing the coverage on your own. You can do this from a major carrier or through a professional or trade association.

---

### Tax Treatment

If you do have a disability policy, through work, through a professional or trade association, or that you've purchased on your own, here is the tax treatment of benefits received under the policy:

- If your employer paid the premiums as a tax-free fringe benefit to you, the benefits are taxable income.
- If you paid the premiums, or your employer paid them as a taxable fringe benefit, the policy's benefits are tax free to you.

### Using Life Insurance for Terminal Illness or Disability

If there is a life insurance policy on someone who has been diagnosed with a terminal illness (death is anticipated within two years) or who has a chronic illness that requires assistance to accomplish daily living tasks, such as eating, dressing, bathing, continence, transferring (e.g., in and out of bed), and toileting; or who has a condition, such as Alzheimer's disease, that requires substantial supervision, cash value in the policy may be a ready source of money. There are two ways to tap into a policy:

1. *Accelerated death benefits.* The insurer may permit the policy owner to take money from the policy to pay for long-term care.

2. *Viatical settlements.* The owner can sell the policy to a third party for a lump-sum payment.

The tax treatment of accelerated death benefits and money received in a viatical settlement depends on the insured's condition.

- For someone who is terminally ill, payments are tax free (they're treated as if the person had received a death benefit under the policy).

- For someone who is chronically ill, payments used to pay long-term care costs are tax free. Payments used for other purposes are subject to a daily dollar limit ($270 per day in 2008).

---

### What to Do Now

Decide whether to tap into a life insurance policy if you would qualify for tax-free treatment. Remember that the funds drawn out of the policy will deplete any death benefits for beneficiaries upon the insured's death.

---

## Workers' Compensation

Workers' compensation is a program designed to compensate workers who are injured on the job or suffer a work-related illness while employed by private companies or state and local government agencies (those employed by the federal government also have a similar type of protection). Workers' compensation can be used regardless of who is at fault for the injury or illness. But job-related injuries are few (less than 10 percent) compared with injuries in general, so workers' compensation can help in only limited circumstances.

Workers' compensation benefits are designed to cover medical costs and wage replacement. They may also pay for vocational rehabilitation and job placement if necessary. While the types of expenses paid through workers' compensation are broad, the benefit amounts are usually modest. For instance, you may receive wage replacement, but only at, say, two-thirds of your pre-injury/illness level.

Those who become permanently unable to work because of a work-related injury or illness will receive a lump-sum benefit. The amount is fixed according to the type of disability.

### Tax Treatment

The tax law looks favorably upon workers' compensation benefits; these benefits, including a lump-sum payment for permanent disability, are tax free.

However, if you retire on disability and receive a lump-sum payment for accrued annual leave, you cannot treat this payment as tax-free income; it's fully taxable to you.

**What to Do Now**

If you're injured or become ill on the job, contact your state workers' compensation board (link to the board in your state through the U.S. Department of Labor (www.dol.gov/esa/regs/compliance/owcp/wc.htm).

Workers' compensation payments can be received only if you waive the right to sue for damages for your on-the-job injuries. Discuss your situation with an attorney before agreeing to accept workers' compensation or any other settlement offered by your employer.

## Social Security Disability Benefits

The term *Social Security benefits* usually connotes payments to retirees. However, the Social Security Administration (SSA) reports that over 6.8 million Americans are receiving Social Security disability income (SSDI), and almost half of these recipients are under the age of 50. The average monthly benefit for SSDI in 2008 is $1,004.

The monthly benefit may be reduced by workers' compensation or public disability benefit (such as a military disability pension). The combined amount of SSDI and workers' compensation/disability payments cannot exceed 80 percent of your average earnings immediately prior to disability, so the SSDI amount depends on your particular situation.

**Example**

Your average current earnings prior to your disability were $4,000 a month. You, your spouse, and your two children are eligible to receive $2,200 a month in Social Security disability benefits. You also receive $2,000 a month from workers' compensation. Because the total amount of benefits you would receive ($4,200) is more than $3,200 (80 percent of your average current earnings), your Social Security benefits will be reduced by $1,000.

It's not easy to qualify for Social Security disability payments. The Social Security Administration says that only about 39 percent of those who apply for them are approved. To qualify for disability benefits, you must show that your disability prevents you from doing any "substantial gainful work," and the condition must be expected to last at least 12 months or to result in death. You can get an idea about whether you'd qualify for SSDI by reading the five-step evaluation process in SSA publication No. 05–10029 at www.socialsecurity.gov/pubs/10029.pdf.

Expect it to take three to five months to get a decision about eligibility. The first five months of disability are not covered; benefits begin for the sixth month.

Even if you qualify, there are frequent reviews of disability to make sure that you continue to qualify for payments. Typically, you receive a letter outlining the steps you must take to continue your disability classification.

Once you reach full retirement age (66 for those born between 1943 and 1954, 66 and 2 months for those born in 1955, 66 and 4 months in 1956, 66 and 6 months in 1957, 66 and 8 months in 1958, 66 and 10 months in 1959, and 67 for those born in 1960 and later), your payments continue, but they are then called retirement benefits instead of SSDI and any improvement in your condition will not impact your benefits at that time.

---

### What to Do Now

You must apply for SSDI, which you can do in person in your local SSA office (call 800–772–1213 to find one near you) or online at www.socialsecurity.gov/applyfordisability/adult.htm. Here you'll find the online application form and disability report that you'll need to complete.

---

### Supplemental Security Income

In addition to SSDI, you may qualify to receive Supplemental Security Income (SSI). This income is designed for those with severe financial need; if SSDI is your only income and isn't enough to keep you above the poverty level, you may receive SSI as well.

The basic SSI payment is the same across the country ($639 per individual, or $956 per couple in 2008). However, nine states (California, Hawaii, Massachusetts, Nevada, New Jersey, New York, Pennsylvania, Rhode Island, and Vermont) and the District of Columbia provide additional payments to their residents.

---

### What to Do Now

You can learn about SSI by reading about it from the Social Security Administration (www.ssa.gov/pubs/11000.html). To learn whether you are eligible for benefits, you must apply through your local SSA office (call 800–772–1213 to find one near you) or online at www.socialsecurity.gov/applyfordisability/adult.htm.

---

### Medicare

Qualifying for SSDI can produce an ancillary benefit. You automatically qualify for Medicare coverage after two years of disability payments. (The 24-month period starts with the first month you are entitled to receive benefits.) Those with amyotrophic lateral sclerosis (ALS or Lou Gehrig's disease) receive Medicare beginning with the month they become entitled to disability benefits.

### Working While Receiving Benefits

Even though the definition of disability implies a permanent condition, you may be able to recover sufficiently to return to work. This may or may not be at your predisability level.

You can continue to receive SSDI and still work under special rules called work incentives. If you have a disabling impairment but return to work under a trial work period, you can continue full SSDI benefits. Only work for which you are paid at least a set amount ($670 per month in 2008) counts for this purpose. The trial period is nine months in total (not necessarily consecutive) within a 60-month period.

Benefits cease once your earnings level is "substantial," which for this purpose means earnings over a set amount ($940 a month in 2008, or for those who are statutorily blind, $1,570 per month).

Benefits can be restarted if earnings drop below the substantial level while you continue to have a disabling impairment. To learn more about continuing to receive SSDI while working, see SSA Publication No. 05–10095 at www.socialsecurity.gov/pubs/10095.pdf.

There is also a Ticket to Work program, which is free and voluntary, and designed to encourage the disabled/blind to return to the workforce without the fear of losing health coverage. The program is administered by an outside company, MAXIMUS, Inc. For information, go to www.yourtickettowork.com or call 866–968–7842.

### Tax Treatment of SSDI

Benefits received because of disability are taxed in the same way as Social Security benefits paid to retirees. They can be fully tax free or included in income at up to 50 percent or 85 percent, depending on your total income picture.

More specifically, the taxable portion, if any, depends on your filing status and your provisional income (your adjusted gross income increased by certain tax-free fringe benefits, one-half of Social Security benefits, and tax-exempt interest).

- Benefits are tax free if provisional income does not exceed $25,000 if single, head of household, qualifying widow(er), or married filing jointly and lived apart from your spouse for the entire year, or $32,000 if married filing jointly.

- Fifty percent of benefits are included in income if provisional income exceeds $25,000, but does not exceed $34,000 for singles, or exceeds $32,000 but does not exceed $44,000 for married filing jointly.

- Eighty-five percent of benefits are included in income if provisional income exceeds $34,000 for singles ($44,000 for married filing jointly), or you are married filing separately and did not live apart from your spouse for the entire year.

For tax purposes, the unreduced SSDI benefit (before reduction for workers' compensation and other disability payments) is taken into account.

## Other Government Disability Programs

Social Security disability income (SSDI) is primarily for those who have worked a sufficient amount of time to be covered by this program. There are other government programs that may provide assistance for disability. These include:

- Disability payments from the Department of Veterans Affairs.
- Pensions for combat-related injuries or injuries from a terrorist attack.
- Disability pensions for anyone who has injuries resulting from terrorist attacks after September 10, 2001.

### Tax Treatment

Payments for disability under government programs other than SSDI are tax free.

## Medicaid

Certain low-income individuals and families may qualify for a special federal-state medical program called Medicaid (Medi-Cal in California); currently, there are about 30 million enrolled in the program. Medicaid is a federal program administered by the states; each state has its own rules for eligibility, benefits, and so forth to supplement federal rules. For instance, federal rules require the states to provide a minimum of 14 types of health coverage, including inpatient hospital care, laboratory services, and transportation. States are permitted to provide up to 34 additional (optional) services, including physical therapy and rehabilitative services.

You don't pay for Medicaid coverage; you qualify for it based on your income, assets (called "resources"), and other conditions. Those who receive SSI because of a disability are automatically covered by Medicaid in 39 states (the other 11 states set their own eligibility rules). Medicare recipients with low incomes and limited resources may also qualify for Medicaid.

For more information about Medicaid, go to the Centers for Medicare and Medicaid Services at www.cms.hhs.gov/Medicaidgeninfo.

## Retirement Plan Distributions

Money you've saved in retirement plans, such as a 401(k) or an IRA, is intended to provide you with retirement income. However, if you find it necessary to use retirement dollars for medical expenses now, you can tap into these resources earlier.

- *401(k) plans.* Generally, contributions and earnings are locked into your 401(k) plan until retirement or you leave the company. However, distributions can be permitted on account of disability. Also, the plan can allow for hardship withdrawals (you don't have to be disabled), which include distributions of elective deferrals to pay for medical expenses incurred by you, your spouse, or any dependents.

- *IRAs and Roth IRAs.* You can take as much or as little as you want from these accounts at any time. There may be tax consequences, though (explained next), and you can't replace the funds, so your retirement pot will be permanently depleted (there is, however, a 60-day window for replacing IRA money by rolling over the distribution into a new IRA).

### Tax Treatment

All withdrawals from qualified retirement plans and IRAs are taxable to the same extent that they would be if you had waited until retirement to begin withdrawals. For Roth IRAs, you can take your after-tax contributions at any time without incurring income tax; a withdrawal of earnings may be taxable (depending on how long the Roth IRA has been open).

In addition to regular income tax on the distributions, there may also be a 10 percent early distribution penalty if you are younger than $59^1/_2$. However, if you are disabled when you take withdrawals, you are not subject to the usual 10 percent penalty on distributions, regardless of your age.

Disability for purposes of avoiding the tax penalty has practically the same meaning as disability for purposes of Social Security disability benefits: You must be able to show that you have a physical or mental condition that can be expected to last indefinitely or result in death and that it prevents you from engaging in "substantial gainful activity" similar to what you were doing before the disability.

## Example

A 45-year-old person who has a terminal illness is considered disabled and so avoids the 10 percent penalty. A 45-year-old person who is clinically depressed but still able to work is not considered disabled and would be subject to the 10 percent penalty.

## What to Do Now

It won't hurt to obtain a doctor's note confirming your condition and your inability to work. Retain this note with your tax records in case the IRS questions your exemption from the 10 percent penalty.

# CHAPTER 11

# Family Breakups

Families can be torn apart because of divorce or death. Both events are highly stressful and can affect health. (On the Holmes and Rahe Stress Scale, which measures the impact of life change events on stress, the two events that produce the greatest amount of stress in life are the death of a spouse and divorce.) Both events can also have a devastating impact on wealth and personal financial security.

The rate of divorce continues to be very high; between 41 percent and 50 percent of first marriages end in divorce. The rate is higher for subsequent marriages, but slightly lower for couples who have children. Divorce rips apart a couple's relationship and can undermine their financial security.

Each year in this country, nearly 2.5 million people die. This fact affects the families who have to deal with the emotional and financial consequences of death. Personal issues about death can be enormous and drain all of your attention from practical and financial matters. This chapter is concerned with those other matters.

For instance, end-of-life health care costs for the last six months of an illness can run to tens of thousands of dollars, much of which may not be covered by insurance. The cost of a funeral can run to thousands or tens of thousands of dollars. In New York, for example, the average cost of a funeral in 2006 was over $7,100 (this included professional service charge, transfer of remains, embalming and other preparation, use of viewing facilities and the facilities for the ceremony, a hearse and limousine, and a casket; the vault or cemetery plot and monument charges were extra).

Then there are the costs of settling the deceased person's estate—going through probate, paying off debts and taxes, and distributing assets to heirs. As a rule of thumb, the costs of settling an estate can run about 5 percent of a person's assets, so if someone has a $1 million estate, it may cost $50,000 in legal fees, court costs, and other administrative expenses to wind up the deceased person's financial affairs.

And then there are the financial decisions that come after death. For a surviving spouse in particular, these decisions are numerous and can impact the rest of his or her life.

In this chapter, you'll learn about:

- Divorce and taxes
- Postdeath responsibilities
- Inheritances
- Income tax treatment of inheritances
- Surviving spouse's finances

## Divorce and Taxes

The rate of divorce peaked in 1981 and, since then, has come down a little. However, 10 percent of the U.S. population is divorced (not counting those who have remarried). Marital dissolutions may be amicable or acrimonious. Either way, divorce can cause serious disruption to the finances of each spouse and can impact their children as well. Studies show that wealth following divorce can decline by 77 percent, with a greater impact on women than men in most cases.

---

### What to Do Now

After a marital dissolution, be sure to review all of your beneficiary designations on life insurance policies, annuity contracts, retirement plans, individual retirement accounts (IRAs), and bank accounts. Even though a marriage may be dissolved, previous beneficiary designations remain valid until specifically revoked.

---

### Alimony

Alimony is a payment made by one spouse to help support the other. It may be called alimony, spousal support, maintenance, or something else. Alimony is less common today than it was in the past, because in many cases both spouses now work and can provide their own support. However, alimony may still be awarded—for life or for a limited time.

## TAX TREATMENT

Whatever the name and however long the term, if certain conditions are met, the payments are treated as taxable alimony. This means that the payments are income to the recipient and deductible by the payer.

To qualify as alimony:

- Payments must be made pursuant to a legal requirement, such as a divorce decree, separation agreement, or court order of support.

- Payments must be in cash. The payments need not be made directly to the spouse as long as they are made for the benefit of the spouse. For instance, if the payer pays the recipient's rent directly to the landlord, this qualifies as a cash payment.

- The couple must live apart. If they share a home (even if they physically live separately under the same roof), they don't live apart.

- The obligation to make payments must terminate on the death of the payer. If the payer's estate is required to continue making payments, then all of the payments (including those made while the payer is alive), are not alimony.

It's important to note that the payer is required to report the recipient's Social Security number on his or her own tax return. The IRS uses this information to check whether the alimony is being reported as income by the recipient.

## Child Support

Child support payments are payments given to the custodial parent to provide support for the child or children in his or her care. The payments may be modest or generous, depending on the financial situations of the noncustodial and custodial parents.

## TAX TREATMENT

Child support payments are not taxable to the parent who receives them, nor to the child they are intended to benefit. The parent who pays child support cannot deduct the payments. From a tax perspective, there is no dollar limit on the amount of child support. From a practical one, however, child support usually is fixed by a separation agreement or divorce decree.

Sometimes it's difficult to discern whether a payment is meant to be alimony (which is taxable to the recipient/deductible by the payer) or child support (which is tax free/nondeductible). How can you tell? The separation or divorce decree may specify that the payment is one or the other. If a payment made to a parent will be reduced upon a contingency related to the child, then that portion subject to the contingency is child support. Contingencies include reaching the age of majority (typically age 18), leaving school, moving out of the parent's home, starting to work and/or attaining a set income level, marrying, or entering military service. Reductions within six months before or after such contingencies are also treated as related to child support even though they may not specify the contingency.

## Example

A child lives with the father, and the mother is required by the divorce decree to pay the father $2,000 per month. The decree further states that when the child is 18 years old, the payments to the father are reduced to $1,200 per month. Under this scenario, it can be deduced that $1,200 is alimony and $800 (the amount subject to the contingency) is child support.

If the paying parent fails to make a full payment, the amount of the payment is first applied toward the child support obligation. Delinquent child support that you are supposed to make can prevent you from receiving a tax refund. Court-ordered child support in arrears can be satisfied by applying a federal tax refund to the obligation. In 2008, the Economic Stimulus payments were similarly applied for this purpose.

### DEPENDENCY EXEMPTION

Taxpayers who support dependents can claim a dependency exemption ($3,500 per dependent in 2008). Paying child support does not automatically entitle the paying parent to the exemption; it belongs to the custodial parent.

However, the custodial parent may waive the exemption to permit the other parent to claim it. The separation agreement or divorce decree may award the exemption to one parent or the other. If it awards the exemption to the noncustodial parent, then the custodial parent must sign the necessary Form 8332, Release of Claim to Exemption for Child of Divorced or Separated Parents, to waive the right to claim the exemption, which is attached to the noncustodial parent's return.

## What to Do Now

Determine which parent could reap the greater tax benefit from claiming the exemption and then follow through to see that this can be done. For instance, if it saves more taxes for the noncustodial parent to claim the exemption, then the custodial parent should sign the waiver.

In assessing tax savings, consider the impact of claiming the exemption on the ability to claim other tax breaks, including the child tax credit and the earned income credit.

### Property Settlements

Who keeps the house, and who gets the car? Who retains the china, and who must give up the antique vase? These and other tricky questions about a couple's property divisions can be decided according to the couple's wishes if they can agree (or if they have a prenuptial agreement spelling out these property rights).

If they can't work things out amicably, state law dictates how the couple's property is to be divided. There are two basic types of rules for dividing a couple's assets:

- *Community property.* Nine states (Arizona, California, Idaho, Louisiana, Nevada, New Mexico, Texas, Washington, and Wisconsin) generally view assets as owned equally, so they are divided equally when a couple splits up.
- *Equitable distribution.* All other states use a rule that allows a court to divide up tangible and intangible assets according to what's deemed to be fair; this may not necessarily result in an even split.

### TAX TREATMENT OF PROPERTY SETTLEMENTS

As a general rule, there are no immediate tax consequences to a property settlement. Each spouse walks away with his or her share of assets.

However, the spouse who obtains an asset from the other also keeps the other spouse's tax basis and holding period. The result: When the asset is sold, the spouse will report any gain on appreciation from the time of the property settlement, plus any appreciation that had accrued up until that date.

### Example

A husband holds title to a vacation home worth $200,000 for which he paid $75,000. The property is awarded to the wife during the divorce settlement. Five years later, when the property is worth $275,000, she sells it. She must pay tax on the $200,000 gain because her tax basis is $75,000 (the husband's basis).

### What to Do Now

When negotiating any property settlement, work with a knowledgeable tax professional who can factor in the after-tax cost of any proposed settlement. For instance, if the couple is to receive a 50–50 distribution of marital assets and one gets $500,000 cash while the other receives property worth $500,000, but with a tax basis of $300,000, this isn't equal. The spouse receiving the $500,000 worth of property would net only $470,000 after tax ($30,000 would be the capital gains tax at the 15 percent rate on the $200,000 profit).

### MARITAL RESIDENCE

Often, one spouse or the other retains the family home, especially when there are young children and the parents want them to remain in the home. Other times, the home is sold and the proceeds divided according to the property settlement. How does this impact the home sale exclusion, which allows up to $250,000 of gain to be tax free for a single individual, or $500,000 on a joint return? Depending on the arrangement, either the smaller or the larger exemption amount will apply.

- If the couple sells the home prior to divorce, the $500,000 can be claimed on their joint return, assuming they owned and used the home as their principal residence for two of the five years preceding the date of sale.
- If the spouses are joint owners and sell the home after divorce (but before they no longer satisfy the ownership and use tests), they each can claim a $250,000 exemption on their personal returns.
- If the home is transferred to one spouse incident to divorce, the time during which the other spouse lived in the home is added to the period of ownership for the spouse who retains the home. However, the spouse-homeowner can claim only a $250,000 exclusion when he or she sells the home, assuming the ownership and use tests are met.
- If the couple jointly own the home, and one spouse receives full possession, a sale entitles each spouse to the home sale exclusion. The spouse who moved is treated as having used the home for any period of time that the spouse in possession uses the home. As long as the resident-spouse meets the ownership and use tests, they each can claim a $250,000 home sale exclusion for their share of the gain.

**RETIREMENT BENEFITS**

The tax law gives a spouse a right in the other spouse's qualified retirement plan benefits. Divorce courts may award a greater share to the nonparticipant spouse. In arranging any transfer of benefits to the nonparticipant spouse, use care to avoid unwanted tax results for the participant.

- *Qualified retirement plan benefits.* Use a qualified domestic relations order (QDRO), which is a court order that directs the plan administrator to transfer benefits to the nonparticipant spouse. Using a QDRO ensures that taxes related to the transferred benefits are the burden of the nonparticipant spouse. Without a QDRO, the participant would be taxed on any benefit transferred to the nonparticipant spouse and, if under age $59^1/_2$, would be subject to a 10 percent penalty.
- *IRAs.* Transfers incident to divorce (made pursuant to a divorce decree or separation agreement) are not taxed to the IRA owner; the

recipient-spouse ultimately bears the tax burden on the transferred IRA funds. The transfer can be done by changing the name on the IRA account from the owner to the recipient-spouse or by directing the trustee to transfer IRA assets to the trustee of an IRA in the name of the recipient-spouse.

# Postdeath Responsibilities

Families who lose loved ones face an array of personal and financial challenges after someone dies.

- The bereavement process, which can last for months or longer; it varies from person to person.
- Handling a funeral and paying outstanding bills for the deceased person.
- Handling probate to see that the deceased person's assets are given to those who are supposed to inherit them.

## Costs of Final Illnesses

Some families have huge medical bills for a loved one's final illness. Costs incurred while the person is alive are deducted as medical expenses on the person's income tax return (see Chapter 10). Even after a person dies, the bills may continue to come in.

If the deceased person's personal representative (an executor, administrator, or personal representative) pays the medical bills within one year of the date of death, there are two options for deducting medical costs:

- Treat them as having been paid in the same year in which the costs were incurred. This would allow the costs to be deducted on the person's final income tax return.
- Treat them as a deduction on the person's federal estate tax return. If they are claimed on the income tax return, the representative must attach a statement to that return waiving the right to claim them on the estate tax return (including the portion covered by the 7.5 percent floor that is not deductible on the income tax return).

---

**What to Do Now**

Figure the deduction both ways if the deceased person's estate is subject to estate tax. In comparing results, remember that the first 7.5 percent of medical costs is nondeductible on the income tax return, but all costs are fully deductible in the estate tax return. The top federal income tax rate is currently 35 percent, compared with the top federal estate tax rate of 45 percent.

### Funeral Costs

Funeral costs can be thousands or even tens of thousands of dollars, depending on the type of service, the burial accommodations, the headstone, and so on. Today, cremation is growing in popularity as a way to keep down the high cost of dying; it costs about one-fifth of the usual burial cost. However, cremation is not an option for everyone (certain religions do not sanction this form of interment).

#### TAX TREATMENT

For tax purposes, none of the expenses related to the funeral can be deducted on an income tax return.

However, if the deceased person's assets were sufficient to require the filing of a federal estate tax return ($2 million in 2008; $3.5 million in 2009), then funeral costs may be a deduction for estate tax purposes. There is no dollar cap on the amount of the deduction that can be claimed.

## Inheritances

Inheritances are windfalls that happen to a few. A study by the Federal Reserve showed that only about 8 percent of the population can expect an inheritance (and half of those will inherit less than $25,000); 92 percent get nothing! Only 1.7 percent can expect to inherit $50,000 or more. These stark statistics are in contrast to the often-quoted statistic that baby boomers as a group would inherit $10 trillion ($135,000 each on average). The point of the Federal Reserve numbers is to show that you can't count on an inheritance.

If you do enjoy an inheritance, money or property may be given to you outright or through a trust in which you are a beneficiary. Spouses in most states have a right to receive a certain portion of a deceased spouse's estate (referred to as a right of election). Children and other relatives generally don't have any right to receive an inheritance if a person leaves property to others through a valid will. If there is no will, then property is distributed to heirs according to state law (called intestacy because there is no last will and testament).

### Probate

Probate is a court-supervised process of collecting a deceased person's property, paying off debts, settling taxes, and distributing what's left to beneficiaries. The process applies only to property titled in the person's name. It does not apply to items that pass automatically to a named beneficiary. Examples of items outside of probate include:

- Annuities (if the contract does not end at the death of the owner, then remaining benefits belong to the named beneficiary).
- IRAs and qualified retirement plan benefits (the benefits belong to the named beneficiary).
- Jointly owned property subject to rights of survivorship (the full property becomes the property of the surviving joint owner).
- Life insurance (the proceeds belong to the named beneficiary).

## Estate Taxes

Currently, there is a federal estate tax, which taxes the right to transfer property. It applies to all assets in which a person had an interest in death—those that are part of probate (probate assets) and those that pass directly to beneficiaries (nonprobate assets).

The estate tax is very different from the income tax. It applies only to large estates—those valued at the time of death at more than $2 million in 2008 ($3.5 million in 2009). There is no federal estate tax in 2010; starting in 2011, the estate tax is set to apply only to estates valued over $1 million.

Many people assume that they are of modest means and don't have an estate worth enough to become subject to estate tax. The truth is that with a home, a retirement plan, a small business, and other assets, you may be surprised at how large the federal government thinks your estate really is. Your estate could become subject to estate tax when you die. Your relatives' estates from whom you may have an inheritance may also be subject to estate tax.

---

**Note**

Congress is considering measures to prevent the old estate tax rules from reemerging in 2011 by increasing the exemption amounts to $5 million, $10 million, or more, so that only very large estates will need to be concerned with this transfer tax after 2010. No immediate action is expected; look to the new Congress to take up the matter in 2009.

---

The estate tax is paid by the estate before assets are distributed to heirs (the terms of a person's will can impose the obligation to pay estate tax directly on a specific heir to reduce his or her share of the estate).

States have their own ways of treating estates. There may be state inheritance taxes and/or estate tax, or there may be no tax at all, depending on where the deceased person lived out his or her life.

> ### What to Do Now
>
> Keep your estate plan flexible to accommodate any federal tax law changes that may occur. For instance, for someone with assets of $2 million or more, the last will and testament should take the exemption amount into account so as not to disinherit anyone you wanted to benefit. It is common practice for wealthy married individuals to use what is called a credit shelter trust, which ensures that both spouses' estates get the full benefit of the exemption amount. However, if Congress were to raise the exemption and the credit shelter trust language were tied into old exemption amounts, the new exemption might be wasted. Work with a knowledgeable estate planning expert to design an estate plan that will serve you now and as tax laws change.

## Income Tax Treatment of Inheritances

When you inherit money or property, count yourself doubly blessed—you've been remembered by the person who died and you don't have to pay any income tax when you receive the inheritance.

However, you are taxed on income that your inheritance earns. For instance, if you inherit a corporate bond, you are taxed on the interest that the bond earns each year. If you are named as the beneficiary of a trust and trust income is distributed to you each year, you are usually taxed on the income, even though it derived from a tax-free inheritance.

> ### What to Do Now
>
> If you inherit property, be sure to obtain information from the estate's representative about the property's tax basis. This is usually the value of the property at the date of death—it is called a stepped-up basis because any increase in value after the time that the deceased person acquired the asset goes untaxed forever; the heir gets a new basis. (For most jointly owned property with a surviving spouse, only the basis for the inherited half is based on the value at the date of death; the other half is the surviving spouse's own basis.)
>
> Your holding period for the property (for purposes of determining short-term or long-term capital gain or loss treatment when you sell) is automatically long-term. This is so regardless of how long the deceased person or you actually own the property prior to a sale.
>
> Keep basis information with your personal tax records; you'll need it to determine gain or loss when you sell the property.

There are some nuances to the basic income tax rule that inheritances are tax free. These rules are complex and include rules related to income in respect of a decedent and savings bonds, discussed next.

## Income in Respect of a Decedent

There is one exception to inheritances being tax free: You must pay income taxes if you inherit an item called income in respect of a decedent (IRD). This is an item that was earned by the deceased person before death but never taxed to him or her; now it's taxed to you. Examples of IRD include IRAs, 401(k) accounts, annuities, savings bonds on which interest was deferred (see next section), and payments to self-employed individuals.

### Example

You inherit your parent's IRA, worth $80,000. The receipt of the inheritance is tax free. However, when you take distributions from the IRA (as you must under the tax law), you are taxed on the distributions to the same extent that your parent would have been taxed if distributions were received prior to death.

If you inherit income in respect of a decedent, you may also get a tax break. If the item was part of a taxable estate, then the portion of federal estate taxes paid on the IRD becomes a tax deduction for you. The deduction is claimed as a miscellaneous itemized deduction; you have to itemize to claim it and can't take the standard deduction, but there is no 2-percent-of adjusted gross income floor on this deduction as there is with other miscellaneous itemized deductions.

## Special Rule for Savings Bonds

Most owners of U.S. savings bonds opt to report interest only when the bonds mature or are redeemed. This deferral of interest saves taxes while the bonds are owned, but eventually tax on the interest must be paid.

If the interest has not been reported prior to the owner's death, then the obligation to pay interest usually belongs to the person who acquires the bonds as an inheritance. (Bonds are transferred automatically if the beneficiary is a co-owner or they must be reregistered in the beneficiary's name if the bonds are left to someone who is not a co-owner.)

There is, however, a special election that can be made to report all of the accrued bond interest on the deceased person's final income tax return. This will relieve the beneficiary of the obligation to report accrued interest; the beneficiary will be taxed only on interest accrued after death. The election to report the accrued interest on the bond owner's final income tax return can make sense if, for example, the bond owner dies early in the year so that interest on the bonds may be most or all of his or her income and may be offset to a large extent by the standard deduction.

---

### What to Do Now

Anyone who inherits savings bonds should work with the deceased person's representative to determine the best way to report bond interest.

If the interest is not reported on the final return and you must report the accumulated interest, you can claim a miscellaneous itemized deduction for federal estate tax on income in respect of a decedent (explained in the preceding section).

---

## Surviving Spouse's Finances

A surviving spouse is faced with dealing with finances—paying bills and making investments—alone. Prior to the other spouse's death, both spouses may or may not have been fully involved with the family's finances. For a spouse who had not been in the loop, postdeath finances can be quite a shock.

### Immediate Actions

After the death of a spouse, the other spouse faces a variety of financial chores, besides participating in the probate process. Certain chores require immediate attention (do them as soon as possible):

- *Obtain 10 to 15 death certificates.* These will be needed for various purposes, including changing title to joint accounts and probate.
- *Contact the Social Security Administration (SSA at www.ssa.gov).* Request the Social Security lump-sum payment. A surviving spouse is entitled to a one-time $255 payment, but must ask for it. Also change Social Security benefits. If the deceased spouse and surviving spouse have been receiving Social Security benefits, inform SSA of the death; this may change the amount of benefits payable to the surviving spouse. If the surviving spouse has not yet been receiving benefits, he or she may be eligible for them.
- *Contact the Veterans Administration (www.va.gov).* If the deceased spouse was a veteran, check for any benefits due the surviving spouse.
- *Inform the employer.* The deceased spouse's employer may have benefits yet to be paid; some benefits may accrue to the surviving spouse. For

instance, find out what steps are necessary to transfer retirement plan benefits where applicable. If the person was a union member, contact the union as well.

- *Cancel credit cards and close bank accounts.* A surviving spouse should have his or her own credit cards and bank accounts.
- *Contact insurers.* Terminate all coverage for the deceased spouse (e.g., health policies, auto policies).
- *Change the name on joint accounts.* Inform banks, brokerage firms, and mutual funds of the death (a death certificate may be required), so that title to the accounts can be changed.
- *Transfer title to the family car and home.* This may have to be done through probate.
- *Cancel services.* If the deceased person had a cell phone, was receiving deliveries that are no longer necessary, or had membership in a health club or other group, cancel them.

### Tax Filing Status

In the year in which a spouse dies, the surviving spouse can file a joint return for income tax purposes (unless the deceased spouse's representative objects). This is allowed regardless of when in the year the spouse died. Filing jointly usually will produce the lowest tax bite possible.

After the year of death, different tax rules apply. The tax law gives certain widows and widowers a break for a limited time. For the two years following the year of a spouse's death, the surviving spouse can use a special filing status called qualifying widow(er) (also called surviving spouse). This tax status lets a surviving spouse use the standard deduction amount and tax rates usually reserved for married persons filing joint returns.

#### ELIGIBILITY

To qualify as a surviving spouse, you must meet three requirements:

1. You did not remarry.
2. You can claim as your dependent a child, stepchild, or adopted child who lived with you for the entire year (except for temporary absences) and you paid over half the cost of maintaining your home. A foster child does not help you be eligible even though you may claim the foster child as a dependent.
3. You were eligible to file a joint return for the year in which your spouse died, whether or not you actually did so.

## Example

Your spouse dies in 2008. In 2009 and 2010, you support your young child in your home; you pay all of the costs. You can file as a qualifying widow(er) for 2009 and 2010, assuming you haven't remarried. Starting in 2011, you no longer are eligible for this filing status. However, if you continue to support your dependent in your home, you may be eligible for head of household status, which is more favorable than the status for single, but less favorable than that of a qualifying widow(er).

### Retirement Plan Elections

As a surviving spouse, if you are the beneficiary of a 401(k) plan or other qualified retirement plan or IRA, you face a unique choice on how to handle these benefits. You can opt to:

- Roll them over into your own account. This allows you to name your own beneficiaries and to postpone taking distributions until you reach age $70\frac{1}{2}$. Retitle the account as your own or direct the current trustee to transfer the funds to your own account. If funds are distributed to you, you have 60 days to roll them over to your own account.
- Treat them as benefits received by a nonspouse beneficiary. You can take distributions now (in full or under required minimum distribution rules); the distributions are usually fully taxable, but you avoid any early distribution penalty if you're under age $59\frac{1}{2}$. Retitle the account as, for example, "Harry Johnson (deceased 6/10/08) Inherited IRA for the benefit of Alice Johnson, Beneficiary."

## What to Do Now

If a surviving spouse is younger than $59\frac{1}{2}$, consider splitting funds into two accounts—one that is treated as the surviving spouse's own account and the other as a nonspouse beneficiary account. This will allow the young surviving spouse to have access to funds without penalty, while preserving some funds for the future.

If the surviving spouse is not the sole beneficiary of an IRA, split the account no later than September of the year following the year of death (in some situations you have until December 31 to act). This will give the surviving spouse the option to treat the account (reflecting his or her share of assets) as his or her own or to take distributions as a nonspouse beneficiary.

## Long-Term Actions

Work with a knowledgeable financial professional to get a handle on your finances. What income sources are open to you? What benefits can you rely on now?

The death of a spouse is an opportunity to review investments, remake budgets, and gain a greater understanding about finances.

A surviving spouse should rethink his or her estate plan. This may include drawing up a new will, and naming new beneficiaries of bank accounts, retirement plans, annuity contracts, and life insurance.

---

### What to Do Now

It's a good rule of thumb *not* to make any major financial decisions for at least six months following the death of a spouse. Emotions during the time immediately following the death of a spouse can cloud your judgment. For instance, don't sell the family home immediately, even if you think this may be the best course of action eventually. Don't make large gifts to family members from your inheritance; you may find that you need this money for your own support. Don't agree to insurance company proposals on what to do with insurance proceeds to which you may be entitled before consulting with a financial adviser.

---

### HOME SALE EXCLUSION

The tax law gives surviving spouses a special tax break. If the surviving spouse sells the couple's home within two years after the death of the spouse, he or she does not pay tax on capital gains up to $500,000 (the same exclusion amount that applies to couples). To qualify for this special tax break, the surviving spouse and deceased spouse must have qualified for the exclusion as of the time of death. This means the couple must have owned and used the home for at least two of the five years before that date. Title to the home can be held in either spouse's name; the home need not be jointly owned as long as both spouses meet the two-year use test.

If the surviving spouse waits more than two years, his or her home sale exclusion is limited to $250,000 (the usual limit for singles).

# CHAPTER 12

# Hard-Learned Lessons

Going through an economic trauma, whether it's losing a home or a bundle of money in the stock market, can have lasting emotional and financial effects. It is hoped that such an experience produces important life lessons that can prevent a reoccurrence of a bad event. Someone whose home had flood damage but no flood insurance would probably be sure to get the coverage as soon as possible. Someone who took on too much debt only to be faced with bankruptcy would probably learn to be more cautious about charging new purchases in the future.

You've heard the advice before—create a budget to live within your means, create an emergency fund, and don't take on too much debt. Now, after you've experienced some financial difficulties, maybe the advice is more meaningful to you.

Whatever your experiences during these difficult economic times, whether beaten down or virtually unscathed, use what you've learned (and what you've seen happen to others) to build a better financial future. In this chapter, you will learn about:

- Living within your means
- Creating an emergency fund
- Managing debt for the long term
- Changing personal emphasis
- Postponing retirement
- Staying healthy

## Living within Your Means

Prior to the 1920s when department stores and other vendors began to sell washing machines and other items on installment plans, most people usually paid cash for the things they needed. They might have had a credit account at the local grocery store, but clothing, cars, and other personal items were purchased only when the funds were in hand. With easy credit terms came mounting debt for many Americans.

Examine your money values. Is it necessary to keep up with the Joneses? Do you really need the latest model car? Spending more than you have simply to create a lifestyle that you think you need is economic suicide. Eventually, your overspending will catch up with you and put you into a serious financial mess.

### *Understand Your Income*

Many people live under a misconception about how much income they really have to spend or save. If their salary is $40,000, they may assume there is $40,000 available to spend or save.

To live within your means, take into account only *after-tax* income. This is your take-home pay after reduction for income taxes (federal and, where applicable, state withholding) and FICA (withholding for Social Security and Medicare taxes).

In addition to taxes that are taken from your paycheck, you may have other subtractions that reduce your available money. These include withholding for:

- Contributions to flexible spending accounts (FSAs) to pay for medical or dependent care expenses.
- Elective deferrals (your contributions) to 401(k) or similar retirement plans.
- Health insurance premiums if your employer does not pay the full cost.
- State disability insurance taxes.
- Transit passes that you pay on a pretax basis.
- Union dues.
- Voluntary savings plans.

If you are self-employed, the fees and other revenue you take in are not the true amount of money you have to spend. From the fees or revenue, you must pay business expenses as well as your personal income taxes (including self-employment tax to cover Social Security and Medicare taxes on your net earnings).

## List Your Goals

Do you want to live debt free? Do you want to be able to afford a home? Think about what you want and how much effort and sacrifice you are willing to put toward achieving your goals. Create a list of short-term and long-term goals:

- *Short-term goals* (goals that can be achieved within a year). Examples of short-term goals include creating a budget, gaining a better understanding of where your money goes, learning ways to improve your financial situation.
- *Intermediate-term goals* (goals that can be achieved in one to five years). An example of an intermediate goal is eliminating credit card debt.
- *Long-term goals* (goals that usually take more than five years to achieve). Typically these involve large purchases or making lifestyle changes. Examples of long-term goals include buying a home, paying for a child's education, and retiring at a targeted age.

Use Table 12.1 to enter your goals. They can include a down payment for a car or a home, eliminating credit card debt, or taking a vacation. Divide the total cost by the number of months in your target date to arrive at your monthly savings requirement to reach your goal on time. For example, say you want to have $5,000 as a down payment on a new car and you want to have it in three years (36 months). Your monthly savings would have to be $138.89. Once you have these goals reduced to dollars, you can build them into your budget (explained in Chapter 5) and make them a reality.

**TABLE 12.1** Your Financial Goals

| Goal | Target Date (in Months) | Total Cost | Monthly Savings |
|------|-------------------------|------------|-----------------|
|      |                         | $          | $               |
|      |                         |            |                 |
|      |                         |            |                 |
|      |                         |            |                 |
|      |                         |            |                 |
|      |                         |            |                 |
|      |                         |            |                 |
|      |                         |            |                 |

### Live on a Budget

A budget is simply a way of planning ahead so you don't use up your income before meeting your monthly obligations and go into debt. Advice on making a budget can be found in Chapter 5.

The key to having a budget is sticking to it. Two ways to stay within your budget:

1. *Review your budget regularly and make needed adjustments.* The budget may or may not be working for you. It's understandable that things won't come out even every month. However, if you continually have a shortfall, you'll need to find ways to make the budget work (e.g., by eliminating some expenditures). If you are fortunate enough to have any excess, determine the best way to use it (e.g., by putting it toward creating an emergency fund, explained later in this chapter).

2. *Make dramatic changes.* Despite your best budgeting efforts, you may not be able to afford your current lifestyle. If you're serious about making ends meet, you may need to relocate to less costly digs or to a new area, sell the second car, or tell your child that going to a private college is out of the question (unless he or she can obtain scholarships and/or grants).

---

### What to Do Now

Eliminate credit card spending—mostly or completely. Not buying items until you have the cash available to pay for them in full can help you live within your means and stick to your budget. For instance, if you plan to spend $600 on back-to-school clothes and shoes for your children (the average for 2000) this means including $50 in your budget each month that can be set aside for the intended purpose.

---

### Budget for Future Events and Expenditures

Plan ahead, and build into your budget the money you'll need for big-ticket items that you anticipate:

- *Holiday spending.* Consider using bank holiday savings accounts to accumulate the money that you plan to spend on gifts, decorations, travel, and holiday events.

- *Vacations.* Create a separate savings account to amass the money you'll need for a planned vacation.

- *Buying a home.* To save up a down payment, create a special savings account for this purpose (you can use a money market account or other savings vehicle).

- *College.* There are various savings vehicles designed specifically for higher education (see Chapter 6).

### Avoid Slipups

Spending money that you didn't include in your budget may be necessary for an emergency (creating an emergency fund is discussed next). But buying a new dress because it's on sale or taking in an extra movie can eat into your budget. Before you spend money you hadn't planned to, ask yourself whether you really need to do it. Like sticking to a diet, you can be successful in sticking to your budget if you let the urge to splurge pass.

## Creating an Emergency Fund

Things happen—a job is terminated, a roof needs to be fixed, there's a sudden medical emergency not fully covered by insurance. Your basic monthly budget probably doesn't have enough elasticity to accommodate a major unexpected expenditure. How will you get through? Create an emergency fund of easily accessible cash to meet the cost of the unexpected.

### Emergency Fund for Personal Living Expenses

An unexpected job layoff can threaten your ability to meet your monthly living expenses. You may have unemployment insurance that will provide benefits for 26 weeks or so. But the amount of benefits may not be enough to meet your needs, and you may not necessarily be employed by the time benefits run out.

How large should your emergency fund be? There's no fixed answer; it depends on your personal situation. For instance, if there are two wage earners and you can get by (even if tightly) on the salary of one, then you only need a small emergency fund for personal living expenses. In a worst-case scenario, with no income coming in, it's a good idea to have an emergency fund that will pay your personal living expenses (the mortgage, utilities, food, etc.) for at least three months (some experts advise six months). In terms of dollars, the size of your fund depends on your monthly costs.

In the old days, people created emergency funds by putting coins or dollar bills in coffee cans or under the mattress. Today, the old strategy is not a good idea. Banks are safe (see Chapter 3 for information about FDIC insurance) and you're wasting money by *not* earning interest. Instead, stash the cash in a savings account that you can access at any time without a penalty. You'll earn interest on the money (even if in today's market the interest is nominal). But you can withdraw what you need when you need it. Be sure that you don't touch the money for any purpose other than an emergency; if you do, you won't have the fund there if an emergency arises.

Start creating the emergency fund in manageable amounts. For instance, set aside $100 or $200 each month until you have amassed your target emergency fund.

Create your emergency fund *before* you put money into investments or spend it on nonessentials. However, you probably want to pay down debt after you've created an initial emergency fund. Carrying debt during an emergency is extremely difficult to do; it's better to be debt free if you experience an emergency.

### Emergency Fund for Home Repairs

If you own a home, you know that it needs repairs from time to time. Some repairs can be postponed, such as a new paint job or upgrading appliances. Other repairs may require immediate attention—a septic system needs to be replaced or the roof is leaking. Do you have the money on hand to make any needed or desired repairs? Do you have other resources that you can turn to for money?

Some people rely on credit card borrowing to pay for emergencies, but this isn't a good idea. The cost of credit card borrowing is very high, compared with other payment methods.

There are two ways to meet these expenses: a special savings fund or a home equity line of credit. One option requires you to prefund the need; the other lets you pay for the need and then repay the money. You can use one or the other, or both of these options:

1. *Special savings account.* Set up a money market account funded to meet emergency home expenses (don't put the money in a certificate of deposit or time savings account, because you'll incur penalties if you need the money before the end of the savings term). The amount you save here depends, of course, on your resources. Generally, it would be wise to aim for a savings fund of $5,000, $10,000, or more; you build up the account over time, stashing away a fixed amount each month if possible until you reach your target fund. Having a savings fund means it does not cost you anything if you need to use the money for repairs. You earn income on the savings and can access the money at any time. Once you use some of the funds, it's a good idea to replace the money as soon as you can so it's available for future needs.

2. *Home equity line of credit (HELOC).* This is a bank loan that you can tap into when and to the extent needed to cover repairs or home improvements. Usually there's no cost to setting up the line; you pay interest on only the amount of money you borrow. However, you can create a HELOC only if the value of your home is greater than your current mortgage balance (depending on the lender, borrowing usually is limited to 75 percent or so of the equity in your home). Using part of your line means you'll have to repay the money, plus interest, which is a drain on your monthly budget.

# Managing Debt for the Long Term

Using credit to buy some types of personal items or property, such as a car or a home, is a useful and necessary tool for having the things you need even though you don't yet have all the money required to own them. But mismanaging debt can lead to serious financial problems and can create personal issues as well. An Associated Press–AOL Health Poll in June 2008 found that people dealing with mounting debt can experience ulcers, severe depression, and even heart attacks—the three key illnesses that can result from high levels of stress.

Debt, in and of itself, isn't a bad thing. It can be the only way to obtain important things, such as owning a home or gaining a college education. However, credit card debt to buy clothing, toys, vacations, and other discretionary items can become a bad thing if it is not managed properly.

## Getting Rid of Unmanageable Debt

Living a life free of worrying about debt collectors and struggling to make ends meet requires that you reduce your credit card debt. It can't be done overnight; it probably took years to get into the financial fix you now find yourself in. Getting rid of unmanageable debt requires some radical action that will produce personal sacrifice. You'll have to do without something; there's no other means to work your way out of debt.

Some people can get rid of unmanageable debt on their own. Others need the assistance of professionals.

### DOING IT YOURSELF

If you think you have the fortitude to work your way out of debt, steel yourself for some hard work and patience.

- *Call your creditors.* Many will work with you if you need to miss a payment because of an illness or other personal event (e.g., divorce, death in the family).
- *Cut up your credit cards.* Some experts advise placing credit cards in the freezer to limit access to their use. Start living on cash so you don't add to your debt burden.
- *Build debt repayment into your budget and stick to it.* Just like creating a savings component to your budget, add a set-aside for debt service.
- *Pay off the higher-interest-rate credit cards first.* Where possible, transfer the balance from these cards to ones with lower interest rates. There may be introductory offers offering no or low interest for balance transfers, but this usually runs for only six months. After then, the interest rate may wind up being higher than the one on the previous card.

### USING HELP

There are numerous consumer credit counselors offering to provide help in managing your debt. Some are good; many are not. Here are some tips to locating a reputable counselor:

- Look for a nonprofit agency offering solid debt management programs. Avoid debt consolidation companies; they usually charge big fees but don't necessarily make big dents in your credit burden.
- Determine the qualifications of the counselors (this can be reflected in how they're paid—on salary or commission).
- Check for fees. The setup fee should be modest ($50 or less) and monthly fees should also be manageable ($25 or less).

Find help through the National Foundation for Credit Counseling (www. nfcc.org). You can locate an agency that belongs to this national association via zip code.

### Limiting Debt in the Future

Limiting debt is taking control of your life. If you need help in limiting your debt assumption, look to professionals and organizations designed for this purpose, such as Debtors Anonymous (www.debtorsanonymous.org), a 12-step program (like Alcoholics Anonymous) with peer group support. To find a local meeting or other organization (Overspenders Anonymous, shopaholic support groups, and spendaholic support groups), check your local newspaper or telephone directory.

### Tax Breaks for Good Debt

Some debt is inevitable for most people and isn't necessarily a bad thing. It can enable you to obtain big-ticket items that would otherwise be impossible to save up for in their entirety within any reasonable amount of time. There are tax breaks for so-called good debt.

### HOME MORTGAGE INTEREST DEDUCTION

The tax law lets you deduct home mortgage interest, which reduces the amount of income on which you pay tax. Interest on a mortgage to buy, build, or substantially improve a principal residence or second home is fully deductible on debt up to $1 million. In addition, you can deduct interest on home equity debt up to $100,000 (home equity debt is discussed in Chapter 2). You can't deduct the principal payments you make every month.

There's no dollar limit on the amount of the home mortgage interest that can be deducted (the limit relates to the amount of the loan). To benefit from the home mortgage interest deduction, you must itemize on your tax return and can't use the standard deduction.

If you've purchased a principal residence using mortgage insurance because you could not come up with the 20 percent down payment, you may be able to treat the premiums as deductible home mortgage interest. The deduction is available only to those who itemize their deductions and meet an income limit. The full premiums are deductible for adjusted gross income up to $100,000 ($50,000 for married persons filing separate returns). The deductible amount is reduced by 10 percent for each $1,000 ($500 on separate returns) over the income limit.

This tax break applies only for 2007 through 2010 unless Congress extends the law. Prepayments for insurance allocable to future years are not deductible.

### STUDENT LOAN INTEREST DEDUCTION

The tax law also lets you deduct interest on student loans. The annual dollar limit on this interest deduction is $2,500. The deduction belongs to the person who is legally obligated to repay the loan.

However, there is a modified adjusted gross income (MAGI) limit on eligibility to use this write-off. The deduction phases out for singles with MAGI between $55,000 and $70,000 in 2008; for married persons filing jointly, the deduction phases out for MAGI between $115,000 and $145,000. The MAGI ranges can be adjusted annually for inflation, so someone who may have been ineligible for the deduction in the past because of his or her MAGI may qualify in light of an increase in the MAGI range.

The deduction cannot be taken by someone who can be claimed as a dependent on another taxpayer's return or by a married person filing a separate return, regardless of MAGI. However, someone who was a dependent in the past but is no longer a dependent can claim the interest deduction now and in the future (assuming the person is within the MAGI limit).

The deduction can be claimed whether or not you itemize your other deductions.

### INVESTMENT INTEREST DEDUCTION

If you use borrowed money to buy or carry investments, the loan is viewed as an investment loan. Interest paid is deductible as an itemized deduction to the extent of net investment income (e.g., dividends and interest received). If investment interest paid exceeds investment income for the year, the excess can be carried forward and used in a future year.

No interest can be deducted to the extent the loan is used to buy or carry tax-exempt bonds. For instance, if you borrow $50,000 to buy $50,000 of municipal bonds, no part of the interest on the loan is deductible.

## Changing Personal Emphasis

Albert Camus said, "It's a kind of spiritual snobbery that makes people think they can be happy without money." Certainly, you need money for all of life's essentials—food, clothing, housing, transportation, education, and more. Without sufficient funds for these essentials, no one can find happiness. But many people are surprised that they can do exceedingly well with a lot less money than they had previously believed. Although each person has his or her own relationship with money and no single fiscal philosophy will meet each person's needs, everyone can reexamine personal attitudes about wealth.

Today's tough economy can be a blessing in disguise for some people. It presents an opportunity to reassess values and find the true joys of life. For example, having less money for some means spending more time at home with family. If a family can't afford to eat out, then dining in (something that had been the rule rather than the exception in previous generations) gives family members a better chance to interact.

It has come to be expected that, except in certain cities, everyone should have his or her own car. With exorbitant gas prices, more families are getting by with a single vehicle. Maybe this type of change is meaningful for you now.

If you don't want to redefine your fiscal philosophy, you can continue your lifestyle with modest modifications. Cutting out little things can produce big monthly savings without seriously impacting your lifestyle. For instance, a latte grande every day would run you about $100 a month. In contrast, it costs only pennies a day to brew your own coffee at home and, if desired, take it with you in a thermos or coffee mug—saving you over a $1,000 a year and you haven't changed your car or moved to a new home!

---

### What to Do Now

If you want to eliminate small expenditures that won't seriously change your lifestyle, do this exercise: Write down every penny you spend for a week or a month so you know where your money is going. Then decide which items you can cut out. Maybe you'll read the newspaper online for free instead of paying for one at the station each morning.

---

## Postponing Retirement

Many people had planned to hang up their hard hats and walk away from their jobs at a relatively young age. For some, that age may have coincided with their full retirement age for Social Security benefit purposes. At that time, they can enjoy full Social Security benefits (retiring and collecting benefits at a younger age results in a permanent reduction in lifetime benefits).

That dream has faded for many Americans today. There are several reasons why it may be difficult if not impossible to retire at an early age:

- *Insufficiency of Social Security benefits.* While only 22 percent of retirees depend solely on Social Security benefits for income, Social Security benefits account for more than half of the retirement income for 66 percent of retirees. Many of those people are struggling financially today. To enjoy a financially secure retirement requires more income than Social Security alone.

- *Smaller retirement savings.* Retirement savings, including 401(k) plans and IRAs, haven't performed as well as expected in view of a poor stock market and low interest rates. And fewer individuals receive fixed pensions from employers; many of these plans have largely been supplanted by 401(k) plans. This leaves less savings available for retirement income.

- *Declining home prices.* Many look upon their home as their retirement income; they plan to sell the home so they can downsize or rent and live off the profits from their sale. Unfortunately, following the housing bubble, home prices have declined by 20 percent or more in some locations.

- *Concern about the economic future.* As prices continue to rise dramatically for many essentials—food, gasoline, health care—many don't expect their savings to be sufficient to meet their future needs.

## What to Do Now

Determine how much money you have for retirement and compare it to your expected needs for the rest of your life. This is easier said than done. The determination requires many assumptions, such as your life expectancy, future health, inflation, tax changes, and other factors that can impact your income and your expenses in the future. However, you can use online calculators to help you with your projections. Link to various retirement planning calculators through ChooseToSave (www.choosetosave.org) or use its BallPark E$timate Calculator to make your projections.

Retire later or retire a little rather than in full. According to an AARP study, most baby boomers don't plan to retire before age 66, and 80 percent say they expect to work during retirement. Of these, 30 percent say financial need is the reason they expect to continue doing some work during retirement. If you need income in retirement, consider part-time work or a sideline business. Both options can bring in additional income to meet any budgetary shortfalls or to provide the extras that can be enjoyed, such as a trip or gifts to family members.

- *Concern about outliving savings.* As longevity increases, so too does the need for additional resources to support you during those added years. When Social Security was instituted in 1935 with the Social Security age fixed at 65, the average life expectancy was only 63; those who lived to age 65 could expect to live only another 14 years. Today, when people reach age 65, they can expect 20 or more years in retirement. One of the biggest fears of seniors today is running out of money because they live longer than they had planned for.

Of course, for many individuals, postponing retirement has nothing to do with money; it's a personal choice. They prefer to stay active by continuing to work.

### Increased Social Security Benefits

While you can begin to receive Social Security benefits at age 62, the full amount won't be paid unless you wait to start benefits until your full retirement age (e.g., age 66 for those born between 1943 and 1954). However, if you delay the receipt of Social Security benefits past your full retirement age, you'll receive greater benefits when you start to collect.

For those born in 1943 and later, you earn an additional 8 percent per year for each year past full retirement age that you wait to start collecting benefits. No additional credits can be earned after age 70, so the maximum credit that can be earned is 32 percent (8 percent × 4 years). Smaller credits apply to those born before 1943.

You can estimate your Social Security retirement benefits by viewing your annual statement, which is sent to you three months before your birthday. You can also project what your benefits will be by using an online calculator (www.ssa.gov/planners/calculators.htm).

---

**What to Do Now**

Whether you start Social Security benefits early, at full retirement age, or at a delayed age, you are eligible for Medicare at age 65. If you fail to sign up for Medicare at this age, you may incur added costs when coverage does begin.

---

## Staying Healthy

One of the biggest costs to financial security and quality of life is the unexpected health issue. No matter how great your medical insurance may be, having an illness or condition usually results in high out-of-pocket costs. And illness can prevent you from working, which cuts down on your income and may end employee benefits on which you've relied.

Of course, there is no way to avoid certain illnesses or conditions; they occur because of genetics, exposure, or other uncontrollable factors. However, the likelihood of contracting certain illnesses or the severity with which they may be experienced can be lessened by maintaining general good health. Fundamental practices can contribute to a healthy you:

- Eating right (getting sufficient nutrients and avoiding obesity).
- Getting enough exercise.
- Avoiding bad habits, like smoking, excessive drinking, and illicit drugs.
- Getting appropriate medical and dental attention. This includes recommended screening for certain conditions (e.g., mammograms to screen for breast cancer in women after age 40; prostate exams to screen for prostate cancer in men after age 50). It also means taking prescribed medications as directed.
- Controlling stress.
- Getting sufficient sleep.

## What to Do Now

Make a commitment to good health, which is its own reward. Staying healthy can also contribute to your financial well-being.

# Glossary

**accelerated death benefit**  A portion of proceeds paid from a life insurance policy while the insured is alive but has a chronic or terminal illness or condition.

**adjustable-rate mortgage (ARM)**  A home mortgage that resets its interest rate annually or at other fixed periods.

**adjusted basis**  The tax basis of a home, securities, and other property (usually the property's cost).

**angel investor**  A private person or group that functions like a venture capitalist to provide funds to businesses.

**at-risk rule**  A tax rule that limits an investment loss to the extent of the investor's economic stake.

**bankruptcy**  A legal process in which a court oversees the liquidation of an insolvent debtor or a repayment plan in which the debtor pays back creditors over time.

**cancellation of indebtedness income**  For tax purposes, the income realized when a creditor forgives some or all of what a debtor owes (also called discharge of indebtedness income).

**catastrophe**  Technically, an event in which there is $25 million or more in insured property losses affecting a significant number of people, but can be any dramatic natural or man-made event that has severe consequences in damage and/or loss of life.

**COBRA (Consolidated Omnibus Budget Reconciliation Act) coverage** Continued health coverage under a former employer's plan, usually up to 18 months after leaving the job.

**commodity** A physical substance that trades on an exchange, such as crude oil, gold, and wheat, which investors buy or sell, usually via futures contracts.

**condemnation** A government action when property is deemed unsafe, a condition that can result after a casualty event.

**Coverdell education savings account (ESA)** A tax-advantaged plan used to save for the beneficiary's education.

**eminent domain** A seizure of private property by a public authority for a public purpose; tax realized on this event can be postponed by acquiring replacement property.

**equitable distribution** A method for dividing up a couple's assets in divorce, which does not necessarily result in an even split.

**equity** The current value of a home after subtracting any existing mortgages (essentially what could be kept after selling a home).

**exchange-traded fund (ETF)** A bundle of securities that trades on the American Stock Exchange.

**exempt asset** Property that cannot be reached by creditors and is protected in bankruptcy.

**FAFSA (Free Application for Federal Student Aid)** The form that must be completed for a student to obtain financial aid.

**529 plan** A tax-advantaged education savings plan that is state-sponsored or available through a private plan; can be a prepaid tuition plan or a savings plan.

**foreclosure** A legal process that occurs when the borrower is in default (has not paid the mortgage for some time) and the lender obtains the property in full or partial satisfaction of the outstanding debt.

**flexible spending account (FSA)** An account funded with employee salary contributions (elective deferrals) that can be used to pay for health costs or dependent care on a pretax basis.

**garnishment** Court action for creditors to obtain a portion of a debtor's paycheck to satisfy the debt.

**health savings account (HSA)** A medical savings plan funded with tax-deductible contributions that can be used to pay health costs on a tax-free basis.

**high-deductible health plan (HDHP)** Medical insurance that meets tax law requirements for minimum deductibles and caps on out-of-pocket costs; a prerequisite to an HSA.

**hobby loss** Hobby expenses, which are tax-deductible only to the extent of income from the activity.

**holding period** The time used to determine whether gains and losses on transactions are short-term or long-term for tax purposes.

**home equity line of credit (HELOC)** A home mortgage that lets you use the credit limit when and to the extent you choose; you pay interest on only the portion actually borrowed.

**income averaging** A tax rule that allows farmers and commercial fishermen to effectively spread income over three years to reduce the tax in high-income years.

**inflation** The upward movement of the cost of goods and services over time, as measured against the consumer price index (CPI); it reduces the buying power of the dollar.

**insolvency** A situation in which your total liabilities exceed your total assets.

**involuntary conversion** A forced disposition of property due to a casualty, theft, or condemnation that results in a taxable gain; gain can be postponed by acquiring replacement property.

**long-term care** Extended personal and/or medical care required by someone with a chronic illness or disease or on account of an inability for self-care.

**margin loan** Borrowing from your brokerage account, using your securities as collateral.

**mortgage workout** Mortgage restructuring by the lender so the homeowner can avoid foreclosure.

**net operating loss (NOL)** A business loss in excess of current income that can be carried back against income in certain prior years and/or carried forward for 20 years to offset future income.

**nondischargeable debt** A debt that cannot be extinguished by bankruptcy.

**outplacement services** A package of benefits provided by an employer to a former employee to help him or her find a new job.

**paper gains and losses** Potential results if holdings were sold.

**ParentsPlus loan** A type of federal loan to parents of dependent undergraduate students.

**passive activity loss (PAL) rule** A special tax rule that limits a deduction for this loss to income from all passive activities, with the unused loss carried forward.

**Perkins loan** A type of federal loan for higher education that is available only to students with exceptional financial need.

**repossession** A legal process in which the creditor obtains ownership of the debtor's property (such as your car) if you can't pay the debt.

**risk tolerance**   The ability (mental and/or financial) to withstand market declines.

**Section 1244 stock**   Small business stock on which a loss qualifies for ordinary loss treatment up to $50,000 ($100,000 on a joint tax return).

**short sale**   A foreclosure avoidance tactic in which the lender agrees to let the home be sold to a new owner for less than the outstanding mortgage balance and extinguishes any remaining debt; alternatively, a type of stock transaction involving the sale of borrowed securities made to freeze the profit or to gain from a declining market.

**Social Security disability income (SSDI)**   Benefits paid to a worker under the full retirement age whose disability prevents him or her from doing any substantial gainful work.

**Stafford loan**   A type of federal loan for higher education that is available without regard to need.

**stagflation**   Rising prices (inflation) and high unemployment without a rising economy (during a recessionary period).

**stimulus payment/stimulus check**   A government check paid to taxpayers and certain other designated individuals under the Economic Stimulus Act of 2008.

**structured settlement**   The result of a successful lawsuit in which damages are paid over a set time.

**subprime mortgage**   An adjustable-rate mortgage given to an individual with a credit history insufficient to qualify for a conventional mortgage.

**Supplemental Security Income (SSI)**   A government program to provide additional income to those in severe financial need.

**supplemental unemployment benefits**   Benefits paid to an unemployed person through a union or other association in addition to state unemployment benefits.

**tax-deferred income**   Income or gains received currently on which tax is delayed until a future time.

**tax efficiency**   The nature of an investment having less costly tax consequences when compared with tax results for other investments.

**viatical settlement**   The sale of a life insurance policy on the life of a terminally ill person to a third party for a portion of the policy's face value.

**wash sale**   A sale of a security at a loss where a substantially identical security is acquired within 30 days before or after the loss sale.

**wrongful termination**   Firing from a job for an impermissible reason, such as on account of age.

# Index